The book of the classic
MV AGUSTA
Fours

Ian Falloon

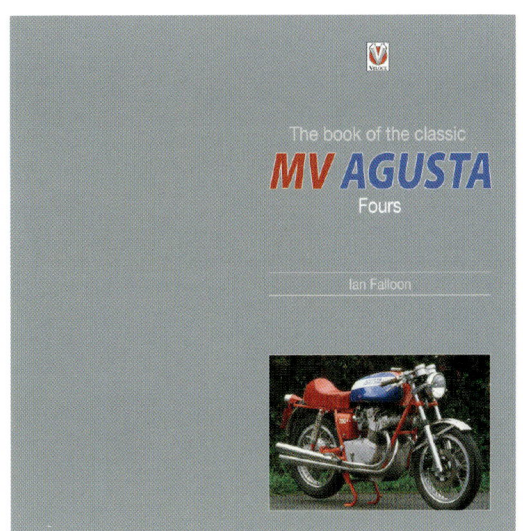

Other great books from Veloce –

Speedpro Series
4-cylinder Engine – How to Blueprint & Build a Short Block For High Performance (Hammill)
Alfa Romeo DOHC High-performance Manual (Kartalamakis)
Alfa Romeo V6 Engine High-performance Manual (Kartalamakis)
BMC 998cc A-series Engine – How to Power Tune (Hammill)
1275cc A-series High-performance Manual (Hammill)
Camshafts – How to Choose & Time Them For Maximum Power (Hammill)
Competition Car Datalogging Manual, The (Templeman)
Cylinder Heads – How to Build, Modify & Power Tune Updated & Revised Edition (Burgess & Gollan)
Distributor-type Ignition Systems – How to Build & Power Tune New 3rd Edition (Hammill)
Fast Road Car – How to Plan and Build Revised & Updated Colour New Edition (Stapleton)
Ford SOHC 'Pinto' & Sierra Cosworth DOHC Engines – How to Power Tune Updated & Enlarged Edition (Hammill)
Ford V8 – How to Power Tune Small Block Engines (Hammill)
Harley-Davidson Evolution Engines – How to Build & Power Tune (Hammill)
Holley Carburetors – How to Build & Power Tune Revised & Updated Edition (Hammill)
Honda Civic Type R, The – High-Performance Manual (Cowland & Clifford)
Jaguar XK Engines – How to Power Tune Revised & Updated Colour Edition (Hammill)
Land Rover Discovery, Defender & Range Rover – How to Modify Coil Sprung Models for High Performance & Off-Road Action (Hosier)
MG Midget & Austin-Healey Sprite – How to Power Tune New 3rd Edition (Stapleton)
MGB 4-cylinder Engine – How to Power Tune (Burgess)
MGB V8 Power – How to Give Your, Third Colour Edition (Williams)
MGB, MGC & MGB V8 – How to Improve New 2nd Edition (Williams)
Mini Engines – How to Power Tune On a Small Budget Colour Edition (Hammill)
Motorcycle-engined Racing Car – How to Build (Pashley)
Motorsport – Getting Started in (Collins)
Nissan GT-R High-performance Manual, The (Gorodji)
Nitrous Oxide High-performance Manual, The (Langfield)
Race & Trackday Driving Techniques (Hornsey)
Rover V8 Engines – How to Power Tune (Hammill)
Secrets of Speed – Today's techniques for 4-stroke engine blueprinting & tuning (Swager)
Sportscar & Kitcar Suspension & Brakes – How to Build & Modify Revised 3rd Edition (Hammill)
SU Carburettor High-performance Manual (Hammill)
Successful Low-Cost Rally Car, How to Build a (Young)
Suzuki 4x4 – How to Modify For Serious Off-road Action (Richardson)
Tiger Avon Sportscar – How to Build Your Own Updated & Revised 2nd Edition (Dudley)
TR2, 3 & TR4 – How to Improve (Williams)
TR5, 250 & TR6 – How to Improve (Williams)
TR7 & TR8 – How to Improve (Williams)
V8 Engine – How to Build a Short Block For High Performance (Hammill)
Volkswagen Beetle Suspension, Brakes & Chassis – How to Modify For High Performance – Updated & Enlarged New Edition (Hale)
Weber DCOE, & Dellorto DHLA Carburetors – How to Build & Power Tune 3rd Edition (Hammill)

Those Were The Days ... Series
Alpine Trials & Rallies 1910-1973 (Pfundner)
American 'Independent' Automakers – AMC to Willys 1945 to 1960 (Mort)
American Station Wagons – The Golden Era 1950-1975 (Mort)
American Trucks of the 1950s (Mort)
American Trucks of the 1960s (Mort)
American Woodies 1928-1953 (Mort)
Anglo-American Cars from the 1930s to the 1970s (Mort)
Austerity Motoring (Bobbitt)
Austins, The last real (Peck)
Brighton National Speed Trials (Gardiner)
British Drag Racing – The Early Years (Pettitt)
British Lorries of the 1950s (Bobbitt)
British Lorries of the 1960s (Bobbitt)
British Touring Car Racing (Collins)
British Police Cars (Walker)
British Woodies (Peck)
Café Racer Phenomenon, The (Walker)
Drag Bike Racing in Britain – From the mid '60s to the mid '80s (Lee)
Dune Buggy Phenomenon, The (Hale)
Dune Buggy Phenomenon Volume 2, The (Hale)
Endurance Racing at Silverstone in the 1970s & 1980s (Parker)
Hot Rod & Stock Car Racing in Britain in the 1980s (Neil)
Last Real Austins 1946-1959, The (Peck)
MG's Abingdon Factory (Moylan)
Motor Racing at Brands Hatch in the Seventies (Parker)
Motor Racing at Brands Hatch in the Eighties (Parker)
Motor Racing at Crystal Palace (Collins)
Motor Racing at Goodwood in the Sixties (Gardiner)
Motor Racing at Nassau in the 1950s & 1960s (O'Neil)
Motor Racing at Oulton Park in the 1960s (McFadyen)
Motor Racing at Oulton Park in the 1970s (McFadyen)
Superprix – The Story of Birmingham Motor Race (Page & Collins)
Three Wheelers (Bobbitt)

Truckmakers
DAF Trucks since 1949 (Peck)

Enthusiast's Restoration Manual Series
Citroën 2CV, How to Restore (Porter)
Classic Car Bodywork, How to Restore (Thaddeus)
Classic British Car Electrical Systems (Astley)
Classic Car Electrics (Thaddeus)
Classic Cars, How to Paint (Thaddeus)
Jaguar E-type (Crespin)
Reliant Regal, How to Restore (Payne)
Triumph TR2, 3, 3A, 4 & 4A, How to Restore (Williams)
Triumph TR5/250 & 6, How to Restore (Williams)
Triumph TR7/8, How to Restore (Williams)
Volkswagen Beetle, How to Restore (Tyler)
VW Bay Window Bus (Paxton)
Yamaha FS1-E, How to Restore (Watts)

Essential Buyer's Guide Series
Alfa GT (Booker)
Alfa Romeo Spider Giulia (Booker & Talbott)
Austin Seven (Barker)
BMW GS (Henshaw)
BSA Bantam (Henshaw)
BSA 500 & 650 Twins (Henshaw)
Citroën 2CV (Paxton)
Citroën ID & DS (Heilig)
Corvette C2 1963-1967 (Falconer)
Fiat 500 & 600 (Bobbitt)
Ford Capri (Paxton)
Harley-Davidson Big Twins (Henshaw)
Hinckley Triumph triples & fours 750, 900, 955, 1000, 1050, 1200 – 1991-2009 (Henshaw)
Honda CBR600 (Henshaw)
Honda FireBlade (Henshaw)
Honda SOHC fours 1969-1984 (Henshaw)
Jaguar E-type 3.8 & 4.2-litre (Crespin)
Jaguar E-type V12 5.3-litre (Crespin)
Jaguar XJ 1995-2003 (Crespin)
Jaguar XK8 (1996-2005) (Thorley)
Jaguar/Daimler XJ6, XJ12 & Sovereign (Crespin)
Jaguar/Daimler XJ40 (Crespin)
Jaguar Mk2 (1955 to 1969) (Thorley)
Jaguar XJ-S (Crespin)
Land Rover Series I, II & IIA (Thurman)
MGB & MGB GT (Williams)
Mercedes-Benz 280SL-560DSL Roadsters (Bass)
Mercedes-Benz 'Pagoda' 230SL, 250SL & 280SL Roadsters & Coupés (Bass)
MG Midget & A-H Sprite (Horler)
MG TD, TF & TF1500 (Jones)
Mini (Paxton)
Morris Minor & 1000 (Newell)
Norton Commando (Henshaw)
Peugeot 205 GTi (Blackburn)
Porsche 911 (964) (Streather)
Porsche 911 (993) (Streather)
Porsche 911 (996) (Streather)
Porsche 911 SC (Streather)
Porsche 928 (Hemmings)
Rolls-Royce Silver Shadow & Bentley T-Series (Bobbitt)
Subaru Impreza (Hobbs)
Triumph Bonneville (Henshaw)
Triumph Spitfire & GT6
Triumph Stag (Mort & Fox)
Triumph TR6 (Williams)
Triumph TR7 & TR8 (Williams)
Vespa Scooters – Classic 2-stroke models 1960-2008 (Paxton)
VW Beetle (Cservenka & Copping)
VW Bus (Cservenka & Copping)
VW Golf GTI (Cservenka & Copping)

Auto-Graphics Series
Fiat-based Abarths (Sparrow)
Jaguar MKI & II Saloons (Sparrow)
Lambretta Li Series Scooters (Sparrow)

Rally Giants Series
Audi Quattro (Robson)
Austin Healey 100-6 & 3000 (Robson)
Fiat 131 Abarth (Robson)
Ford Escort MkI (Robson)
Ford Escort RS Cosworth & World Rally Car (Robson)
Ford Escort RS1800 (Robson)
Lancia Delta 4WD/Integrale (Robson)
Lancia Stratos (Robson)
Mini Cooper/Mini Cooper S (Robson)
Peugeot 205 T16 (Robson)
Saab 96 & V4 (Robson)
Subaru Impreza (Robson)
Toyota Celica GT4 (Robson)

WSC Giants
Ferrari 312P & 312PB (Collins & McDonough)
Gulf-Mirage 1967 to 1982 (McDonough)
Matra Sports Cars – MS620, 630, 650, 660 & 670 – 1966 to 1974 (McDonough)

Biographies
André Lefebvre, and the cars he created at Voisin and Citroën (Beck)
Cliff Allison, The Official Biography of – From the Fells to Ferrari – (Gauld)
Edward Turner: The Man Behind the Motorcycles (Clew)
Jack Sears, The Official Biography of – Gentleman Jack (Gauld)
Jim Redman – 6 Times World Motorcycle Champion: The Autobiography (Redman)
John Chatham – 'Mr Big Healey' – The Official Biography (Burr)
Pat Moss Carlsson Story, The – Harnessing Horsepower (Turner)
Virgil Exner – Visioneer: The Official Biography of Virgil M Exner Designer Extraordinaire (Grist)

General
1½-litre GP Racing 1961-1965 (Whitelock)
AC Two-litre Saloons & Buckland Sportscars (Archibald)
Alfa Romeo Giulia Coupé GT & GTA (Tipler)
Alfa Romeo Montreal – The dream car that came true (Taylor)
Alfa Romeo Montreal – The Essential Companion (Taylor)
Alfa Tipo 33 (McDonough & Collins)
Alpine & Renault – The Development of the Revolutionary Turbo F1 Car 1968 to 1979 (Smith)
Alpine & Renault – The Sports Prototypes 1963 to 1969 (Smith)
Alpine & Renault – The Sports Prototypes 1973 to 1978 (Smith)
Anatomy of the Works Minis (Moylan)
Armstrong-Siddeley (Smith)
Art Deco and British Car Design (Down)
Autodrome (Collins & Ireland)
Autodrome 2 (Collins & Ireland)
Automotive A-Z, Lane's Dictionary of Automotive Terms (Lane)
Automotive Mascots (Kay & Springate)
Bahamas Speed Weeks, The (O'Neil)
Bentley Continental, Corniche and Azure (Bennett)
Bentley MkVI, Rolls-Royce Silver Wraith, Dawn & Cloud/Bentley R & S-Series (Nutland)
Bluebird CN7 (Stevens)
BMC Competitions Department Secrets (Turner, Chambers & Browning)
BMW 5-Series (Cranswick)
BMW Z-Cars (Taylor)
BMW Boxer Twins 1970-1995 Bible, The (Falloon)
BMW Custom Motorcycles – Choppers, Cruisers, Bobbers, Trikes & Quads (Cloesen)
Britains Farm Model Balers & Combines 1967-2007, Pocket Guide to (Pullen)
Britains Farm Model & Toy Tractors 1998-2008, Pocket Guide to (Pullen)
Britains Toy Models Catalogues 1970-1979 (Pullen)
British 250cc Racing Motorcycles (Pereira)
British at Indianapolis, The (Wagstaff)
British Cars, The Complete Catalogue of, 1895-1975 (Culshaw & Horrobin)
BRM – A Mechanic's Tale (Salmon)
BRM V16 (Ludvigsen)
BSA Bantam Bible, The (Henshaw)
Bugatti Type 40 (Price)
Bugatti 46/50 Updated Edition (Price & Arbey)
Bugatti T44 & T49 (Price & Arbey)
Bugatti 57 2nd Edition (Price)
Caravans, The Illustrated History 1919-1959 (Jenkinson)
Caravans, The Illustrated History From 1960 (Jenkinson)
Caring for your 50cc Scooter – Your guide to maintenance & safety checks (Fry)
Carrera Panamericana, La (Tipler)
Chrysler 300 – America's Most Powerful Car 2nd Edition (Ackerson)
Chrysler PT Cruiser (Ackerson)
Citroën DS (Bobbitt)
Classic British Car Electrical Systems (Astley)
Cobra – The Real Thing! (Legate)
Concept Cars, How to illustrate and design (Dewey)
Cortina – Ford's Bestseller (Robson)
Coventry Climax Racing Engines (Hammill)
Daily Mirror 1970 World Cup Rally 40, The (Robson)
Daimler SP250 New Edition (Long)
Datsun Fairlady Roadster to 280ZX – The Z-Car Story (Long)
Diecast Toy Cars of the 1950s & 1960s (Ralston)
Dino – The V6 Ferrari (Long)
Dodge Challenger & Plymouth Barracuda (Grist)
Dodge Charger – Enduring Thunder (Ackerson)
Dodge Dynamite! (Grist)
Draw & Paint Cars – How to (Gardiner)
Drive on the Wild Side, A – 20 Extreme Driving Adventures From Around the World (Weaver)
Ducati 750 Bible, The (Falloon)
Ducati 750 SS 'round-case' 1974, The Book of the (Falloon)
Ducati 860, 900 and Mille Bible, The (Falloon)
Ducati Monster Bible, The (Falloon)
Dune Buggy, Building A – The Essential Manual (Shakespeare)
Dune Buggy Files (Hale)
Dune Buggy Handbook (Hale)
East German Motor Vehicles in Pictures (Suhr/Weinreich)
Efficient Driver's Handbook, The (Moss)
Electric Cars – The Future is Now! (Linde)
Fast Ladies – Female Racing Drivers 1888 to 1970 (Bouzanquet)
Fate of the Sleeping Beauties, The (op de Weegh/Hottendorff/op de Weegh)
Ferrari 288 GTO, The Book of the (Sackey)
Fiat & Abarth 124 Spider & Coupé (Tipler)
Fiat & Abarth 500 & 600 2nd Edition (Bobbitt)
Fiats, Great Small (Ward)
Fine Art of the Motorcycle Engine, The (Peirce)
Ford F100/F150 Pick-up 1948-1996 (Ackerson)
Ford F150 Pick-up 1997-2005 (Ackerson)
Ford GT – Then, and Now (Streather)
Ford GT40 (Legate)
Ford In Miniature (Olson)
Ford Model Y (Roberts)
Ford Thunderbird From 1954, The Book of the (Long)
Formula 5000 Motor Racing, Back then ... and back now (Lawson)
Forza Minardi! (Vigar)
Funky Mopeds (Skelton)
GM In Miniature (Olson)
GT – The World's Best GT Cars 1953-73 (Dawson)
Hillclimbing & Sprinting – The Essential Manual (Short & Wilkinson)
Honda NSX (Long)
Intermeccanica – The Story of the Prancing Bull (McCredie & Reisner)
Jaguar, The Rise of (Price)
Jaguar XJ 220 – The Inside Story (Moreton)
Jaguar XJ-S (Long)
Jeep CJ (Ackerson)
Jeep Wrangler (Ackerson)
Karmann-Ghia Coupé & Convertible (Bobbitt)
Kawasaki Triples Bible, The (Walker)
Kris Meeke – Intercontinental Rally Challenge Champion (McBride)
Lamborghini Miura Bible, The (Sackey)
Lamborghini Urraco, The book of the (Landsem)
Lambretta Bible, The (Davies)
Lancia 037 (Collins)
Lancia Delta HF Integrale (Blaettel & Wagner)
Land Rover Series III Reborn (Porter)
Land Rover, The Half-ton Military (Cook)
Laverda Twins & Triples Bible 1968-1986 (Falloon)
Lea-Francis Story, The (Price)
Lexus Story, The (Long)
little book of smart, the New Edition (Jackson)
little book of microcars, the (Quellin)
Lola – The Illustrated History (1957-1977) (Starkey)
Lola – All the Sports Racing & Single-seater Racing Cars 1978-1997 (Starkey)
Lola T70 – The Racing History & Individual Chassis Record 4th Edition (Starkey)
Lotus 49 (Oliver)
Marketingmobiles, The Wonderful Wacky World of (Hale)
Mazda MX-5/Miata 1.6 Enthusiast's Workshop Manual (Grainger & Shoemark)
Mazda MX-5/Miata 1.8 Enthusiast's Workshop Manual (Grainger & Shoemark)
Mazda MX-5 Miata: The Book of the World's Favourite Sportscar (Long)
Mazda MX-5 Miata Roadster (Long)
Maximum Mini (Booij)
Mercedes-Benz SL – 113-series 1963-1971 (Long)
Mercedes-Benz SL & SLC – 107-series 1971-1989 (Long)
MGA (Price Williams)
MGB & MGB GT– Expert Guide (Auto-doc Series) (Williams)
MGB Electrical Systems Updated & Revised Edition (Astley)
Micro Caravans (Jenkinson)
Micro Trucks (Mort)
Microcars at Large! (Quellin)
Mini Cooper – The Real Thing! (Tipler)
Mitsubishi Lancer Evo, The Road Car & WRC Story (Long)
Montlhéry, The Story of the Paris Autodrome (Boddy)
Morgan Maverick (Lawrence)
Morris Minor, 60 Years on the Road (Newell)
Moto Guzzi Sport & Le Mans Bible, The (Falloon)
Motor Movies – The Posters! (Veysey)
Motor Racing – Reflections of a Lost Era (Carter)
Motorcycle Apprentice (Cakebread)
Motorcycle Road & Racing Chassis Designs (Noakes)
Motorhomes, The Illustrated History (Jenkinson)
Motorsport In colour, 1950s (Wainwright)
MV Agusta Fours, The book of the (Falloon)
Nissan 300ZX & 350Z – The Z-Car Story (Long)
Nissan GT-R Supercar: Born to race (Gorodji)
Northeast American Sports Car Races 1950-1959 (O'Neil)
Nothing Runs – Misadventures in the Classic, Collectable & Exotic Car Biz (Slutsky)
Off-Road Giants! (Volume 1) – Heroes of 1960s Motorcycle Sport (Westlake)
Off-Road Giants! (Volume 2) – Heroes of 1960s Motorcycle Sport (Westlake)
Pass the Theory and Practical Driving Tests (Gibson & Hoole)
Peking to Paris 2007 (Young)
Plastic Toy Cars of the 1950s & 1960s (Ralston)
Pontiac Firebird (Cranswick)
Porsche Boxster (Long)
Porsche 356 (2nd Edition) (Long)
Porsche 908 (Födisch, Neßhöver, Roßbach, Schwarz & Roßbach)
Porsche 911 Carrera – The Last of the Evolution (Corlett)
Porsche 911R, RS & RSR, 4th Edition (Starkey)
Porsche 911, The Book of the (Long)
Porsche 911SC 'Super Carrera' – The Essential Companion (Streather)
Porsche 914 & 914-6: The Definitive History of the Road & Competition Cars (Long)
Porsche 924 (Long)
Porsche 928 (Long)
Porsche 944 (Long)
Porsche 964, 993 & 996 Data Plate Code Breaker (Streather)
Porsche 993 'King Of Porsche' – The Essential Companion (Streather)
Porsche 996 'Supreme Porsche' – The Essential Companion (Streather)
Porsche Racing Cars – 1953 to 1975 (Long)
Porsche Racing Cars – 1976 to 2005 (Long)
Porsche – The Rally Story (Meredith)
Porsche: Three Generations of Genius (Meredith)
Preston Tucker & Others (Linde)
RAC Rally Action! (Gardiner)
Rallye Sport Fords: The Inside Story (Moreton)
Roads with a View – England's greatest views and how to find them by road (Corfield)
Roads with a View – Wales' greatest views and how to find them by road (Corfield)
Rolls-Royce Silver Shadow/Bentley T Series Corniche & Camargue Revised & Enlarged Edition (Bobbitt)
Rolls-Royce Silver Spirit, Silver Spur & Bentley Mulsanne 2nd Edition (Bobbitt)
Runways & Racers (O'Neil)
Russian Motor Vehicles – Soviet Limousines 1930-2003 (Kelly)
Russian Motor Vehicles – The Czarist Period 1784 to 1917 (Kelly)
RX-7 – Mazda's Rotary Engine Sportscar (Updated & Revised New Edition) (Long)
Scooters & Microcars, The A-Z of Popular (Dan)
Scooter Lifestyle (Grainger)
Singer Story: Cars, Commercial Vehicles, Bicycles & Motorcycle (Atkinson)
Sleeping Beauties USA – abandoned classic cars & trucks (Marek)
SM – Citroën's Maserati-engined Supercar (Long & Claverol)
Speedway – Auto racing's ghost tracks (Collins & Ireland)
Standard Motor Company, The Book of the
Subaru Impreza: The Road Car And WRC Story (Long)
Supercar, How to Build your own (Thompson)
Tales from the Toolbox (Oliver)
Taxi! The Story of the 'London' Taxicab (Bobbitt)
Tinplate Toy Cars of the 1950s & 1960s (Ralston)
Toleman Story, The (Hilton)
Toyota Celica & Supra, The Book of Toyota's Sports Coupés (Long)
Toyota MR2 Coupés & Spyders (Long)
Triumph Bonneville!, Save the – The inside story of the Meriden Workers' Co-op (Rosamond)
Triumph Motorcycles & the Meriden Factory (Hancox)
Triumph Speed Twin & Thunderbird Bible (Woolridge)
Triumph Tiger Cub Bible (Estall)
Triumph Trophy Bible (Woolridge)
Triumph TR6 (Kimberley)
TWR Story, The – Group A (Hughes & Scott)
Unraced (Collins)
Velocette Motorcycles – MSS to Thruxton New Third Edition (Burris)
Volkswagen Bus Book, The (Bobbitt)
Volkswagen Bus or Van to Camper, How to Convert (Porter)
Volkswagens of the World (Glen)
VW Beetle Cabriolet (Bobbitt)
VW Beetle – The Car of the 20th Century (Copping)
VW Bus – 40 Years of Splitties, Bays & Wedges (Copping)
VW Bus Book, The (Bobbitt)
VW Golf: Five Generations of Fun (Copping & Cservenka)
VW – The Air-cooled Era (Copping)
VW T5 Camper Conversion Manual (Porter)
VW Campers (Copping)
Which Oil? – Choosing the right oils & greases for your antique, vintage, veteran, classic or collector car (Michell)
Works Minis, The Last (Purves & Brenchley)
Works Rally Mechanic (Moylan)

From Veloce Publishing's new imprints:

Battle Cry!
Soviet General & field rank officer uniforms: 1955 to 1991 (Streather)
Red & Soviet military & paramilitary services: female uniforms 1941-1991 (Streather)

Hubble & Hattie
Animal Grief – How animals mourn for each other (Alderton)
Clever Dog! (O'Meara)
Complete Dog Massage Manual, The – Gentle Dog Care (Robertson)
Dinner with Rover (Paton-Ayre)
Dog Cookies (Schops)
Dog Games – Stimulating play to entertain your dog and you (Blenski)
Dogs on wheels (Mort)
Dog Relax – Relaxed dogs, relaxed owners (Pilguj)
Exercising your puppy: a gentle & natural approach – Gentle Dog Care (Robertson)
Fun and games for cats (Seidl)
Know Your Dog – The guide to a beautiful relationship (Birmelin)
Living with an Older Dog – Gentle Dog Care (Alderton & Hall)
My dog has cruciate ligament injury – but lives life to the full! (Häusler)
My dog has hip dysplasia – but lives life to the full! (Häusler)
My dog is blind – but lives life to the full! (Horsky)
My dog is deaf – but lives life to the full! (Willms)
Smellorama – nose games for dogs (Theby)
Swim to Recovery: Canine hydrotherapy healing (Wong)
Waggy Tails & Wheelchairs (Epp)
Walking the dog – motorway walks for drivers and dogs (Rees)
Winston ... the dog who changed my life (Klute)
You and Your Border Terrier – The Essential Guide (Alderton)
You and Your Cockapoo – The Essential Guide (Alderton)

www.veloce.co.uk

First published in August 2011 by Veloce Publishing Limited, Veloce House, Parkway Farm Business Park, Middle Farm Way, Poundbury, Dorchester, Dorset, DT1 3AR, England.
Fax 01305 250479/e-mail info@veloce.co.uk/web www.veloce.co.uk or www.velocebooks.com.
ISBN: 978-1-84584-203-1 UPC: 6-36847-04203-5
© Ian Falloon and Veloce Publishing 2011. All rights reserved. With the exception of quoting brief passages for the purpose of review, no part of this publication may be recorded, reproduced or transmitted by any means, including photocopying, without the written permission of Veloce Publishing Ltd. Throughout this book logos, model names and designations, etc, have been used for the purposes of identification, illustration and decoration. Such names are the property of the trademark holder as this is not an official publication.
Readers with ideas for automotive books, or books on other transport or related hobby subjects, are invited to write to the editorial director of Veloce Publishing at the above address.
British Library Cataloguing in Publication Data – A catalogue record for this book is available from the British Library.
Typesetting, design and page make-up all by Veloce Publishing Ltd on Apple Mac. Printed in India by Replika Press Ltd.

The book of the classic
MV AGUSTA
Fours

Ian Falloon

CONTENTS

Foreword by Arturo Magni 5

Introduction 6

1. Birth of the MV Four 8

2. The 600 (MV4C6) 61

3. The 750 S 1970-1973 (MV4C75) 93

4. The 750 GT 1972-1974 (MV4C75) 130

5. The 750 S 1974 (MV4C75) 145

6. The 750 America 1975-76 (MV4C75) 167

7. The 850 SS (Monza) 1977 189

8. Modified MV Fours.. 199

9. Living with an MV Four 226

Index 238

FOREWORD BY ARTURO MAGNI

I am very pleased to be able to write the foreword to Ian Falloon's book covering the classic MV Agusta four-cylinder motorcycle. For me personally, the MV Agusta four-cylinder is the most significant of all motorcycle engines. In 1947 I began work at Gilera in Arcore under Piero Remor, and the first job he gave me was the assembly of a four-cylinder Gilera racing engine. So my career as a motorcycle mechanic began with this engine, and continued after I moved to MV Agusta in 1950.

I am fortunate to have worked on all racing four-cylinder MV Agustas, from the beginning until it was pensioned from racing in 1966, and then the triples, and later fours until 1976. Even after it was outclassed, the spirit of this racing engine lived on with the production 600, 750 S and America. After production at Cascina Costa ended in 1977, my son Giovanni and I have endeavoured to keep the legend of the four-cylinder MV Agusta alive. None of this would have been possible without the enthusiasm and passion of Count Domenico Agusta. Although the many stories of his difficult personality are true, Count Domenico was totally involved and committed to racing and production bikes. We had to work long hours, and every evening I would be summoned to his office to explain and justify any new development or modification. He always had to give the final word before any changes could be implemented. I believe that if Count Domenica had not died so prematurely, the racing and production would have continued.

The four-cylinder MV Agusta is not only a great engine, but in the hands of many leading riders it established a legacy unparalleled in the motorcycle world. For this reason, it is important to preserve the history of these bikes, and I am happy to be able to contribute to Mr Falloon's comprehensive and detailed history.

Arturo Magni
Samarate

Two of the most important names in the history of the MV four-cylinder are Giovanni Magni (left) and Arturo Magni. Here, they pose with Giovanni's MV Magni special.

INTRODUCTION

Few production motorcycles enjoy the legend bestowed upon the MV Agusta four. Only MV Agusta has produced a production motorcycle powered by an engine virtually identical to that which won 13 World Manufacturers' Championships and took victories in 91 Grands Prix. In the world of production motorcycles the MV Agusta four's legacy is unparalleled. Further adding to the myth of the MV Agusta four was its excessive expense at the time. As an MV four cost more than double that of any comparable motorcycle, few could savour it. The MV four may not have represented the pinnacle of performance, but it exuded an aura of unattainable exoticism. The MV four was a luxury product more than a motorcycle. In many ways it reflected an earlier world than the 1960s and 1970s when it was produced. Engineering-wise, the engine had its roots in the 1930s, as did Count Agusta's vision of the production four as a limited edition motorcycle for the very few.

Producing the MV Agusta four today as MV did between 1967 and 1977 would be inconceivable. Even if a stratospheric price was asked, there is no way building three or four motorcycles a week would be profitable. These were truly motorcycles of an earlier era, and this, along with the racing legend surrounding the MV four, is part of the appeal of these motorcycles. Also contributing to the appeal was that the production MV four was intentionally flawed. Count Agusta didn't want privateers racing MV fours against his factory bikes, so all production bikes had shaft final drive, rather than the chain drives of racing bikes. Thus, the MV four was too heavy to be a really effective sporting motorcycle, and the engines on early examples were very mildly tuned. Other motorcycles were undoubtedly faster and better handling, but somehow, with the MV four, this didn't matter. The MV four had nothing to prove. The MV Agusta four was more than a motorcycle, it was the production realisation of a racing legend.

Until recently, the MV four was always an enigma for me. I had ridden several 750 Sports and Americas over the years, and been unimpressed when compared back-to-back with my Ducati Super Sport. I always found the MV to be heavy, short, and with a high centre of gravity that inhibited spirited cornering. But now I realise I was missing the point, as the MV four was never meant to be a razor-sharp sporting bike. And if ridden conservatively, powering through corners the MV handles well. It will never be a svelte sporting motorcycle, but it was never meant to be. In 2002 I finally bought a 1974 750 Sport, and have learnt to appreciate the MV as a worthy exponent of one of the finest eras in motorcycling; the early to mid-1970s.

Much mystery surrounds the production four-cylinder MV and, although it was produced in moderate quantities over a ten year period, very little has been effectively documented in the past. There has also been considerable misinformation espoused over the years, and I have endeavoured to rectify this. Although the MV Agusta four was always a compromised motorcycle, I also believe examples should be preserved in their original state, so this book is also a guide to originality. Another characteristic peculiar to the MV four is the importance of modified bikes in its history. Of total production of around 1300 bikes, a large proportion (possibly 20 per cent) have been modified for improved handling and performance, and it is appropriate that these are also dealt with in this book.

Without any extensive personal hands-on experience with MV Agusta fours, I have had to engage several noted experts to help, especially regarding technical details. Particular thanks must go to Arturo Magni for agreeing to write the foreword to this book and answering many questions. Many thanks also go to Giovanni Magni for his translation and willingness to share his knowledge. More than anyone else, the Magnis have perpetuated the legend of the MV four-cylinder, and their enthusiasm and my warm welcome into their Samarate workshop was much appreciated. Dave and Mark Kay may be controversial within the close-knit MV world, but their hands-on experience with MV fours is unquestioned. I am particularly grateful for their technical expertise and analysis of problems with MV fours. The Kays also provided access to original engine drawings and supplied many engine components for photography. Although I was unable to visit Albert Bold personally, Albert was extremely forthcoming in answering my many technical questions. Former MV Agusta Concessionaires (GB) mechanic Richard Boshier was another

INTRODUCTION

with extensive practical experience who was extremely agreeable in answering technical questions. Without the support of Dorian Skinner of the MV Agusta Owners' Club in the UK I doubt much of my research would have been possible. Dorian allowed invaluable access to archives and also provided many useful pictures. Another whose enthusiasm and support was invaluable was Raphaël David of the MV Owners' Club France. Raphaël facilitated an introduction to King Vittorio Emanuele living in Geneva, and also established the connection with Giovanni Magni. Bill Irwin in New Zealand made his exceptional collection of MV fours available for photography.

Other thanks must be extended to: Alessia Riboni at MV Agusta; Enrico Sironi and Dario Paganini of Museo Agusta; Jeremy Bowdler of *Two Wheels* magazine; Mark Hoyer of *Cycle World* magazine; King Vittorio Emanuele de Savoie; Arnaud Andrieu; Peter Calles; James Feery; Michael Furman; Erik Hakstege; Reuben Hoggett; Roy Kidney; Gary Kohs; Rob Labordus; Ian Mackay; Ben Morris; Luc Meersmans; Russ Murray; Dave Rodd; André and Bryan Thompson; and Marco Vittino. Finally, I must thank my wife Miriam and sons Ben and Tim, who willingly visited MV Agusta collections and people throughout Europe in the course of researching this book.

Ian Falloon

The final factory MV four was the 850 Monza.

1 BIRTH OF THE MV FOUR

In the wake of World War II Italy faced many problems, not in the least cheap and reliable mass transportation. And with public transport awry, cars unaffordable and unobtainable, Agusta was one of many Italian companies to embark on the production of lightweight motorcycles. Located in the tiny village of Cascina Costa di Verghera, between Gallarate and Malpensa near Milan, Agusta was a highly successful aviation company, but, under the terms of surrender, was forbidden to produce aviation products. Count Domenico Agusta anticipated this scenario; as early as the autumn of 1943 recognising the need for postwar diversification. He had his engineers draw up the plans for a 98cc two-stroke single, and when Meccanica Verghera Agusta was formed on 12 February 1945 its first product was the 98cc Vespa (Wasp). Demand far exceeded supply, and this modest machine soon heralded a range of larger displacement motorcycles. It also propelled MV Agusta into the world of motorcycle sport, and soon the little 98 was achieving considerable success in the hands of enthusiastic owners. This success prompted MV to present its first factory racer (98 two-stroke) at the 1946 Milan Show. By 1948 the bike had grown to 125cc, and although Franco Bertoni won the 125cc race at the 1948 Italian Grand Prix, the little two-stroke was overwhelmed by the Mondial in the new FIM World Championship of 1949.

Although not a successful year for racing, 1949 was significant for MV Agusta. Production of motorcycles flourished, and the signing of the North Atlantic Pact on 4 April 1949 opened the door for Agusta to recommence its aviation business. Business was initially slow, but an agreement was signed with Bell in 1952 to produce the Bell Model 47G helicopter under licence. This was a masterstroke and soon Agusta found itself in a position of financial security that ensured the continuation of its expensive racing program.

Count Domenico Agusta was the driving force behind MV's racing program, here with the 1952 team at Monza. From left to right: Alfredo Copeta, Carlo Bandirola (on the bike), the Count, Tito Forconi, Arturo Magni, and Les Graham. (Courtesy Museo Agusta)

BIRTH OF THE MV FOUR

PIERO REMOR

More mathematician than mechanical engineer, Piero Remor was born in Portovenere on the Ligurian coast in 1896, later studying engineering in Rome under the eminent Professor Bordoni. Well known for his argumentativeness, Remor left OPRA (Officine Romane di Precisione Autoveicole) in 1930 after a disagreement with Bonmartini and went to work for the automotive company OM in Brescia. There he designed a 1500cc four-cylinder engine (Tipo M), but after Fiat bought OM in 1938, phasing out car production in favour of trucks, Remor began to look for alternative employment. In 1939 Piero Taruffi persuaded Remor to join Gilera, primarily to produce the next generation 500cc racer, but initially Remor worked on a supercharged 250 and a new rear suspension system for the existing supercharged 500 Rondine. Although not raced, many features of the supercharged 250 were incorporated in the later Gilera 500 four. Remor also had access to Alfa Romeo's technical department and incorporated details of its celebrated straight-eight design in his work. As soon as the Gilera 500 was launched Remor had difficulties with the riders complaining about its handling. Remor blamed the riders for the initial engine problems (caused by faulty lubrication), and his confrontation with Nello Pagani was particularly bitter as Pagani was deprived of a ride on the 500 for the best part of 1948. His abrupt departure from Gilera to MV Agusta at the end of 1949 was also acrimonious. But Remor's career at MV Agusta was also brief, and in 1954 he moved to the Motom motorcycle company where he designed the 9ST; a moped far removed from the exotic Gilera and MV Agusta fours. In 1957 Remor became a consultant, and died in Rome in 1964.

Piero Remor at Monza in 1949. Still with Gilera, he was about to move to MV Agusta.

The success of the 125 during 1948 also led to Count Domenico Agusta developing a passion for motorcycle racing. Thus, the disappointment of the 1949 racing season was a bitter pill to swallow, and he was determined this failure would not be repeated. Towards the end of 1949 he approached Ing Piero Remor, designer of the remarkable postwar Gilera four, and in November 1949 Remor left the neighbouring Gilera factory in Arcore.

Remor's initial brief at MV Agusta was to create a new 125cc four-stroke double overhead camshaft racing twin. This heralded a change in emphasis for MV as it was designed purely as a racer with no connection to any production model. Remor also provided MV with a racing 500cc four that was remarkably similar to the 1948-49 Gilera, and it was no surprise that it took only 15 weeks from design drawings to the test bench. The Gilera 500 four had its origins in the Rondine liquid-cooled supercharged four Gilera acquired in 1936, but was originally an air-cooled design by Carlo Gianini and Remor of 1923. Both recent graduates from Rome University, Gianini and Remor reasoned that an across-the-frame layout would solve the problem of excessive length and inadequate cooling of the in-line four. Their design came to the attention of wealthy industrialist Count Giovanni Bonmartini, and in 1924 they formed the company GRB (Gianini Remor Bonmartini). This first engine displaced 500cc and featured a single overhead camshaft and exposed valve springs. While it produced a reputed 28 horsepower at 6000rpm the design languished until 1927 when Bonmartini, along with Count Lancelotti, formed a new company OPRA (Officine Romane di Precisione

By 1928 the GRB engine gained double overhead camshafts and was called the OPRA.

Autoveicole). A complete motorcycle was created, and in 1928 the engine gained double overhead camshafts and power was increased to 30.6 horsepower at 6400rpm, over 10 horsepower more than most of the competition at that time. In the hands of Piero Taruffi the OPRA won the 1928 Italian 500cc Championship, but disappointing results during 1929 resulted in its retirement.

Earlier (in 1919), Bonmartini had established the aircraft company CNA (Compagnia Nazionale Aeronautica), and with the Fascist government's encouragement of the aviation industry he had Gianini design experimental aeroplane engines. But in 1933, Bonmartini again became enthused with motorcycle racing, and instructed Gianini to resurrect the OPRA. The resulting racing engine was only loosely based on the OPRA as it was now water-cooled and supercharged, and had bore and stroke dimensions of 52x58mm instead of 51x60mm. The valves were inclined at 96 degrees instead of 90 degrees, with the cylinders inclined at 60 degrees. The cylinder head design was inspired by the Bugatti Type 51 Grand Prix engine, itself a copy of an American Miller, as was the use of a gear-driven Roots supercharger. The CNA Rondine (or Swallow) made its debut at the Tripoli Grand Prix in 1935 – Taruffi providing a surprising victory after the fancied Moto Guzzis retired. But in the process Bonmartini earned the ire of Tripoli Governor Italo Balbo by protesting the entry of Guzzi start Stanley Woods. A few months later Balbo became minister of aviation, and made life so difficult for Bonmartini in 1936 he sold CNA to the Caproni Aircraft Company in Milan.

With no interest in motorcycles at that stage, Caproni asked Taruffi to find a buyer for the six Rondine racers. He found a willing purchaser in Giuseppe Gilera at Arcore on the other side of Milan. Taruffi went to Gilera, and over the next few years the Rondine was developed into one of the most competitive 500cc racers of the era. Producing more than 70 horsepower at 8800rpm the 170kg Gilera was a formidable machine; Dorini Serafini beating the supercharged BMWs to win the 1939 European Championship. Although Gilera resurrected the

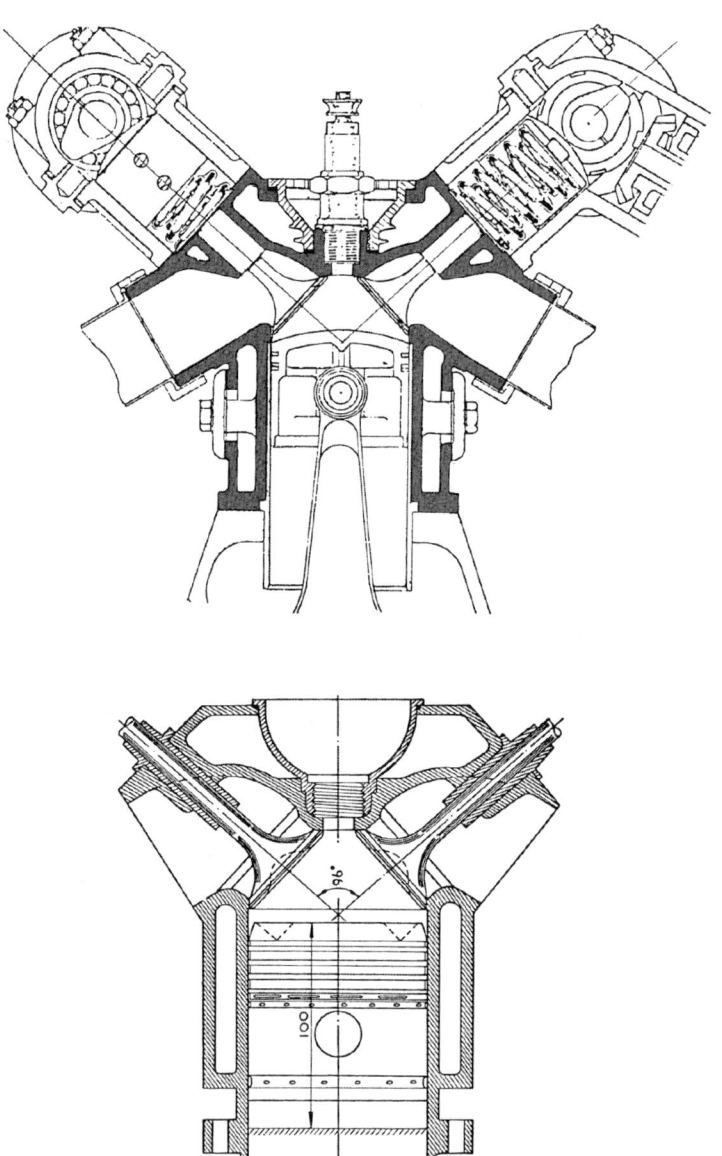

Although water-cooled, the Rondine engine had its origins in the earlier OPRA.

The Rondine cylinder head featured double overhead camshafts and a wide included valve angle.

BIRTH OF THE MV FOUR

supercharged racers briefly after the war, in November 1946 the FIM banned supercharging, and Gilera was forced to redesign its 500. But with Remor fully occupied with prototypes, it wasn't until 1947 that he was able to produce the new design. Unveiled in the Spring of 1948, Gilera's new 52x58mm 500 was now air-cooled, had separate

In 1939 the supercharged Gilera Rondine won the European Championship.

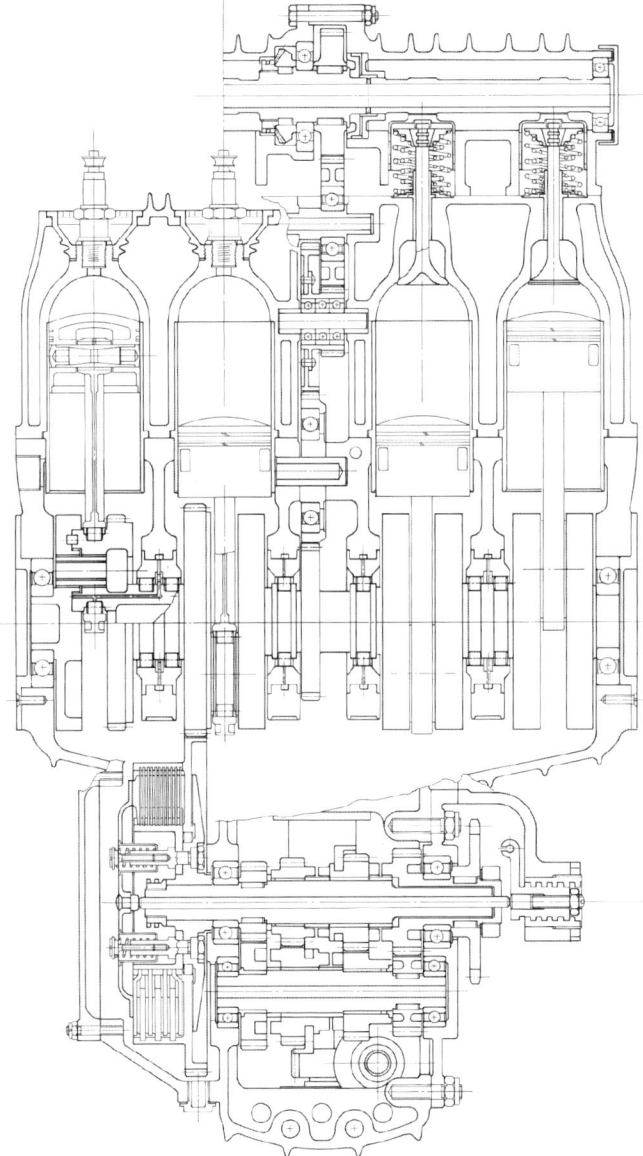

The origins of the MV Agusta four are clearly evident in the Rondine. The camshaft drive was from the centre of the crankshaft and primary drive to the multi-plate clutch between cylinders one and two.

Serafini at speed on the Rondine in the 1939 Ulster Grand Prix.

11

MV AGUSTA FOURS

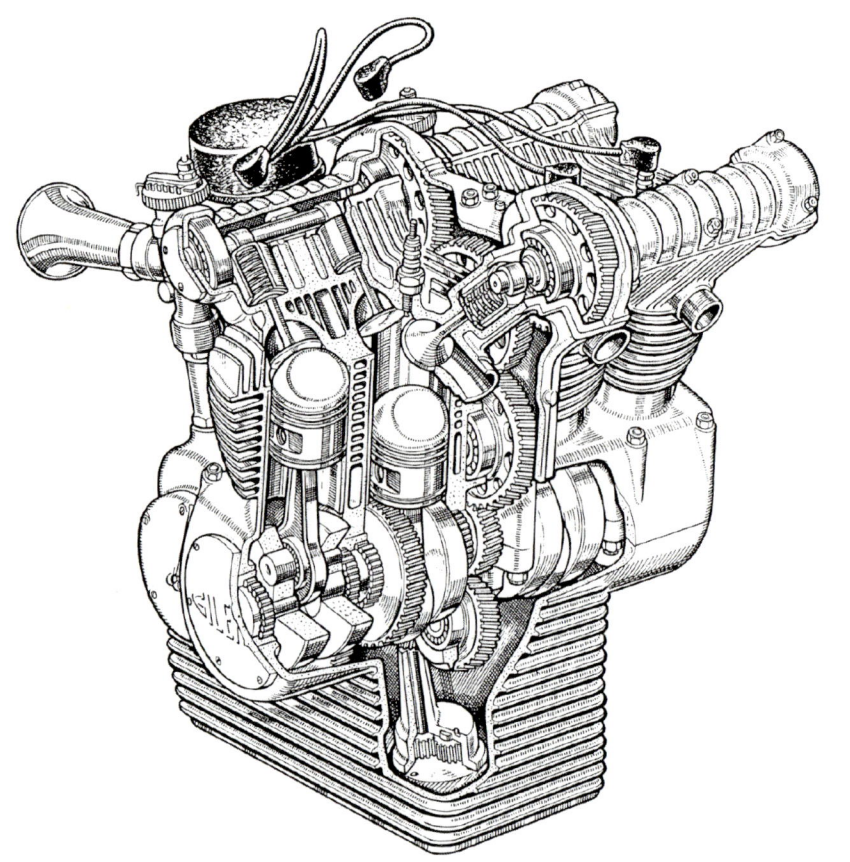

Remor's 500 Gilera design would form the basis of the MV four. The cylinders and cylinder head were in one piece.

joined by short forged rods. This allowed the final drive housing to arc along a straight line, and was an extremely advanced concept for the time. Torsion bars and adjustable friction dampers controlled the rear assembly, and the bike rolled on 20in wheels.

Unlike the chassis, the wet sump engine was very similar to the Gilera design; with light alloy cylinders cast in a block canted 30 degrees. This reasonably large inclination aided airflow over the top of the engine to helped cooling, but precluded the use of downdraft induction that would limit power later in the engine's development. Double overhead camshafts were driven by a train of centrally located spur gears, and the valves set at a 90-degree included angle closed by coil springs. At this time hairpin valve springs were generally preferred, but Remor claimed hairpin springs weighed four times more than coils. Although the Gilera four featured a one-piece casting

cylinders inclined at 30 degrees, dual 28mm Weber carburettors, power taken by gears between cylinders one and two to a wet clutch and four-speed gearbox, separate cylinders, paired heads, and one-piece camboxes. The two valves were inclined at 100 degrees. The early Gilera 500 was extremely light (at around 135kg) but, although fast, was initially unreliable due to a crankshaft lubrication problem. Remor's assistant Colombo solved the lubrication problem, and Remor took a set of blueprints that included these improvements with him to MV Agusta. The Gilera design continued with little revision until 1953, dominating Grand Prix racing for a decade until Gilera withdrew from competition at the end of 1957.

MV'S FIRST FOUR

When MV displayed the 500 four at the Milan Trade Fair in April 1950 it differed from the Gilera by featuring shaft final drive instead of chain and unusual torsion bar suspension front and rear. The front fork was a girder unit with chrome-molybdenum steel blades and four 6mm torsion bars, while the rear suspension consisted of doubled arms on each side

MV's 500 appeared only a few months after Remor left Gilera. The front fork was a girder type, with a torsion bar and a dual swingarm at the rear.

BIRTH OF THE MV FOUR

incorporating the cylinders and cylinder head, the MV cylinder head was detachable. The crank carrier and cylinders were cast as one-piece. The five bearing crankshaft and con rods were supported on roller bearings, the bore and stroke a square 54x54mm (as favoured by Remor), carburetion by a pair of Dell'Ortos, and ignition by a Vertex magneto with rotary magnets. This early engine also had central sparkplugs, as on the Gilera. Unlike the Gilera, the four-speed transmission was mounted longitudinally; the power transmitted from the engine by a pair of bevel gears and clutch downstream from the gearbox. Another unusual feature was the gear lever, which was a transversely-mounted rocking pedal. Upward changes were on the left and downward changes on the right. From the outset the MV 500 made competitive power, with 50 horsepower produced at 9000rpm. But although the engine was an immediate triumph, the eccentric chassis was flawed. Despite a light dry weight of only 118kg, the shaft drive combined with unusual suspension provided

The debut of the MV four at Belgium in 1950. The young Arturo Magni is on the left with his hand on the seat.

MV AGUSTA FOURS

Les Graham's first acquaintance with the MV four at Monza late in 1950. From left to right: Piero Remor, Bertacchini, Count Domenico Agusta, Bandirola Bertoni, Graham, the Count's mother Giuseppina, and Vincenzo Agusta.
(Courtesy Museo Agusta)

run on the factory test bench, ex-Gilera rider Artesiani managed a creditable fifth on the untested and ungainly MV 500. His race average speed of 99.83mph (160.66km/h) was impressive, but the remainder of the season proved difficult and the MV failed to live up to expectations. Artesiani's third place at Monza in the Nations Grand Prix was the highlight of the season, and Artesiani finished eighth overall in the World Championship. Count Agusta knew that without a top rider his dream of a 500cc World Championship would remain unattainable. During the off-season the 500 was redesigned, and 1949 World 500cc Champion Les Graham signed for 1951. In the meantime, a Grand Turismo version was produced and displayed at the Milan Show at the end of 1950.

500 GRAND TURISMO R19

By the end of 1950 the postwar resurgence of the Italian motorcycle industry was well under way, and the Milan Show was its showcase to the world. The 28th Milan Show opened on 3 December 1950, in the traditional prewar venue of the Palazzo Triennale. Count Domenico Agusta was determined to steal the show, and he did so with style by unveiling a street version of the 500cc Grand Prix four; the R19. Compared to every other motorcycle available at the time the R19 was unbelievably exotic, but, despite a list price of 950,000 Lire, was destined to remain unobtainable. MV Agusta continued to display the R19 at shows for several years but never put it into production.

Although only one example was built, the R19 was one of the most

awkward handling. It was at this stage that Remor requested a technician familiar with the four and able to appreciate its level of technological sophistication. Arturo Magni had worked with Remor at Gilera since 1947, and on 1 May 1950 Magni joined MV Agusta. Magni proved everything Remor and MV Agusta expected, and he would supervise the technical development of the racing bikes from 1950 until 1976. Although much credit has been given to the riding talent MV Agusta had available, without Magni's genius it is doubtful the MV racers would have been as dominant over such a long period.

MV was scheduled to appear at the first Grand Prix at the Isle of Man, to be ridden by Arcisco Artesiani (also from Gilera), Bertoni, and Magi, but the 500 wasn't ready. The first race for the MV four was the Belgian Grand Prix at the very fast Spa Francorchamps circuit on 5 July 1950. After a short twenty-minute

The spectacular R19 of 1951 was destined to remain a prototype.

BIRTH OF THE MV FOUR

Carburetion was by a pair of Dell'Orto 27mm SS 1 carburettors. The ignition distributor is behind the cylinders.

The R19's rear suspension arrangement included a double swingarm with torsion bar and friction dampers.

The R19 engine architecture would form the basis of all MV fours. Unlike the Gilera, the sparkplugs were centrally located.

MV AGUSTA FOURS

A speedometer and tachometer were positioned in the R19's fuel tank.

spectacular street motorcycles of the 1950s. The double overhead camshaft 494.4cc (54x54mm) four-cylinder engine was shared with the racer, and the cylinder head, including three outer vertical fins and three horizontal fins, would later feature on the GP bikes. Also like the later racing bikes, the cylinders and carrier were cast in one-piece, although this layout did make for more complicated assembly. Carburetion was by a pair of Dell'Orto 27mm SS1 D carburettors, but the ignition was by battery and coil (with a distributor behind the cylinders) and the exhaust system a two-into-one on each side. The sparkplugs were now angled and not centrally located as on the Gilera, a feature that would characterise all MV fours. The claimed power output was 38-40 horsepower at 8500rpm, providing a top speed of nearly 180km/h. These were astonishing figures for a production bike in 1950.

Some features of the 1950 GP bike were retained, including a four-speed gearbox, shaft drive, duplex cradle frame, and double swingarm with torsion bar and friction dampers. New for the R19 was a telescopic front fork, 230 and 220mm drum brakes, and Borrani light alloy 19in wheel rims shod with a Pirelli 3.00 tyre on the front and 3.50 on the rear. Rolling on a 1520mm wheelbase, the R19 was long and low, and stunning looking in metallic silver. The weight was only 155kg, and minimalist styling cues extended to the speedometer and tachometer incorporated in the 18-litre fuel tank. The original show bike had twin headlights, but a single unit later replaced these. After tantalising the public for several years with the prospect of a production version, eventually the R19 was forgotten, and it took 15 years for a street MV four to eventuate.

BIRTH OF THE MV FOUR

GRAND PRIX FOURS OF THE 1950S & 60S
1951

Possessing considerable developmental ability, Les Graham spearheaded a formidable rider line-up for the 1951 Grand Prix season. This included Artesiani, another former Gilera rider Carlo Bandirola, and, later in the season, ex-Moto Guzzi factory rider Bruno

Les Graham on the 500 MV in April 1951 at the Spanish Grand Prix. This was his first outing. While the front fork was now telescopic, the rear suspension was still by torsion bar and friction dampers.

Artesiani testing the 500 at Ospedaletti (San Remo) in October 1950. (Courtesy Museo Agusta)

Bertacchini. The 500 four was slightly redesigned; a telescopic front fork replacing the earlier girder type. The parallelogram swingarm and shaft final drive remained. According to Arturo Magni, the first test was in October 1950 at San Remo and at its first appearance in the opening round in Spain in early April 1951. The 500 still included torsion bar rear suspension with friction dampers, and the four-cylinder engine was very similar to the R19, with a one-piece cylinder block and carrier, and forward rotating crankshaft. It had full circle flywheels and steel con rods supported in roller bearings. According to Arturo Magni, "all the racing fours, right until 1966, had the one-piece cylinder and carrier casting. It made engine rebuilding more difficult, but we got used to it." Double coil valve springs operated the two valves (set at a 90 degree included valve angle) via short inverted bucket tappets. The Lodge 10mm sparkplugs were angled, and a narrow sump allowed the exhaust pipes to tuck in close to the engine. Carburetion was by a pair of Dell'Orto carburettors

Arcisco Artesiani testing the 500 at Monza late in 1950. (Courtesy Museo Agusta)

17

MV AGUSTA FOURS

Graham at the Isle of Man TT 1951. The MV 500 now had twin shock rear suspension.

with separate float chambers, ignition by a Lucas racing rotating magnet magneto driven by bevel gears and a shaft from the clutch pinion on top of the gearbox. The four exhaust pipes merged into two 457mm megaphones, and with a 9.5:1 compression ratio the power from the square 54x54mm design was 52 horsepower at 9000rpm. A more conventional gearshift arrangement was incorporated, and the 230mm front brake was the usual full width design (although still only single sided). Rolling on a pair of 20in wheels with 3.00 tyres, the 155kg 500 was capable of around 200km/h.

Artesiani finished third and Bandirola fifth in the Spanish GP, but that was the best result of the season. Bandirola managed fourth at the next round in Switzerland, and for the Isle of Man TT the 500 gained a pair of hydraulic shock absorbers. After a string of DNFs, four carburettors (no longer with individual external float chambers) and a fairing that encased the steering head and front section of the fuel tank appeared for the final race, the Nations Grand Prix at Monza, but the MV was still underdeveloped. While there had been some isolated victories in Italian Championship events (Bandirola winning at Ferrara on May 6 followed by Bertacchini at Varese) and in the UK (Les Graham at Thruxton), on the world stage the bikes were outclassed. The Gileras were still faster than the MVs, and handling of all the fours inferior to the Norton singles. But the woeful reliability during 1951 was the MV's downfall and Graham failed to score a single point. Although Artesiani salvaged some of MV's reputation with a class victory in the Milano Taranto road race, it was obvious the MV four needed considerable development. Remor left MV on his own volition at the end of 1951, and the 500 was extensively redesigned for the 1952 season.

Another view of Graham in the 1951 Senior TT.

BIRTH OF THE MV FOUR

1952

1952 was a landmark year for MV Agusta, Cecil Sandford providing its first world title – the 125cc World Championship. Alongside the 125, the 500 was also considerably more successful this year, mostly attributable to Les Graham's input into the design. According to Arturo Magni, "Les Graham was the best tester of all MV's riders. He

The 500 was redesigned for 1952, with a single swingarm and small fairing that blended into the tank.

MV also contested the Italian Championships. Here is Guglielminetti on the start line for the 1952 Monza GP.

was very technical and also a fantastic rider. He was the greatest of all MV's riders." Graham also managed to earn the respect of the difficult Count Domenico, who usually demanded control of every aspect of development. The Count provided Graham a free

Bandirola's 500 at the 1952 Swiss Grand Prix in April, with four carburettors and chain final drive. He finished third.

MV AGUSTA FOURS

Domenico Agusta making a movie of Graham, Sandford, and Lomas during a 1952 practice session at Monza. Two versions of the 500 four are evident. (Courtesy Museo Agusta)

Graham narrowly missed winning the 1952 Senior TT.

Graham testing the early Earles fork 500 at Monza in 1952.

hand in development, and he set about resolving the 500's handling and reliability problems. Graham engaged an old associate from his Velocette days, Ernie Earles, to assist in the design of the forks and frame, and engineers Mario Montoli and Mario Rossi undertook a redesign of the engine. The bore and stroke was changed to the 53x56.4mm of the 125cc racer, and the gradual shift to smaller bores and longer strokes during this period was to reduce piston failure as power and heat increased. With a compression ratio of 11:1, 34 and 32mm valves set at 90 degrees, four carburettors (although mostly two carburettors still featured in races), and siamesed exhausts, the power rose to 58 horsepower at 10,500rpm. But the most notable development was the incorporation of a transversely-

BIRTH OF THE MV FOUR

Graham flying through the air at the bumpy 1952 Ulster GP.

mounted five-speed gearbox and chain final drive on the right. The updated 500 also received a new duplex cradle tubular steel frame with single swingarm and hydraulic shock absorbers. Seeking an improvement in high-speed directional changing resulted in a gradual move to smaller diameter wheels, and the tyres were now a 3.00x19in on the front and 3.50x18in on the rear. With Graham leading the development of the chassis, for the first time MV (and Gilera) began to use Avon tyres (as used by the British manufacturers and preferred by British riders) in preference to its usual Pirelli. At some races, a small streamlined fairing was incorporated with the fuel tank, covering the steering head.

The redesign resulted in the MV four being considerably more competitive. Graham was holding second in the opening event in Switzerland before retiring when the rear tyre fouled the mudguards, but Bandirola finished third. Graham still found the handling wanting, and for the next race at the Isle of Man had an Earles fork installed. He went on to take second in the Senior TT, but he could easily have won if it wasn't for a long pit stop after missing a gear resulting in a loss of 800rpm, and also being slowed by an oil leak. A stroke of luck for winner Reg Armstrong occurred as his Norton primary chain broke while crossing the line – if the race had been a fraction longer Graham would have won.

With no points earned in Holland and Belgium, Graham battled bravely in the German Grand Prix at Solitude to finish fourth (although he had the consolation of setting the fastest lap at 135.962km/h (84.483mph). By now Masetti's Gilera was leading the title chase, but Graham led a determined charge at the Ulster Grand Prix before being forced to retire while in the lead. The rear tyre disintegrated after fouling the mudguard on the bumpy Clady course, but, again, Graham set the fastest lap (162.299km/h/100.848mph). New MV recruit Bill Lomas finished third.

Graham ended his season with two fine victories; at the Nations Grand Prix at Monza on September 14 (race average 171.158km/h/106.353mph), and the Spanish Grand Prix at the tight Montjuich circuit of Barcelona (race average 95.882km/h/59.578mph). The Monza win was particularly gratifying as it was MV's home circuit

The heavy landings destroyed the rear tyre.

MV AGUSTA FOURS

The shaft drive 500 was mainly used in the Italian Championships. Here is Bruno Francisci in practice at Monza during 1952. (Courtesy Museo Agusta)

and Graham led the 201km race from start to finish, earning an overwhelming ovation from the Italian crowd. Gilera protested, but after measuring Graham's machine for displacement the protest was disallowed. With the best five results counting towards the championship Graham needed Masetti to DNF at Barcelona, but he finished second. So MV missed its first 500cc World Championship by three points.

1953

For 1953 Les Graham moved his family to Italy, staying in Count Agusta's holiday home in the mountains near Verghera. Graham enjoyed an extremely close relationship with the Count and much was expected during 1953. There were only a few updates to the 500: the small fairing around the steering head was discarded, and exposed spring rear shock absorbers tested. Sandford joined Graham on the 500 and they, along with new signing Carlo Ubbiali, were also to ride 125s. Occasionally the earlier mounted four was also raced, now with an updated Earles fork layout.

The season began brilliantly for MV, Graham winning the 125 TT at the Isle of Man and MV occupying five of the top six positions.

Graham was an extremely brave rider, unperturbed by the bumps on the Clady course.

22

BIRTH OF THE MV FOUR

Graham also rode the earlier shaft drive four occasionally, here at Mettet early in 1953.

Then disaster struck. At the beginning of the second lap of the Senior TT Graham crashed the 500 MV heavily at the bottom of Bray Hill. It was assumed a retaining bolt for one of the Earles fork suspension legs had come loose, resulting in the suspension locked on full compression at the dip, but Arturo Magni says "He came down the hill at high speed and found two slower riders on his line. He lost control while changing line to avoid them." Graham crashed at around 210km/h (130mph) and was killed instantly. Australian Norton rider Ken Kavanagh was behind Graham on the road and said, "I came down Bray Hill and saw the MV on the ground so I stopped, but Les was dead." At that

MV AGUSTA FOURS

The 1953 team with the new 500 four. From left to right: Copeta, Dale, Bandirola, Ubbiali, Francisci, Lomas, Sandford, and Franzosi. (Courtesy Museo Agusta)

point Kavanagh retired. Although MV continued to contest the 125cc series, Count Agusta was devastated and withdrew the 500s until Monza in September. The Count was also determined to ascertain the cause of Graham's accident and had his riders test a variety of 500s at Monza. According to Cecil Sandford, "Dozens of different types of frames were tested and we went round and round Monza. We nearly made a groove we went round so many times. We weren't able to find out anything, but there was a feeling that it was something to do with the front forks." Sandford rode the 500 to 5th place in the Nations Grand Prix at Monza, with the German Hans Peter Müller sixth. Bandirola provided some hope for MV with a fine second in the

The 1953 version of the shaft drive four had an updated Earles fork layout.

BIRTH OF THE MV FOUR

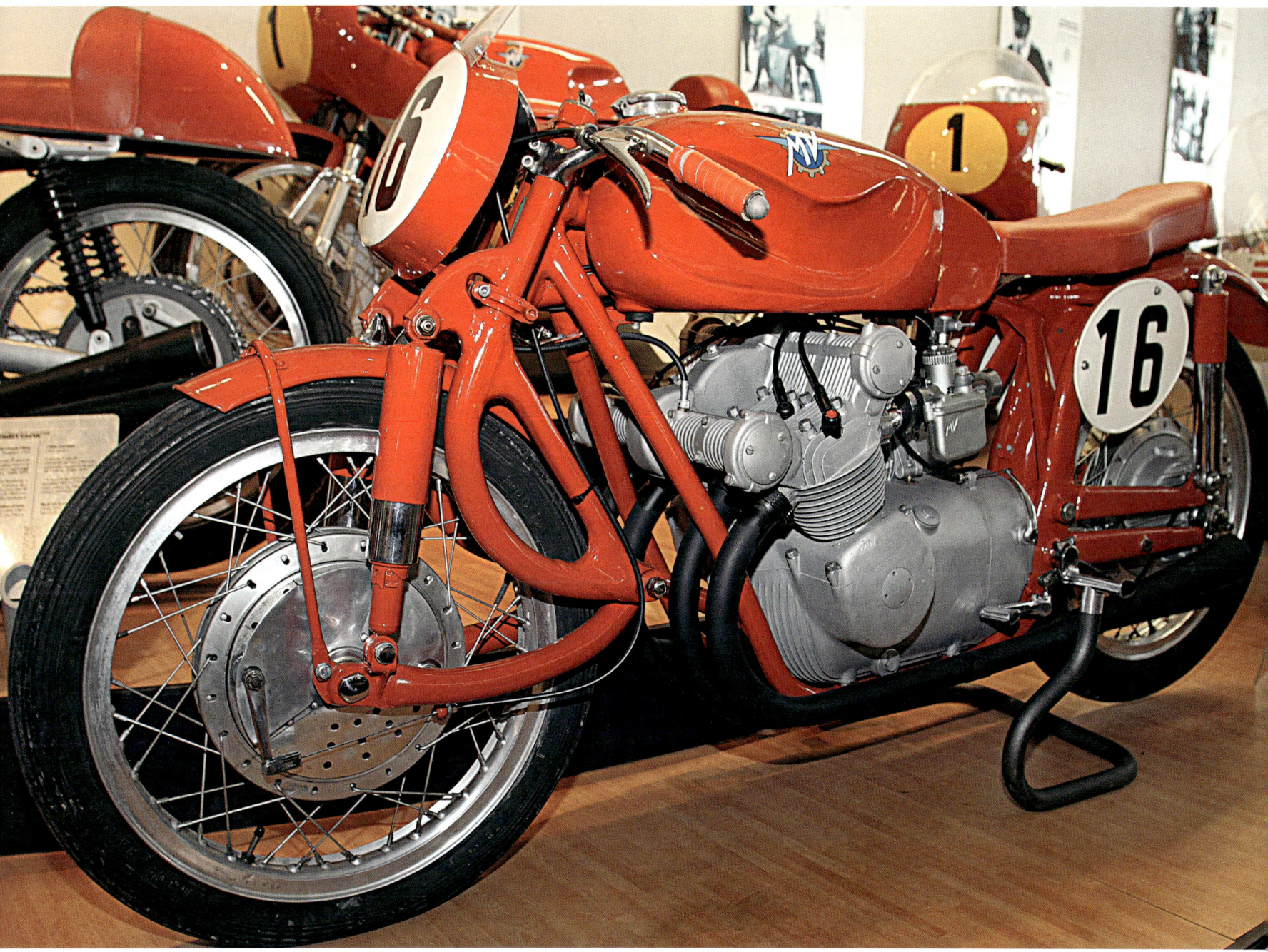

The 1953 500 in Museo Agusta. Apart from the remote float bowl carburettors and exhaust system, this is identical to Graham's bike in the previous photos.

final Grand Prix of the 1953 season at Barcelona. Sandford said later, "After testing tall ones, low ones, short ones and long ones, I finished with a short, low one, which suited me. But I realised that without Les my chances of getting an engine comparable to those of the Italian riders was fast diminishing."

Although 1953 was marred by Graham's death, it did see the unveiling of a new 350cc four-cylinder racer. Ostensibly a downsized 500, this was never originally intended as a serious racer and conceived as a training model, mainly because the 350cc class was virtually unknown in Italy. At that time 350 racing was dominated by

25

MV AGUSTA FOURS

Graham (right) with Arturo Magni and the 350 at the weigh-in for the 1953 Junior TT. Graham was killed in the Senior TT a few days later.

BIRTH OF THE MV FOUR

Bandirola gave the 350 its first victory at the 1953 German Grand Prix, but the results were later declared invalid.

Norton and AJS singles. Graham rode the 350 for the first time in the Junior TT a few days before his fatal accident, but was forced to retire early in the race with persistent clutch slip. Bandirola gave the 350 its first victory in the German Grand Prix at Schotten in July, but MV was denied an official victory when the results were declared invalid, as many top riders had boycotted the event on the grounds of safety.

This first 350 was simply obtained by sleeving the 500 engine to give a bore and stroke of 47.5x49.3mm. With four Dell'Orto SS1 28A carburettors like the 500, the power was 42 horsepower at 11,000rpm. While this was more than the British singles, the 350 was handicapped by being heavier, weighing 145kg. The 350 retained an Earles fork, and experimentation with straight arm linkages would see these adopted on the 500 during 1954.

1954

Searching for a Graham replacement, young British riders Bill Lomas

MV AGUSTA FOURS

Bill Lomas was signed as Graham's replacement for 1954. (Courtesy Museo Agusta)

Dickie Dale also rode the 500 during 1954. Here he is at Stockholm. (Courtesy Museo Agusta)

and Dickie Dale were signed alongside Bandirola and Pagani for 1954. Bandirola was nearly forty but still surprisingly competitive, while Pagani was approaching 43 years and in the twilight of a fine career. Pagani was chief tester during 1954 and would eventually become team manager. Continued development of the 500 four saw it producing nearly 60 horsepower, and a six-speed gearbox was installed. Girling or Armstrong rear shock absorbers replaced the earlier MV type, and the exhaust pipes were often straight, without megaphones. During the season, the Earles fork gained straight arms

The early 1954 version of the 500 with a small screen and open exhausts.

Bandirola was a new signing for 1954, riding in both the Italian and World Championships. (Courtesy Museo Agusta)

BIRTH OF THE MV FOUR

and fairings appeared. Although top speed approached 230km/h, MV was reluctant to follow the trend towards fairings because they made the tall, heavy 500s difficult to handle. Early season development was confined to the Italian Championships, and while Bandirola won at Modena without a fairing, by Ferrara a dolphin type unit covering the steering head appeared. At Monza Pagani won the 500 race with a half-dustbin type fairing. In the World Championships the 500 was fitted with different fairings to suit different riders and circuits, and at the Isle of Man Dale used another variation of the dolphin style (on the 350 as well as the 500), while Lomas' 500 had only a flyscreen for protection. Lomas' machine appeared with a 'fish mouth' fairing at Monza, while, in the only Grand Prix victory that season at the tight Barcelona circuit, Dale raced without a fairing. He won at 107.689km/h (66.915mph). Apart from this win, the 1954 season was one to forget for the 350 and 500 MV fours, Dale ending fourth in the 500cc World Championship.

MV experimented with a number of fairings during 1954. This is Bandirola's 500 at the Dutch TT, where he finished third.

Bill Lomas on the 500 at Faenza in 1954. The fairing is an early dolphin type.

MV AGUSTA FOURS

Dickie Dale on the 350 in the Isle of Man 1954 Junior TT. The Earles fork now had straight arms and the fairing was more abbreviated.

1955

Dale departed MV at the end of 1954, and in his place Count Agusta signed Rhodesian Ray Amm. Amm finished runner-up in both the 350 and 500cc classes on a Norton in 1954, and headed the normal line-up that included Bandirola, Pagani, and Ubbiali alongside another new recruit Tito Forconi. Lomas was still a member of the team, riding the new 250, while Luigi Taveri and Remo Venturi were signed to ride the 250 and 125. Pagani became team manager, and development to the 500 four resulted in an increase to 65 horsepower at 11,000rpm. Following Gilera's example, MV lengthened the stroke again, with bore and stroke now 52x58mm. The smaller piston reduced piston temperature, but the longer stroke design was delicate and fragile if over revved, as valve float remained a problem. According to Arturo Magni, "the MV always had a little more power than the Gilera, but still didn't handle as well."

Considerable time and effort was spent in chassis and streamlining development and 1955 saw a lower frame with detachable cradle to assist engine removal. The lower frame resulted in a lower riding position and allowed for a longer fuel tank. Early in the season an MV-designed and built telescopic leading axle fork with external coil springs above the fork sliders replaced the Earles fork, while twin MV or Girling shock absorbers controlled the rear. The steering head angle was 26 degrees, with the trail 115mm. Many fairings were tried this year; from the 'fish mouth,' a half-dustbin, to a full dustbin type, with or without air intakes. At some events unfaired bikes were raced.

Unfortunately, the season began

BIRTH OF THE MV FOUR

Ray Amm and the 350 MV prior to the 1955 Imola Gold Cup. It was his first race on the MV. Amm crashed during the race and was killed instantly.

Count Agusta at Monza in 1955 with (left to right) Pagani, Masetti, and Bandirola. (Courtesy Museo Agusta)

tragically for MV when Ray Amm crashed the 350 at Rivazza bend in his first race with the manufacturer, the Imola Gold Cup on 11 April 1955. Chasing former Norton team-mate Kavanagh on a Moto Guzzi, Amm hit a metal fence post and was killed instantly. It was another major blow for Count Agusta, who had already earmarked Amm as a successor to Les Graham. MV then engaged former Gilera double world champion Umberto Masetti, who rewarded them with a fine third behind Bandirola in the season opener, the Spanish Grand Prix at Montjuich. But this year Geoff Duke and the Gilera were dominant, and it wasn't until the final Grand Prix at Monza that MV tasted success in the 500cc class. After Duke retired Masetti battled with Reg Armstrong's Gilera, narrowly taking the victory at a race average of 177.395km/h (110.228mph). Count Agusta was so pleased with this victory he presented Masetti a one million Lire bonus.

MV AGUSTA FOURS

After the death of Amm, former World Champion Umberto Masetti assumed the position of lead rider in the MV team.

1956

MV Agusta mounted its largest offensive on the World Championships yet, entering all four solo classes in 1956. Although Ubbiali and Taveri were to dominate the smaller classes, Count Agusta was still searching for a Graham and Amm replacement. In the wake of these tragic deaths a question mark still hung over the handling of the MV four, and many established riders were wary. But British privateer racer and businessman Bill Webster persuaded the young up-and-coming John Surtees to visit Count Agusta at Gallarate at the end of 1955. Surtees was only 21-years-old but had already established an impressive

John Surtees signing with Count Agusta at the end of 1955. (Courtesy Museo Agusta)

BIRTH OF THE MV FOUR

John Surtees developed the MV 500 four into a World Championship winner for 1956. (Courtesy Roy Kidney)

The 1956 MV 500 epitomised elegance and function. (Courtesy Roy Kidney)

The engine for 1956 was largely unchanged. (Courtesy Roy Kidney)

Four Dell'Orto carburettors fed the engine, and ignition was by Lucas magneto. (Courtesy Roy Kidney)

MV AGUSTA FOURS

The front brake was by MV, and the front fork a leading axle type with exposed springs. (Courtesy Roy Kidney)

Surtees' first appearance on the MV four was at Crystal Palace in April 1956. Using a 1955 machine, Surtees comfortably won the race.

The 1956 500 frame was heavily braced around the steering head. This version also has additional bracing for the rear shock absorbers supports.

BIRTH OF THE MV FOUR

reputation on British short circuits on a works supported Norton. With no Norton ride on offer, Surtees accepted a contract to ride 350 and 500 MV fours during 1956. It would be the beginning of one of the most fruitful periods in MV racing history.

Surtees' first ride on the MV was at Modena in February, and he soon proved to be a superb developmental rider and worthy successor to Les Graham. According to Arturo Magni, Surtees exhibited extraordinary analytical racing intelligence. "He would analyse the lines of other riders and see how it affected carburetion. Surtees was always searching for improvements. He would even stop during a lap to change sparkplugs so we could check the mixture." After this initial testing at Modena and Monza Surtees was impressed with the four-cylinder engines, but suggested a modest frame redesign. Surtees also wanted reduced suspension travel, as he found the 150mm of travel detrimental to high-speed handling. New MV-built brakes included air scoops, the front 220mm still a single leading-shoe. The six-speed four-cylinder engine was largely unchanged from 1955, and with a compression ratio of 11:1 the power increased slightly to 67 horsepower at 10,500rpm. With an 11,000rpm redline there was still a very small over-revving margin. Although Gilera went to a wider 100-degree included valve angle in 1954, MV stayed with its 90-degree angle. For the Italian Championship round at Monza, ram-air intakes

Surtees at the start of the 1956 Junior TT. He retired in the race.

MV AGUSTA FOURS

Surtees on his way to MV Agusta's first 500cc victory at the Isle of Man in 1956, here rounding Parliament Square at Ramsey. This was the same 1955 machine that was raced at Crystal Palace.

for the carburettors were incorporated into the fairing. Rolling on 19 and 18in wheels with Avon tyres, the weight was now 164kg, the wheelbase a short 1360mm, and, with the new dustbin fairing, the 500 was capable of around 245km/h. The 350 was now producing around 48 horsepower, but still weighed 156kg, considerably more than the 120kg Moto Guzzi single.

In April 1956 Count Agusta sent Surtees to England with a 1955 500. After two victories at Crystal Palace and another two at Silverstone, the team went to the Isle of Man with high expectations. It was well rewarded. Although Surtees collided with a cow during the Senior TT final practice session, rendering the bike too damaged to race, he rode the 1955 bike to victory at an average speed of 155.413km/h (96.569mph). Surtees also set the fastest lap, at 157.331km/h (97.761mph), and it was very nearly a Junior/Senior double victory. Set to take victory in the Junior TT, Surtees' 350 four ran out of fuel with a quarter of a lap to go.

At the Dutch Grand Prix at Assen, Surtees took an easy victory at 132.651km/h (82.426mph), also finishing second to Lomas' Moto Guzzi in the 350cc race. A double 350/500 victory at Spa Francorchamps sealed the 500 World Championship for Surtees. The Belgian Grand Prix victory was particularly gratifying as it signalled the return of Geoff Duke and the Gilera after an FIM suspension for refusing to ride in the 1955 Dutch TT. Duke was out to prove the Gilera's superiority, and, although faster, was forced to retire while comfortably in the lead. Surtees won at a race average of 184.076km/h (114.380mph), backing this with a victory in the 350 race at 176.466km/h (109.651mph). Ubbiali's winning both the 125 and 250 races accompanied Surtees' two victories. 8 July 1956 was a great day for MV Agusta, with victories in all four classes, a record at the time.

After Belgium the season turned slightly

BIRTH OF THE MV FOUR

sour. At the next round, the German Grand Prix at Solitude, Surtees crashed in the 350 race, badly breaking his arm. Masetti managed second in the 500 race, but Surtees was ruled out for the rest of the season. Fortunately, he had enough of a lead in the 500 Championship, as only the best four results were counted. Ultimately, Surtees won by 8 points and, with Ubbiali taking the 125 and 250 titles, 1956 was the greatest season yet for MV Agusta, and Surtees' 500 World Championship the first for the double overhead camshaft four.

1957

After the success of 1956 much was expected during 1957, but the competition was hotting up, not only in the 500cc class but also in the smaller categories. Moto Guzzi's V8 threatened to obliterate the fours, so MV retaliated with a six-cylinder 500. The 48x46mm across-the-frame six had the cylinders canted forward 10 degrees, chrome-plated cylinder bores, and a central gear drive for the twin overhead camshafts. The cylinder head design, wet sump, and magneto ignition were similar to the four. With a 10.8:1 compression ratio and six Dell'Orto SS1 26A carburettors the power was 75 horsepower at 15,000rpm. A six-speed gearbox transmitted this power, and the double cradle frame design was similar to the four, also including a detachable lower cradle to facilitate engine removal. With 18in wheels front and rear, a 260mm four leading-shoe front brake, and 190mm twin leading-shoe rear brake, the 145kg six materialised too late. It didn't appear until the Nations Grand Prix at Monza in September; Pagani trying it in practice but it wasn't raced. Unfortunately, the unveiling of the six coincided with Gilera, Moto Guzzi and FB Mondial's announcement to retire from GP racing. With no competition the six was left without a raison d'être, but there were a few isolated outings during 1958.

Limited development of the 500 four for 1957 saw the frame, again,

A new lower frame was produced for 1957, but the 500 wasn't as successful as in the previous year. The distinctive arms for the rear shock absorbers remained.

37

Surtees finished fourth in the 1957 Junior TT on a bike fitted with a dustbin fairing.

Ken Kavanagh rode the 500 with a dustbin fairing at Monza in 1957. (Courtesy Museo Agusta)

lowered. The front fork remained the previous leading axle type, and throughout the season new versions of the dustbin fairing were tried, with the usual small fairing for tighter circuits. MV also produced a 350 twin and single, but their failure saw the perseverance with the heavier 350 four. MV's main problem this year was Surtees' slow recovery from injury and the team's gradual disillusionment as Gilera's four again established superiority. It wasn't only in the larger classes that MV suffered during 1957, as the new 125 and 250cc Mondials were faster than the MVs.

Surtees elected to ride with a half-fairing in the 1957 Senior TT, but couldn't match McIntyre's Gilera.

BIRTH OF THE MV FOUR

After a dismal German Grand Prix, where new signing Terry Shepherd's fifth in the 500 race was the best placing, Surtees took the 350 and 500 to the Isle of Man. Racing with a dustbin fairing, this year he finished fourth in the 350 Junior TT, but was forced to undertake two long pit stops to rectify sparkplug trouble. In the Senior TT Surtees elected to race without a fairing as gusty conditions were predicted. Surtees was never happy with the dustbin fairing on the MV. He found it unsafe as it meant the bike tended to take-off. He always felt that Moto Guzzi (with its wind tunnel) and Gilera managed to design a superior dustbin fairing to MV Agusta (despite MV's aeronautical connection). On race day for the Senior TT the weather was perfect, and Surtees couldn't match Bob McIntyre on the fully faired Gilera. McIntyre set the first 100mph lap ever on the TT course and Surtees was second, more than two minutes in arrears. Surtees wouldn't score any more points on the 350 this year, but won the next 500 GP at Assen easily, at 132.851km/h (82.550mph). This was to be his only victory of the season, retiring with piston problems at Belgium and Ulster. He did have the consolation of setting the fastest lap at Ulster (154km/h/95.691mph). For Ulster, Surtees persuaded Count Agusta to incorporate a new front fork and this improved the handling, but with only the Nations Grand Prix at Monza remaining the championship was lost. Surtees did manage to dice with Liberati for the lead for half the 500 race, but engine problems saw him finish fourth, just ahead of Masetti and Shepherd. Ken Kavanagh also rode the 500 at Monza. Lured from Moto Guzzi, Kavanagh somehow spent more time watching the MVs than riding them.

So MV Agusta finished the 1957 season with no World Championships, not even a manufacturer's award. Surtees was third in the 500cc Championship, only bettered by Taveri's second in the 125 title. But with its three main rivals no longer racing, MV looked forward to a new era of domination.

1958

Over the winter of 1957 considerable effort was expended to overcome the mechanical problems that had plagued the MV four during the previous season. Different pistons and valve springs were tried, and power was 70 horsepower for the 500 and 45 horsepower for the 350. A wider power band, now from 4500-10,500rpm, allowed Surtees to control rear wheel drift on bumpy circuits. Surtees designed a new frame, and MV produced a new four leading-shoe

In an otherwise unsuccessful year, Gilberto Milano (left) provided MV with the 1957 Junior Italian Championship. (Courtesy Museo Agusta)

39

MV AGUSTA FOURS

John Hartle (right) joined Surtees on the 350 and 500 MV fours in 1958.

front brake similar to the type Gilera had in 1957. This year saw the banning of full dustbin fairings, so the MV fours ran with new red and silver dolphin fairings. John Hartle (who had joined MV to ride a 250 after Colombo's death in Belgium in 1957) moved up to be Surtees' support rider in the 350 and 500cc championships. Without any competition from the other Italian factories, they proved an unbeatable combination; the MV fours far superior to the British singles. But the fours were still relatively heavy and bulky machines and although Surtees made winning look easy, the results were as much a tribute to his expertise in developing the machine as to its

BIRTH OF THE MV FOUR

Surtees setting off in the 1958 Senior TT. Dustbin fairings were banned this year. (Courtesy Two Wheels)

MV AGUSTA FOURS

Hartle had a less successful year than Surtees, but still finished second in the 350 and 500cc World Championships. Here he is on his way to finishing third at Ulster. His 500 MV four retains the earlier fork with external springs.

inherent superiority. Surtees pioneered a new cornering style to suit the MV four; hanging inside the bike to keep it more upright and prevent the wide engine grounding, while introducing controlled rear wheel drift. This way Surtees overcame the deficiencies of the greater weight and higher centre of gravity.

Surtees also responded to the gradual improvement in Avon tyres by improving the chassis. The single backbone duplex frame included a swingarm braced to the engine by the gearbox lugs. Although a leading axle fork with external springs was sometimes fitted, Surtees mostly raced with a centre axle fork with internal springs. The Girling shock absorbers still connected to the frame by individual extensions on either side. The wheels were now 18in front and rear, although rim width remained at a narrow WM2 (1.85in) because wider rims increased the tyre's rolling resistance and reduced top speed.

At the Isle of Man Surtees led the Junior TT from start to finish, at 151.230km/h (93.970mph), while Hartle retired with piston failure. In the Senior TT, Hartle's MV caught fire at Governor's Bridge after the fuel tank split, but Surtees went on to win at 158.735km/h (98.633mph). Surtees' double victory was simply a prelude to total dominance that year. He repeated the 'double' in Holland, Belgium, Germany, Ulster, and Italy, securing both World Championships with maximum points. Hartle finished second to Surtees in every 350 race after the Isle of Man, and in two 500 GPs, to finish second in both championships. Hartle also rode the 500 six at the Nations Grand Prix at Monza but retired. MV Agusta won all four World Championship categories contested in 1958, heralding the beginning of a golden era for the racing motorcycles from Casina Costa. Veteran rider Carlo Bandirola also won the 1958 500cc Italian Championship.

Celebrating victory in the 1958 Senior TT – the beginning of a successful season. Surtees' MV is flanked by the Nortons of second-placed Bob Anderson (right), and Bob Brown. (Courtesy Two Wheels)

BIRTH OF THE MV FOUR

allow a different position for the Girling shock absorbers, and the front brakes received larger air scoops. The compression ratio was over 11:1, carburetion still by four 26mm Dell'Orto carburettors, and the maximum power of 70 horsepower was produced at 10,700rpm. This provided only a 300rpm margin between peak power and valve float.

As the 350 was still a sleeved down 500, it came in for some serious weight reduction through the use of materials from Agusta's aeronautical division. This resulted in a reduction of 20kg, virtually ensuring the 350 was unassailable, especially in the hands of Surtees. In the first Grand Prix of the season (at Clermont-Ferrand) Surtees won the 350 and 500 races by over a minute in each. This year Remo Venturi replaced Hartle on the 500, although Hartle remained on the 350, and rode the 500 at the Isle of Man.

At the Isle of Man Surtees became the first to equal Stanley

Tino Brambilla rode in the 1958 Italian Championship. Here he is before the start at Cattolica. (Courtesy Museo Agusta)

1959

As the only factory team contesting the 350 and 500cc classes, MV could have simply rested on its laurels and raced the 1958 bikes for another season. But although the 350 and 500 fours were clearly superior to the Norton singles and BMW twins that filled most of the Grand Prix grids, MV continued to develop the fours, in particular the 350. The 500's frame was again modified, with detachable lower tubes further improving rigidity. The rear frame section was also modified to

Surtees on his way to victory in the 1959 French Grand Prix. (Courtesy Museo Agusta)

Surtees on his way to a comfortable victory in the 1959 Senior TT.

Woods' Junior and Senior TT Double in successive years. He romped to victory in the Junior TT at 153.530km/h (95.399mph), with Hartle second, but bad weather delayed the start of the Senior TT 24-hours. In cold and uncomfortable conditions Surtees set an astonishing fastest lap of 162.839km/h (101.183mph), winning by more than 5 minutes after most of his competitors crashed or retired in the gusty conditions.

The 1959 season was incredible for Surtees. He won all seven 350 and 500 Grands Prix, finishing at Monza where he shattered the lap record at 191.844km/h (119.206mph) and won the 500cc race at 185.436km/h (115.225mph). Venturi came second, and finished second in the 500cc World Championship. Hartle again finished second in the 350cc championship, and Ubbiali won both the 125 and 250cc titles. It had been another season of dominance for MV and while some treated Surtees' success with scepticism because the MV was so superior to the competition, he was undoubtedly the class rider.

1960

There were few changes to the MV Agusta team for 1960. Emilio Mendogni was signed to ride 500s alongside Surtees, Hartle, and Venturi. Hartle was also to ride the 350, and the Rhodesian, Gary Hocking, was signed alongside him. Hocking had impressed Count Agusta by finishing second in the 1959 250cc World Championship on the temperamental MZ, and was to ride the 125, 250, and 350. Although they were so dominant during 1959, the MV fours were further developed by Surtees and featured a new twin loop frame. This followed the style of the final Gilera four,

Hartle only rode the 350 during 1959, here on his way to second (behind Surtees) in the Junior TT. The 350 benefited from considerable development this season and was much more compact than before.

BIRTH OF THE MV FOUR

Remo Venturi was Surtees' team-mate on the 500 during 1959, finishing second in the World Championship. Venturi's bike also retained the earlier fork. (Courtesy Museo Agusta)

with more bracing and revised shock absorber mounts, and during the season an eccentric chain adjuster was incorporated at the swingarm pivot. As before, the wheels were narrow rimmed 18in, with Avon tyres. This year MV also took a step down a different road by producing a 350 (actually 286cc) out of one of its all-conquering 250 twins. Although 10 horsepower down on the 350 four, the twin was 30kg lighter and Hocking won the 350 race at the first Grand Prix at Clermont-Ferrand. Surtees was expected to triumph on the four and finished third after setting the fastest lap. Surtees easily won the 500cc race, with Venturi second. Both Surtees and Hocking favoured the new twin on tighter circuits, but MV continued with the downsized 500 four until Honda finally beat it with its enlarged 250.

At the Isle of Man Surtees was denied the opportunity to be the first rider to win the Junior/Senior double three times in a row when mechanical problems forced him to slow in the 350cc Junior TT. Although Surtees set the fastest lap of 159.646km/h (99.199mph), Hartle took the lead on the fifth lap and won by nearly two minutes at a record speed of 155.620km/h (96.698mph). In the 500cc Senior TT Surtees was untroubled, setting both a new lap record of 167.506km/h (104.083mph) and race record at 164.326km/h (102.445mph). Surtees became the first rider to win the Senior TT three times running, and equalled Stanley Woods' record of four Senior victories. Hartle was

The four-cylinder engine was largely unchanged, but continually refined.

Emilio Mendogni on the MV 350 during 1959. (Courtesy Museo Agusta)

MV AGUSTA FOURS

Despite its clear superiority, Surtees continued to develop the MV four and a new frame was produced for 1960.

second and had lost favour with Count Agusta, so was dropped. Always a talented rider, his two years playing second fiddle to Surtees hadn't proved very satisfactory and he missed many races through injury.

At the next round at Assen Surtees beat Hocking in the 350cc event, winning at 134.522km/h (83.588mph), but retired in the 500cc race, allowing Venturi to win. Venturi's winning speed of 134.652km/h (83.669mph) was barely faster than Surtees' 350 race average, and

Although he had lost favour with Count Agusta, Hartle still won the 1960 Junior TT. (Courtesy Museo Agusta)

Venturi also finished second in the 1960 500 World Championship.

was an indication of the disparity between Surtees and the rest of the field. Without a 350cc GP at Belgium, Surtees romped away in the 500cc event to win at an incredible average speed of 198.982km/h (120.535mph). His new lap record was an equally staggering 197.433km/h (122.679mph). Next it was to Solitude in Germany where, again, there wasn't a 350cc race. This time Surtees led an MV clean sweep, Venturi and Mendogni completing the podium. This event was marred by the death of Hocking's friend, Australian rider Bob Brown, killed practising a 250 Honda.

With the 500cc World Championship already sealed, Surtees now had only to win the 350cc GP at Ulster to complete his third 350/500cc

BIRTH OF THE MV FOUR

Hocking won the 1960 350 Grand Prix at Monza on the new 350 four. (Courtesy Museo Agusta)

double World Championship in a row. This he did comfortably, but had a more difficult race in the 500. Hartle, now on a private Norton, won after a broken gear lever resulted in a lengthy pit stop for Surtees. With 18 laps to go Surtees joined the race three minutes behind and in 42nd place, finally finishing second, only 19 seconds in arrears.

At the final GP of the season, the Nations Grand Prix at Monza, a new version of the 350 appeared, with a larger sump, smaller fairing, and a space-frame rear section. At the same meeting Emilio Mendogni tested a 500 with a new triangulated rear section to the frame. This was to be Surtees' final race for MV, and he won the 500 race at 185.105km/h (115.019mph), but retired in the 350 event. On the new 350 Hocking won the 350cc race at 176.587km/h (109.726mph). 1960 was the third successive year MV had won all four Grand Prix classes, and in only ten years had secured 17 individual World Championships, 82 classic victories, and 19 manufacturers' titles. It was a remarkable achievement, but big changes were afoot.

1961

At the end of 1960 Surtees retired from motorcycle racing to concentrate on racing cars, and in 1964 became the only person ever to win the 500cc Motorcycle World Championship and Formula One car title (with a 1.5-litre Ferrari). Carlo Ubbiali also hung up his leathers and these retirements, along with the increasing competitiveness of the new Hondas, prompted Count Agusta to retire from World Championship racing and concentrate on the Italian Championships. Although recently promoted to ride the MV 350 and 500, Gary Hocking was left stranded. He unsuccessfully sought a ride with Honda, but eventually the Count agreed to provide 350 and 500cc machines, along with a couple of mechanics, for the World Championships. Hocking jumped at the chance, the bikes carrying 'Privat' tank decals to indicate they were no longer full works bikes. There was also little development, and the fours were much the same as for 1960. Four 28mm Dell'Orto carburettors fed the engine, the

47

MV AGUSTA FOURS

compression ratio was 11.5:1, and power was up to 72 horsepower at 10,700rpm.

The MVs may have been carrying 'Privat' badges but there was no denying they were still superior to the predominately Norton (and Jawa in the 350) mounted field. And while Hocking's relationship with the Count was uneasy, he proved a worthy successor to Surtees, totally dominating the 500cc class. In the opening round at Hockenheim he won by more than a lap at 193.552km/h (120.268mph), following this with another easy victory at Clermont-Ferrand. But after years of dominance, the 1961 Isle of Man TT was a disaster for MV. The 350 went off song after Hocking set the fastest lap and he finished second to Phil Read's Norton, while Mike Hailwood's Norton was untouchable in the Senior TT. Hocking again set the fastest lap at 165.15km/h – slower than Surtees' record set the previous year – but he failed to finish.

Controversy surrounded Hocking's tactics in the Dutch TT are Assen, and Count Agusta was infuriated. In the 350 race Hocking was determined to beat Bob McIntyre's Bianchi, elbowing his way past the Scottish rider on the final lap. Although his tactics were frowned upon, he won the race and led the World Championship. Hocking also won the 500cc event, following this with victories in Belgium, East Germany, and Ulster. He also won the 350cc races at Sachsenring (East Germany) and Ulster, sealing both world titles. But Hocking had such little opposition that his victories at Spa and Ulster were considerably slower than Surtees in 1960.

Not only was Hocking's relationship with Count Agusta strained, the Count was looking out for another rider of the 'Privat' fours for 1962. Again he turned to Bill Webster as his talent scout, and Bill recommended Mike Hailwood. Honda was fresh from three TT

After Surtees' retirement, Gary Hocking raced the MVs without official factory support, but easily won the 350 and 500cc World Championships. Here he is on the 350 on his way to victory at Assen. (Courtesy Museo Agusta)

BIRTH OF THE MV FOUR

Hocking set the fastest lap in the 1961 Senior TT, but failed to finish. (Courtesy Museo Agusta)

Hocking at speed at Imola in 1961. (Courtesy Museo Agusta)

great era. Surtees had given MV dominance for four years and Hailwood would repeat this. Between 1962 and 1965 Hailwood won all but three of the 500cc races he entered, while at the same time competing in two, or even three, GP races in other classes on the victories and, after Ulster, Hailwood was on track to winning the 250cc World Championship on a Honda. He also wanted to move into the heavier classes. During 1957 Hailwood began his racing career on one of Webster's 125 MVs, and Webster convinced the Count to offer Hailwood a ride on the 350 and 500 for Nations Grand Prix at Monza. This was a blow to Hocking as he didn't really need to win at Monza, and he soon came to resent Hailwood. In the 500 race at Monza Hocking crashed after his footpeg dug into the ground, leaving Hailwood to win at a new record speed of 187.490km/h (116.501mph). Hocking managed to overcome Hailwood's challenge in the 350cc event, winning at a new record of 181.590km/h (112.835mph). Although Hocking impressed with new lap records in both the 350 and 500 races, his days of easy victories were quashed when the Count told Hailwood he wanted him on the team for 1962.

1962

With the signing of Mike Hailwood, MV Agusta entered into its next

The 1962 Junior TT saw a tremendous battle between Hailwood (3) and Hocking (6), with Hailwood winning by 5.6 seconds. (Courtesy Museo Agusta)

49

MV AGUSTA FOURS

Hocking made amends by winning the 1962 Senior TT, but it was his final race on the MV. (Courtesy Museo Agusta)

same day. With two top riders on equal machinery, the 1962 season promised to be exhilarating. Honda was also to compete in the 350cc class for the first time, its new RC170 four a larger version of the successful RC162 250. The 350cc World Championship would be a battle between a scaled up 250 (285cc later enlarged to 339cc) Honda and the scaled down 500 MV four. With little competition in the 500cc class the larger MV four was essentially unchanged from the previous year.

From the outset it was obvious there would be little cooperation between the two MV riders and, after Hocking won the Imola Gold Cup Grand Prix, the season started off with an incredible duel in the Junior TT at the Isle of Man. Racing each other on the road for most of the six laps, Hailwood eventually won by only 5.6 seconds, setting new lap and race records in the process. Hocking had his revenge in the Senior TT when Hailwood was forced to slow with clutch trouble. Hocking won at a new race record speed of 166.583km/h (103.510mph), also setting a new lap record of 170.193km/h (105.753mph). But this was to be his final race for MV. Following the death of his friend, 125cc World Champion Tom Phillis in the Junior TT at the Isle of Man, Hocking decided to quit motorcycle racing, return to Rhodesia and switch to car racing. Unfortunately, his dream of success on four wheels never eventuated as, during practice for the Natal Grand Prix in South Africa on 21 December 1962, his Lotus 24 failed to take a corner. The Rob Walker Racing Team Lotus somersaulted and Hocking died of head injuries.

With the departure of Hocking, the great Mike Hailwood was MV's only rider in the 350 and 500 classes. But, even with Hailwood in the saddle, the 350 was no match for Redman's Honda. After the Isle of

BIRTH OF THE MV FOUR

Man Hailwood didn't win another 350 event, eventually finishing third in the Championship. It was another story in the 500cc class, Hailwood winning at Assen, Spa, Ulster, Sachsenring and Monza. He also set new race records in the last three, culminating in a race average at Monza of 187.563km/h (116.540mph). With the title won, MV didn't even contest the final two events in Finland and Argentina.

1963

A surprising move at the beginning of 1963 saw Gilera resurrect its 1957 500cc fours. In this unofficial comeback, Gilera provided the fours to former champion Geoff Duke, who formed Scuderia Duke and signed Derek Minter and John Hartle as riders. Duke had tried to persuade Gilera to lend him the machines as early as 1961 and eventually it agreed, on the condition that Bob McIntyre rode them. McIntyre had earned the respect of Giuseppe Gilera after setting

Hailwood with Carrano and father Stan at Monza 1962. (Courtesy Museo Agusta)

Mike Hailwood with Carrano and the 500 at Mallory Park in 1963. (Courtesy Two Wheels)

Hailwood on the 350 four in 1962. Still ostensibly a downsized 500, the 350 was no match for Redman's Honda. (Courtesy Museo Agusta)

51

MV AGUSTA FOURS

Hailwood won the 1963 Senior TT in record time. (Courtesy Museo Agusta)

the one-hour record in 1957. After McIntyre was killed in August 1962, Duke was lent one of the fours for a lap of honour at Oulton Park in his memory. Minter and Hartle then went to Monza where they lapped close enough to Surtees' record to persuade Gilera to continue to lend Duke the fours.

Although Minter provided some morale boosting victories at Brands Hatch, Oulton Park and Imola prior to the Grand Prix season, the much-anticipated Grand Prix challenge didn't materialise. The MV four was still remarkably similar to the 1957 version, but years of development by Surtees and Hailwood resulted in a finer handling motorcycle. The Gilera was arguably superior to the MV back in 1957, but it had not benefited from any rider development. Other problems beset the Gilera challenge, too. Minter claimed Hartle's machine was faster, and he had a disagreement with Duke, but a more serious impediment occurred in May at Brands Hatch. Minter's Gilera was hit by Dave Downer's Dunstall Norton 650 on the final lap, Minter breaking his back and Downing being fatally injured. Phil Read was drafted in to replace Minter for the first three Grands Prix.

BIRTH OF THE MV FOUR

Hailwood at speed on the 350 MV at Assen in 1964. He finished second, his only result for the season in this class on the ageing four. (Courtesy Museo Agusta)

At the first round, the Isle of Man, Hailwood was untroubled. He won the Senior TT at a record 168.402km/h (104.640mph) with a fastest lap of 171.259km/h (106.415mph), ahead of Hartle's Gilera by more than a minute. Read was third. Although Hartle won at Assen (after Hailwood's engine expired on the second lap), Hailwood demolished the field at Spa with a blistering race average of 199.539km/h (123.988mph). His fastest lap was an astonishing 202.151km/h (125.611mph), amazing when you consider the narrow Avon tyres and rudimentary suspension of the early 1960s. Record race victories at Ulster, Sachsenring, Tampere (Finland), Monza and Argentina ensured Hailwood's second 500cc title. At Monza he won by two laps from Jack Findlay's Matchless at 190.008km/h (118.065mph) with a fastest lap of 193.097km/h (119.985mph). Ultimately, the Gilera challenge faded, but much of this was due to circumstance and the brilliance of Hailwood. But Hailwood had to work harder than usual for his victories.

Again Redman's Honda outclassed the 350 MV. Although little changed for 1963, the Honda RC171 now produced 52 horsepower, just enough to see off Hailwood on the old MV and John Hartle on the even older Gilera. Breathing through four Dell'Orto 25mm carburettors, and with a compression ratio of 10.4:1, the MV 350 four produced 52 horsepower at 11,000rpm. The tyres were 3.00x18in on the front and 3.50x18in on the rear, and at 145kg it was capable of around 240km/h. Although Hailwood won at Sachsenring and Tampere, managing second in the 350cc World Championship, Redman again proved an enlarged 250 was still a better formula for a 350 than a downsized 500.

1964

Still entered under the 'Privat' banner, by 1964 Count Agusta had lost interest in the 350cc class and Hailwood rode the 350 occasionally only. He finished second to Redman at Assen and rode an MZ at Suzuka after the 500cc season was completed. The 350 MV may have been outclassed, but Hailwood was still untroubled in the 500cc class, winning all seven races he entered. Hailwood may have claimed to be technically ignorant but he ensured MV constantly tested new brakes, forks, rear suspension, and frames so the 500 handled acceptably. By now suspension damper design had progressed, and the Girlings were more sophisticated than the older two-orifice, one-way valve types. These

Again Hailwood won the 'Race of the Year' at Mallory Park on the 500. (Courtesy Museo Agusta)

53

MV AGUSTA FOURS

Hailwood on his way to victory in the 1964 US Grand Prix at Daytona. (Courtesy Museo Agusta)

new shocks improved low speed bump control and paved the way for the big, heavy MV four to adjust to the next technical revolution; Dunlop's new triangular tyres. The rear tyre was initially the only one triangulated, but soon this profile predominated front and rear. The Dunlop triangular tyres provided a wider footprint while leaned over, but the narrow central region resulted in a tyre that responded very quickly to steering input, leading to instability. MV began to experiment with steering head angle and trail – varying the trail with axle clamps to provide different offsets – and settled on around a 27-28 degree steering head angle to best provide stability.

The 1964 results were also a tribute to the incredible reliability of the MV four, a feature emphasised at Daytona prior to the opening United States Grand Prix. Hailwood decided to take advantage of the Daytona Speedbowl that was being used for the first time in a Grand Prix to attempt two speed records (see sidebar on page 60). A shipping mix-up saw only one bike arrive, which also had to serve in the Grand Prix in the afternoon following the morning record attempt. For the first time in several years Hailwood was pushed hard in the race, and from a surprising competitor. Little know Argentinean Benedicto Caldarella, whose family worked for Gilera in South America, obtained one of the Duke Gileras at the end of 1963. In the race, Caldarella stayed close to Hailwood for 14 laps of the Daytona Speedbowl before gearbox trouble forced his retirement. Hailwood went on to win at 161.168km/h (100.145mph) but the prospect of more close racing kept the series alive. Unfortunately, industrial disruption ruined Caldarella and the Gilera's prospects for much of the season, but they still provided competition for Hailwood at Assen and Monza.

At Assen the Argentinean stuck close to Hailwood before losing control on the long curve leading onto the front straight and careering onto the grass. He re-mounted but Hailwood was now long gone and

BIRTH OF THE MV FOUR

won easily. The closest race of the season was the Nations Grand Prix at Monza, and again it was Caldarella who hounded Hailwood. Ultimately, Hailwood won by 11 seconds at a record average speed of 191.758km/h (119.153mph), although Caldarella was credited with the fastest lap. Apart from the Nations Grand Prix, Hailwood's race winning speeds this season were slower than for 1963. That he still won by large margins (up to 4½ minutes) was indicative of the superiority of both Hailwood and the MV four. But it was only the 500 MV that was competitive, as Japanese manufacturers now controlled all the smaller classes, once MV Agusta's preserve. The 350 four was now outclassed, but Count Agusta remained reluctant to lend the new triple to Hailwood for fear he would crash it and jeopardise his chance of winning the 500 title. Hailwood chose to race an MZ at the final 350 Grand Prix of the 1964 season, and there were already signs of Hailwood's discontent at MV Agusta.

1965

By 1965 MV Agusta had won the 500cc title seven consecutive times, but the monopoly they once had in the 350cc class was now relinquished to Honda. Although some observers expected Count Agusta to finally capitulate and retire from racing, MV resurrected the challenge for the 350cc title. Determined to win back the 350cc

Following a crash in treacherous conditions, Hailwood re-mounted to win the 1965 Senior TT. The windscreen was shattered and a footrest bent. (Courtesy Museo Agusta)

Hailwood leading Agostini in the 1965 500cc German Grand Prix. Hailwood went on to win. (Courtesy Museo Agusta)

Championship, Count Agusta engaged riding prodigy Giacomo Agostini, and finally released the new three-cylinder 350 that was lighter, had a narrower frontal area, and handled better than the four. Only 22-years-old, Agostini was fresh from winning the 1964 Italian Senior Championship on a Morini and, because he was Italian, Count Agusta was grooming him to be his future star rider. But in 1965 that had to wait. Although Hailwood enjoyed a somewhat turbulent relationship with the Count, he was still the number one rider.

The 1965 season was to be the final full season for the

Another 500cc victory for Hailwood, this time at the 1965 Dutch TT. (Courtesy Museo Agusta)

BIRTH OF THE MV FOUR

venerable 500 four, and, as before, it was totally dominant. Largely unchanged from 1964, during the season a square section swingarm was tested and this would eventually make its way onto the next generation of racers. Hailwood won eight Grands Prix, and Agostini one (at Imatra when Hailwood retired). Hailwood said later of the MV four that it was the most enjoyable bike he ever rode. "The MV develops so much power that I am not sure that anyone has yet succeeded in getting the best out of it, simply because the rider's limitations are greater than those of the bike." His victory in the Senior TT that year was one of his most memorable. In wet conditions Agostini fell at Sarah's Cottage, as did Hailwood. Hailwood then kicked the battered machine straight and rode back to the pits where the mechanics ripped off the broken screen. He then set off again and, although suffering a sticking throttle and hitting 240km/h in the rain without a screen, won at 147.550km/h (91.683mph). It was the slowest Senior win in 15 years but is still one of the most talked about.

Although Agostini also rode the 500 during 1965, finishing second to Hailwood six times, Hailwood's victories were generally as untroubled as in the past. Apart from Monza, Hailwood won every race by nearly a minute or more, and wasn't pressured to set race or lap records. Only at Assen did he set a new race record (142.242km/h/88.385mph).

By the end of 1965, Hailwood's four years at MV resulted in four 500cc World Championships, 27 Grand Prix victories, and a string of race and lap records. But Hailwood was restless. He found the lack of 500cc competition irritating, wanted to compete in more classes, and was also contemplating following John Surtees with a move to four wheels. Between 1963 and 1965 Hailwood entered twelve Formula One car Grands Prix and managed six top ten finishes in a Lotus or Lola. With the rise of Agostini at MV, and Honda eyeing the 500cc World Championship, at the end of the season Hailwood switched camps.

The new 350 triple was also a harbinger of the future, as MV finally realised the Japanese threat couldn't be ignored, and the two-valve cylinder head had had its day. The 56x47mm engine now featured four valves per cylinder like the Honda, and the cylinders inclined at only 10 degrees to promote intake downdraft. 127mm narrower than the four, with 62.5

horsepower at 13,500rpm, the compact 116kg triple was nearly as fast as the 500 four. Capable of 240km/h, it appeared at Imola early in 1965. Without the 'Privat' badge, and in the hands of Agostini, it won the first 350cc Grand Prix of the year at the Nürburgring. Trouble with his new triple saw Hailwood ride the older four, and he finished second. Hailwood's triple suffered a bad oil leak at the Isle of Man (although Agostini rode to third), and throughout the season it suffered from unreliability. Agostini ultimately ended second in the 350cc World Championship (with three victories), and Hailwood third (with a victory at Suzuka). Although Redman still won the title on the Honda, the success of MV's 350 triple in its maiden year was so encouraging it hastened the retirement of the all-conquering four in the 500cc class.

1966 ONWARDS

With Hailwood's departure Agostini became MV's only rider in the 1966 350 and 500 classes, and the 350 MV 3 came close to matching Hailwood's 70 horsepower Honda RC173. Despite a power deficit, it was narrower, lighter, and handled better, and this formula would serve MV well in its next phase. But, with two wins to Hailwood's six, Agostini could only manage second in the 350cc World Championship. The 500cc title was also hard fought. At the first Grand Prix of the season at

Agostini is more associated with the MV triple, but he rode the 500 four occasionally in 1966. (Courtesy Museo Agusta)

MV AGUSTA FOURS

Hockenheim, Agostini fronted with the older 500 four and he finished second to Redman's Honda. Outclassed by the new Honda, this prompted MV to build a 420cc 12-valve triple for the next race at Assen. But Agostini reverted to the venerable four in the final race of the season, the Nations Grand Prix at the power circuit of Monza. This final version of the 53x56.4mm four produced 75 horsepower at 9000rpm, the brakes were still a drum (250mm front and 220mm rear), and, rolling on 19in wheels, the 150kg four was capable of around 265km/h. Hailwood went to the final GP at Monza needing to win to take the championship, but the RC181 broke a valve. Agostini on the older four bike was untroubled, winning at a comfortable 191.46km/h (118.97mph). The 500cc four finished its career in style, also providing Agostini the 1966 500cc World Championship after Honda made an early season tactical error: allowing Redman to ride the 500 RC181 in preference to Hailwood early in the season saw Hailwood miss the first few races, and the championship decider come down to the last race at Monza.

So, on 11 September 1966 at Monza, one chapter opened and another closed. Agostini won his first World Championship, going on to become the most successful rider in Grand Prix history, and the older racing four was finally pensioned off. The 500 four had provided MV Agusta nine World Manufacturers' Championships in the hands of Surtees, Hocking, and Hailwood, seven Italian Championships (Bandirola, Venturi, Grassetti and Agostini), and one Italian Junior Championship (Milano). Before it was pensioned off in 1964, the 350 four also gave MV four manufacturers' World Championships. The 500's record of 66 Grands Prix wins and 175 victories, and the 350's 25 Grands Prix wins (and 32 victories) was admirable, but time had

A harbinger of the future. This Campagnolo front disc brake from the 600 tourer was tested on racing bikes during 1966.

John Surtees still demonstrates his style on the MV four at modern historic events.

58

BIRTH OF THE MV FOUR

caught up with the four. The racing era for two-valve cylinder heads with a wide included valve angle was over, as were air-cooled engines with the cylinders inclined 30 degrees. The future lay in lighter, more compact designs with four-valve cylinder heads and a more upright cylinder inclination. The 500 four was now 40-years-old and, while no longer competitive as a racing design, it would have another life as a limited quantity production engine.

Agostini on a 1974 four at an historic event at Phillip Island in Australia in 2000.

MV AGUSTA FOURS

HAILWOOD'S 1964 DAYTONA SPEED RECORDS

With an additional Grand Prix scheduled at Daytona for 1964, journalist Charlie Rous suggested to Stan and Mike Hailwood this could be an opportunity to attack Bob McIntyre's 143mph One Hour record set at Monza in 1957 on the Gilera 350 four. Rous specialised in record-breaking attempts, and although Mike was enthusiastic, Count Agusta was less so. MV only had two 500s and the Count placed more emphasis on winning the Grand Prix, so he vetoed the idea. But Stan Hailwood was determined the attempt would take place, and the Daytona authorities enthusiastically endorsed the idea. Stan told mechanic Vittorio Carrano that he had cabled the Count and it was OK to go ahead, and, with little time for organisation, it had to be so on the morning of the Grand Prix, 2 February.

Stan Hailwood (wearing the cowboy hat) watches as Mike prepares to set a new one-hour record at Daytona in February 1964. Charlie Rous is on the left. (Courtesy Museo Agusta)

Hailwood at speed on the Daytona banking. The bike carries a 'Privat' sticker. (Courtesy Museo Agusta)

Another problem was tyres. Before leaving England, Dunlop competition manager Dickie Davies had warned against using ordinary racing tyres at sustained high speed in the Florida heat, so the tyres were changed to a Dunlop front and Avon rear. The 500 four retained the minimal racing dolphin fairing and 24-litre fuel tank, but the gearing was raised so it would pull 10,000rpm in top running on petrol. From a standing start, Mike set a new one-hour record of 233.081km (145.675m) and a 100km record at 233.047km/h (144.809mph). Hailwood rode the same machine to 500cc Grand Prix victory in the afternoon.

Visit Veloce on the web – www.veloce.co.uk
Details of all books in print • Special offers • New book news • Gift vouchers • Forum

THE 600 (MV4C6)

Although Agostini raced the 500 four early in the 1966 season it was already destined for replacement by the triple. And with the 500 four about to be pensioned off for racing, Count Agusta reasoned it was time to finally release a production version. By the early 1960s everyone had tired of waiting for the R19, but more rumours began to emerge regarding a production four. However, the early 1960s were still a grim time for Italian manufacturers, and the Italian motorcycle industry sank further into the mire that had begun in the late 1950s. This was now exacerbated by the influx of small capacity Japanese motorcycles, and all the major Italian manufacturers began to look at larger displacement models and export to the US for salvation. Ducati produced a V4 1260cc Apollo, Moto Guzzi the 700cc V7, and Laverda the 650 twin, but it was the MV Agusta 600 that stole the headlines at the Milan Show at the end of 1965.

The most surprising aspect of the 600 was its design orientation. Here was the venerable Grand Prix four, undoubtedly the highest performing, most technically advanced and sophisticated production motorcycle engine in the world, placed in a touring chassis. Determined that no one would convert his four into a racer that could embarrass the factory machines, Count Agusta wanted the 600 to be a luxury grand tourer rather than a high-performance motorcycle. The 600cc capacity, electric start and shaft drive ensured the four wouldn't be raced, and the prototype was displayed at the 39th Salon di Milano. However, when the show opened on 4 December 1965 there were two empty plinths on the MV stand, delays in the preparation of the 600s seeing them arrive on 9 December.

According to Mario Rossi, MV's technical director between 1943 and 1978, it took only one year to develop the prototype 600. The first version as displayed at Milan had a bore and stroke of 56x60mm, 590cc, and a pair of Dell'Orto SS1 carburettors. The compression ratio was 9:1 and power was 52 horsepower

The prototype 600 displayed at the 1965 Milan Show differed from the eventual production version in a number of details.

MV AGUSTA FOURS

The prototype had a different final drive unit, and rear brake operation was from the right.

at 8000rpm. The technical department for developing the street bikes was the same as for racing, and the main feature not shared with the racing engines was the four individual cylinders and separate crank carrier – changed from the racing one-piece cylinder and carrier arrangement to make the engine easier to manufacture. The 600 cylinder head featured three horizontal fins like the Grand Prix 500, but the valve shims on the 600 were on top of the bucket and the intake and exhaust ports were threaded to accept pipes and carburettors. The camshaft end caps were also similar to those of the racing 500, but the racing cases were modified to house the electric dynastart and shaft drive. To improve aesthetics, a bulge was introduced at the front of the crankcase and the timing gear housing was cast iron instead of aluminium as on the GP bikes. Ignition was by a horizontal distributor instead of magneto, with a softer timing curve, and the main bearing housing was made in two halves to ease assembly. As the Count wanted to maintain a strong technological link with the factory racers, he stipulated the basic engine architecture remain unchanged.

Many other details distinguished this bike from the production version. These included front-mounted brake callipers, cable operated rear brake set up on the right, chrome-plated steel wheel rims, shorter mufflers, smaller battery side cover, and a shorter rear mudguard. The front mudguard included a double pinstripe on the front only, and turn signals were incorporated in the sides of the headlight shell. The final drive casting was also unique, and quite different to the production version.

THE PRODUCTION 600 (1967-73)

The 600 didn't immediately make it into production, and it wasn't until April 1967 that the definitive version was displayed at the Fiera Campionara di Milano. The first example (engine 199-001, frame 199001) was built on 26 June 1967. Only 28 were manufactured in 1967, and initially sold only to purchasers approved by the Count. The first went to Renato Galtrucco of Busto Anzio. Galtrucco was a wealthy textile industrialist and motorcycle enthusiast that later raced this machine. Other early examples went to the US, UK,

The Campagnolo brake callipers were mounted ahead of the fork legs.

THE 600 (MV4C6)

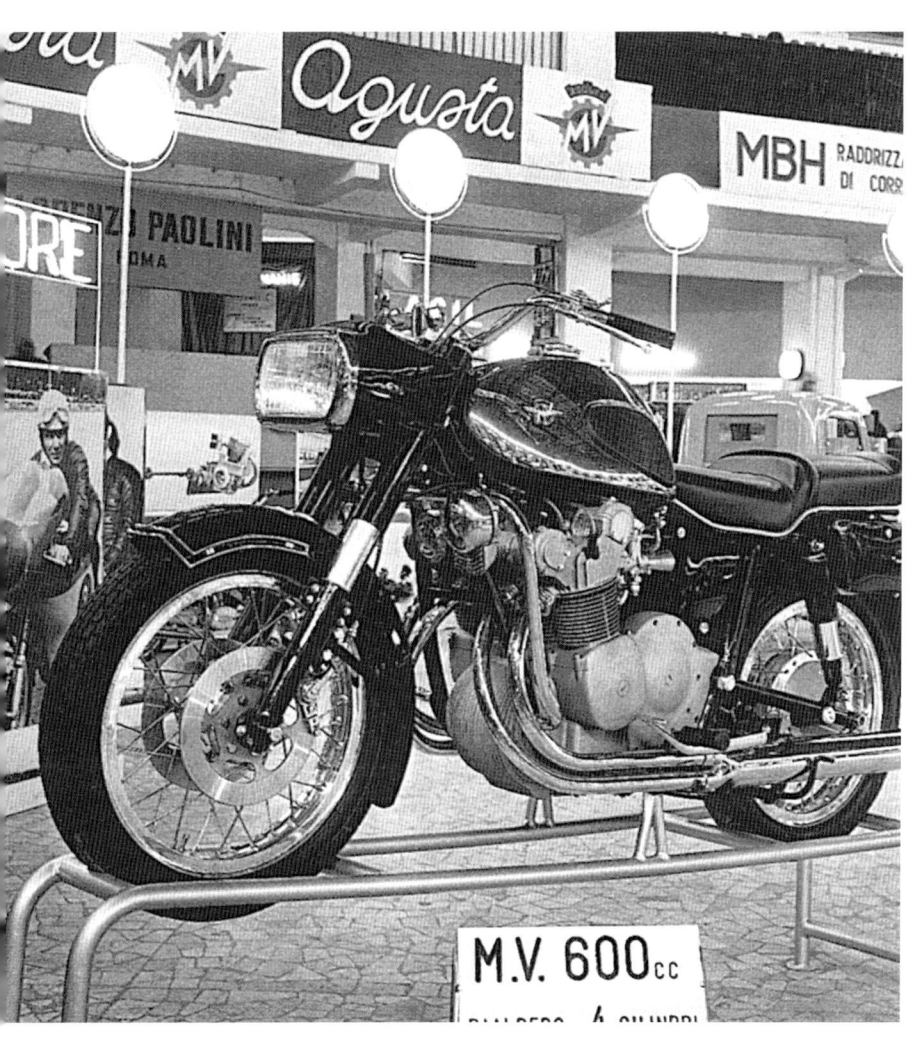

The definitive production 600 appeared at the Fiera Campionario di Milano in April 1967. This has the dual rib front mudguard and was possibly the same bike as tested by Motociclismo magazine.

Count Agusta in tandem on a 600 with a Bell helicopter representative. (Courtesy Museo Agusta)

France, Sweden, and Japan, the list price in the UK being £665. The one UK example (engine 199-009, frame 199006) was used for a publicity exercise in the *Motorcycle News* 'Spot the Ball' competition. As the Count didn't appreciate criticism he was reluctant to allow a press test bike. Most early tests were confined to US magazines *Cycle* and *Cycle World*, the machines lent by individual owners.

As the four-cylinder engine was essentially a racing design hand-built in extremely small numbers the 600 was never going to suit mass-production. After racing the four for 15 years, MV engineers knew this

When the production 600 appeared early in 1967 it had new longer mufflers but retained the disc front brakes. This example had frame number 199011 (engine 199-008) and was featured in the owners' manual of January 1968. The production date was 8/9/67.

Cycle World magazine tested the first 600 in the US, featuring it on the cover of its March 1968 issue with a Ferrari 275 GTB. This bike (engine 199007, frame 199009) was sold to a buyer in Miami on 7 July 1967. (Courtesy Cycle World)

THE 600 (MV4C6)

Another view of the 600 with the Ferrari. (Courtesy Cycle World)

engine demanded skilled assembly. Each unit was handmade, with all components matched by selective assembly to provide acceptable running tolerances. Valves, valve buckets, pistons and piston rings were all individually selected so assembly was time-consuming. Although the early examples were not perfect, compared with other designs of the 1960s, the MV engine was stronger, more reliable, and provided a vastly superior operating life.

MV AGUSTA FOURS

ENGINE

Because the four-cylinder engine wasn't really suitable for general production only a small number of 600s were built each year between 1967 and 1973. Engine numbers began at 199-001 and finished at 199-0134, and were stamped at the base of the distributor on the crankcase, on the right behind the cylinders. MV always added a 0 after the model designation (the 600 model designation 199), so only the first 100 examples had a six-digit number. Although engine numbers went up to 134, production records indicate only 127 600s were built.

The engine's strength came from its design, with bearings in every conceivable position, and all components

The Cycle World 600 bike, still almost the same more than 40 years later, only now in Bill Irwin's collection in New Zealand.

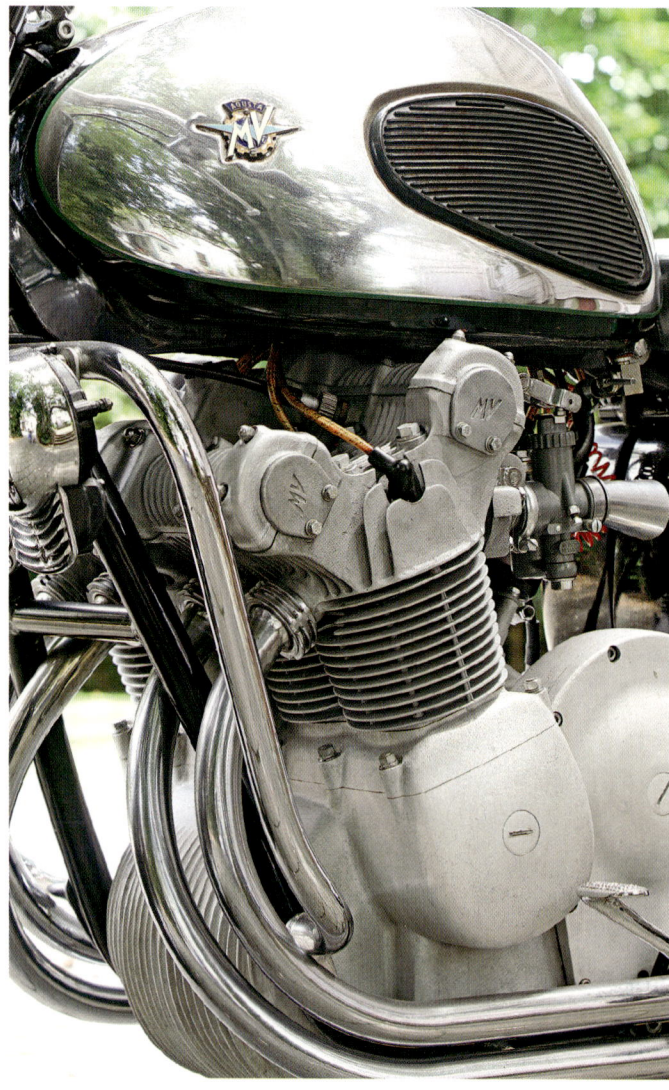

The Grand Prix ancestry of the 600 engine is clearly evident.

THE 600 (MV4C6)

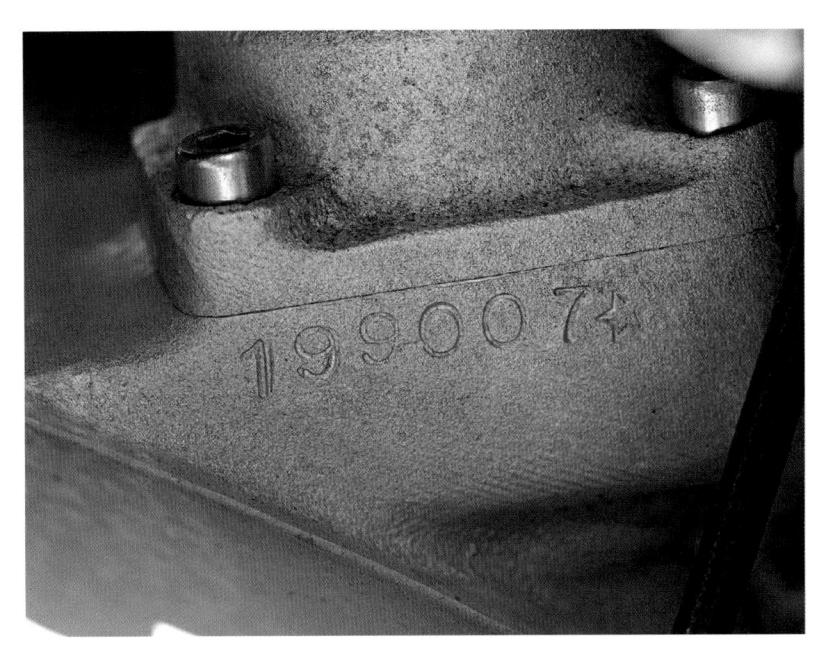

The engine number was stamped at the base of the distributor; this early example with engine number 7.

generously proportioned. The 600 was also in a very mild state of tune, producing a modest 50 horsepower at 8200rpm. There were ten updates to the engine design between 1966 and 1971, most to the valves, guides and seats. The first design was dated 22/7/66, with other updates occurring on 10/10/66, 19/11/66, 26/4/67, 15/6/67, 1/9/67, 15/6/67, 1/9/67, 5/4/68, 12/6/68, 9/6/69, and 9/6/71.

600 Engine specifications

Type	Four-stroke, four-cylinder, air-cooled
Bore	58mm
Stroke	56mm
Capacity	592cc
Compression ratio	9.3:1
Maximum power	50hp at 8200rpm

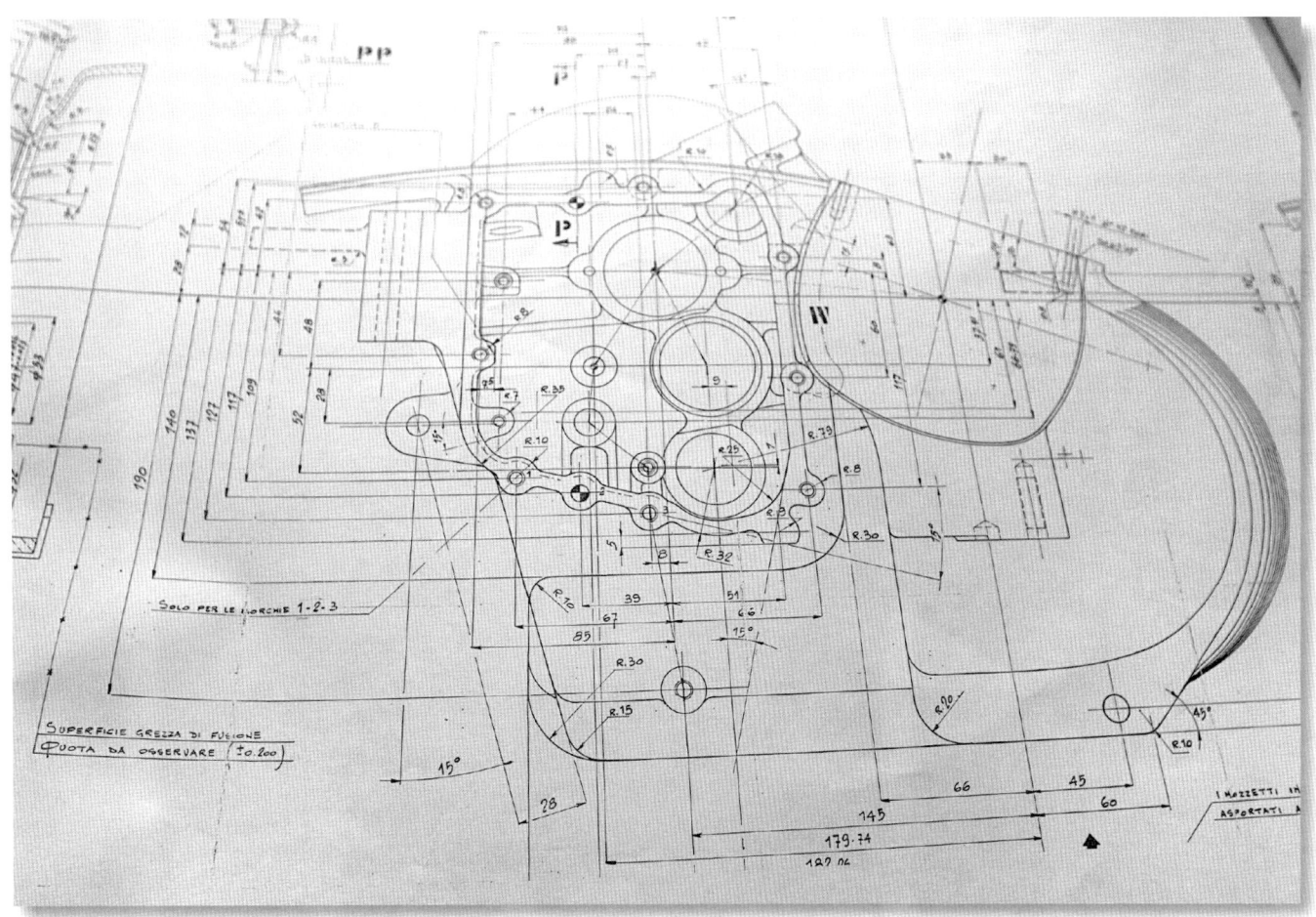

The original drawings for the 600 crankcase show a deeper sump than that of the Grand Prix engine.

MV AGUSTA FOURS

The sump of the 600 had 15 fins, compared to the 750's 21.

CRANKSHAFT AND CRANKCASE

The crankshaft design followed that of the racing bikes, with two outer main ball bearings (25x52x15mm on the 600) to take up any endfloat and four special split internal bearings. These were divided bearings with external rings, the outside rings weakened in two opposite places by drilling and being cracked open. At the time, MV used to crack them with a hammer. The two parts fitted

Most 600s had a helical primary gear like the 750.

The crank assembly was one of the most complex components in the engine.

THE 600 (MV4C6)

The aluminium crank rack supported the crankshaft.

The crankcase was essentially a large hollow casting. This is a modern Kay casting.

correctly as the broken parts matched perfectly, and the result was an extremely durable crank if correctly assembled with very close tolerances. This divided bearing construction wasn't new, Zündapp used it in its 1951 twin cylinder 600 KS601 'Green Elephant,' and the manufacturing process is common today in the construction of two-piece con rods running plain bearings (although not using hammers; modern con rods are frozen then snapped in a controlled environment). Unlike the prototype's 60mm stroke, the production 600 had a 56mm stroke (providing 592cc with the 58mm pistons), and this stroke would feature on the later fours from 750 to 862cc. The nine-piece crankshaft was pressed together, the one-piece con rods running on 16x5mm caged needle roller bearings with a plain bushing small end. Crankpin diameter was 31mm, small end diameter 17mm, and eye-to-eye con rod length 120mm. This provided a stroke to con rod length ratio of 1:2.143. The crankpins were set at 180 degrees, and circular grooves incorporated in the crank counterweights for con rod lubrication. The diameter of the steel crank flywheel was 112mm. MV four-cylinder crankshafts were built by Maurizio Mazzucchelli & Figli of Cavaria (Varese) and assembled exclusively with Durkopp cages. Mazzucchelli also supplied gearbox and final drive components.

Engines until 199-023 had straight-cut primary gears (56/98) with a ratio of 1.75:1, which also fitted to engines 199-024 to 199-026 and 199-036, 199-038, and 199-039. After engine 199-042 a helical geared

The 600 conrod, split bearing shell, and crankpin. This was identical to the 750.

7mm studs held the crankcase and crank rack together. The 600 had no rib on the crank carrier.

The 600 cylinder head bolts were not recessed as on later engines.

primary drive was fitted (same ratio), and on all engines the drive was between cylinders one and two (as on the MV racers and Rondine and Gilera fours). Apart from the early 600 with straight cut primary gears, all the crankshafts were interchangeable, and balanced identically.

Also similar to the 500 racer was the sand-cast, horizontally-split crankcase, but the sump was deeper to incorporate the automotive-like oil filter. As on the 500 the crankcases were produced by Genevoise, and according to Mario Rossi only ten were initially produced. Albert Bold confirmed the 600 crankcases were very good quality with strong castings. The sump had 15 fins. Empty inside, the only role for the crankcase casting was that of a sump for 3 litres of oil, as the crankshaft bolted to a bearing rack by 12 8x104mm studs. This sub-assembly bolted into the main engine casting with split caps and 12 5x50.5mm studs, and was a carry-over from the MV racing engine design. Particularly suitable for limited production, it provided incredibly strong support for the crankshaft, minimised thermal distortion, and eliminated the need for more complex and intricate casting and machining operations.

The individual cylinders and cylinder head also attached to the crank sub-assembly by 12 longer waisted 7mm studs with slip-washers and 9mm hexagonal nuts. A design weakness meant these waisted studs tended to shear when being undone. The 600 crankshaft rack didn't have a rib around the edge like later 750 racks, but matching to the crankcase was more difficult. Another feature of the 600 was a second inspection plug, on the right side of the crankcase.

CAMSHAFT DRIVE

The alloy crankshaft rack also supported the trio of camshaft drive gears. These were riveted to three 35x62x9mm roller bearings, and locked by end caps into the one-piece cast iron housing. This enabled the timing relative to each gear to be

THE 600 (MV4C6)

maintained, while the entire gear train could be removed as a unit by removing the two bolts (8x35 and 8x45mm) holding the gear unit to the crankshaft rack. Wear was minimised by the different sizes of the gears (28, 37 and 32 teeth) and generous bearing support. The gears were 40-tooth modulo 2, marked with a grinding tolerance of 27.55 or a slightly larger 27.64. Nine Ø5m holes in the gear face working as three sets of three allowed 1 degree increments at the camshaft and 2 degree increments at the crank for valve timing. The red marked tooth was at 90 degrees to the initial setting tooth, and the cam drive casting was sealed in the cylinder head by a 1.78x19.77mm O-ring. Although the camshaft drive was well proven, the 9mm cam drive gears were problematic on the 600. The top gears were also 9mm thickness.

CYLINDERS AND PISTONS

Unlike the racing 500, the cylinders were inclined at 20 degrees and cast individually. The interchangeable cylinders were cast in pairs with

The 9mm 600 camshaft gears (left) were narrower than those on the 750.

The 58mm 600 piston was cast aluminium.

MV AGUSTA FOURS

All production four-cylinder MVs had individual cylinders. (Courtesy Dorian Skinner)

two separate cylinder base gaskets (but no O-ring on the 600 as on the 750). Providing a compression ratio of 9.3:1 the three-ring solid skirt Borgo 58mm cast alloy pistons were matched to the barrels, and for each barrel size there were two pistons, 'A' and 'B.' The 'A' piston was 0.01mm smaller than the 'B' and both types weighed 170 grams. On many four-cylinder engines with identical bores, cylinders two and three sometimes had 'A' pistons, while cylinders one and four had 'B' pistons. This was because the two central cylinders ran hotter – an expedient way of allowing a greater tolerance. When installed, the tolerance length for the cylinders had to be within 0.02mm.

CYLINDER HEAD AND CAMSHAFTS

The production double overhead camshaft cylinder head was recast from the prototype but remained a complex casting. A three-piece aluminium cylinder head gasket sealed the two pairs of cylinders and central cam gear drive. Now with two horizontal cooling fins, the two valves per cylinder were set at an 80-degree included angle (40 degrees inlet and 40 degrees exhaust). This was slightly wider than the final 500 racer. The outer vertical fin near the sparkplug was cut away and, as on the prototype, the exhaust ports were threaded (although the 24mm inlet ports were now flanged). Also as on the prototype, on the production 600 the valve shims

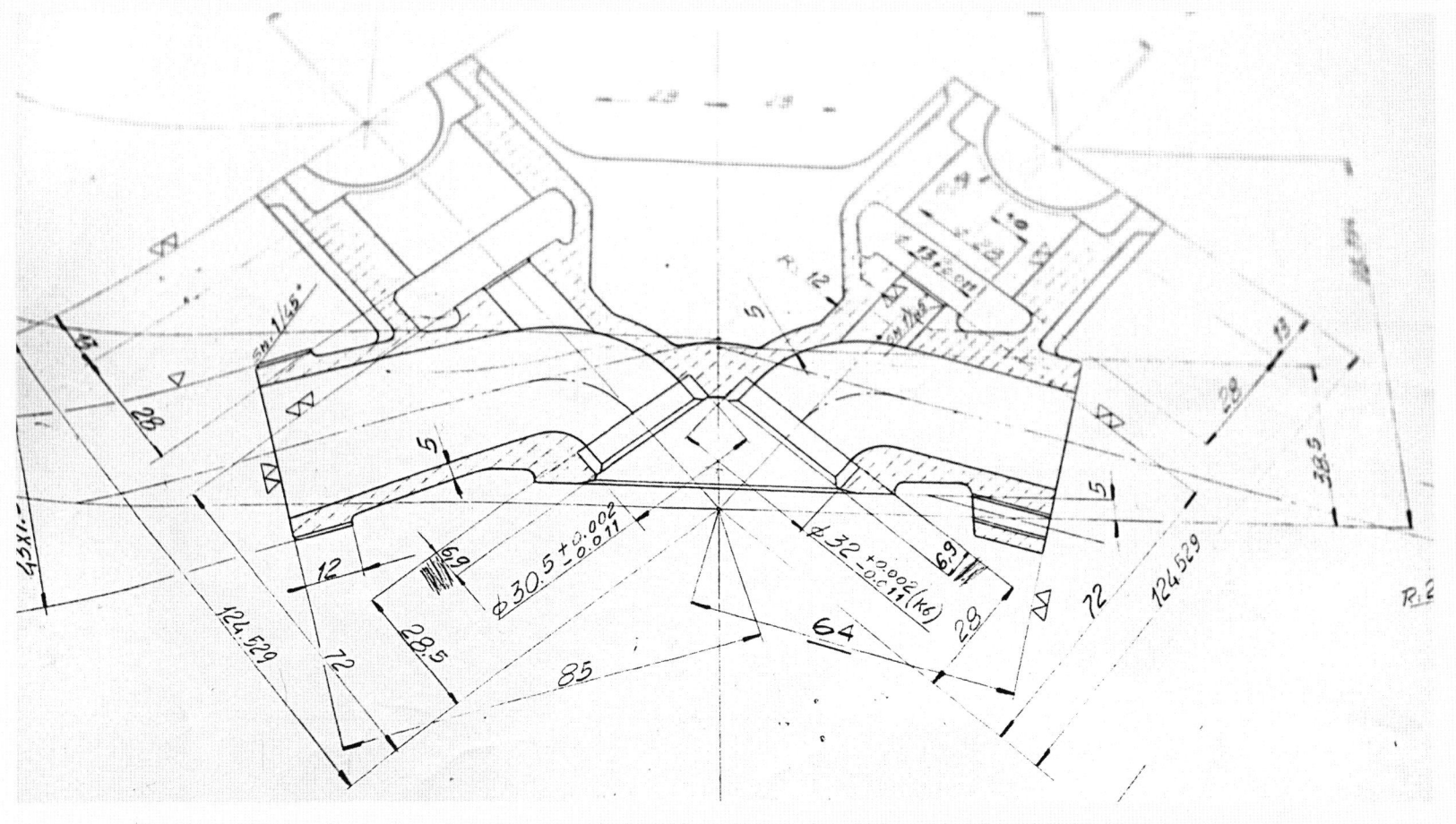

The two-valve cylinder head design was derived from the racing 500 and had a wide included valve angle.

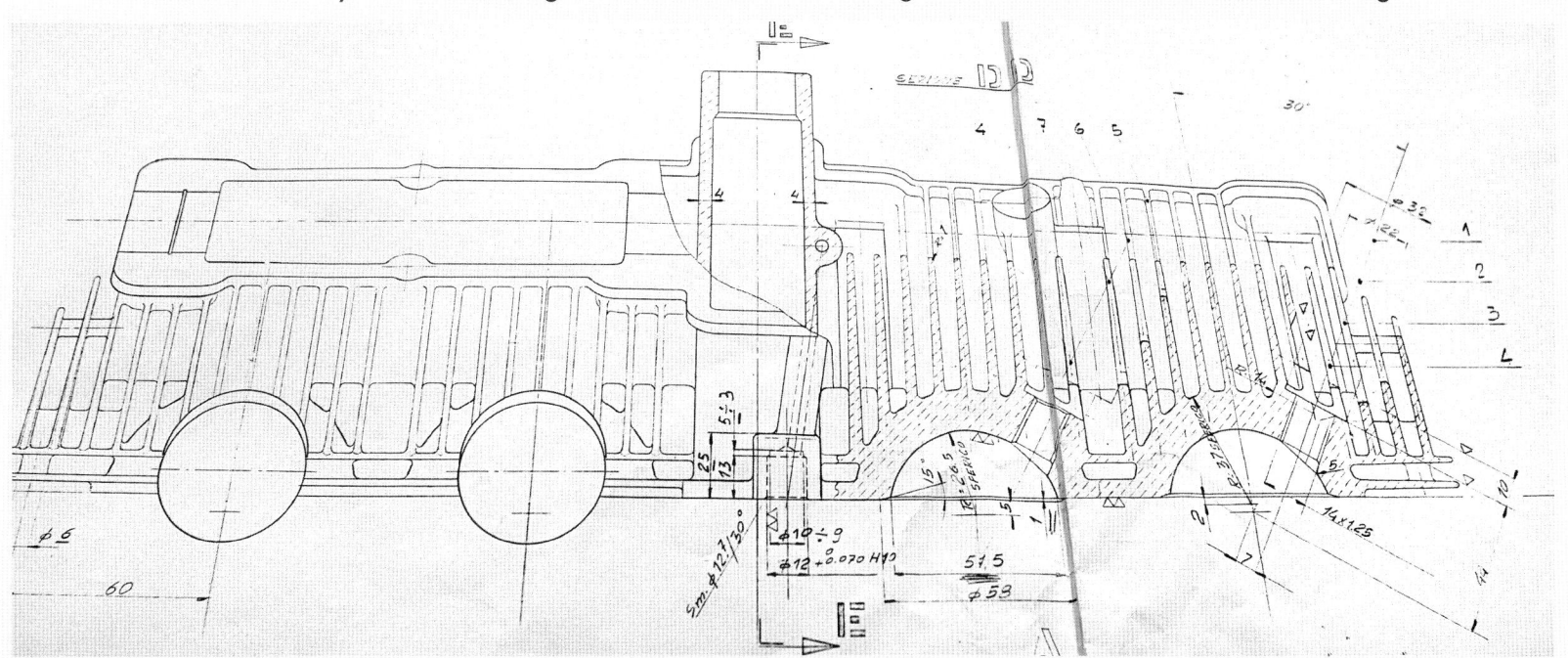

MV AGUSTA FOURS

The MV four cylinder head; essentially the same for all models. (Courtesy Dorian Skinner)

were above the buckets. It has been stated in other publications that only the first 50 600cc engines featured above-bucket shims, but this isn't substantiated in the 1st edition (January 1970) 600 parts list that shows only above-bucket shims. Noted MV tuner Albert Bold also says, "As far as I'm concerned, all 600s had shims above the buckets, the 750 Sport was the first to put the shim below the bucket." This is confirmed by Dave Kay in the UK, but some of the very last 600s, those built alongside the 750 S, may have had under-bucket shims. Richard Boshier, who worked for MV Agusta Concessionaires, certainly believes this. The buckets were a two-hole type prone to cracking. The valve sizes were 29.4mm inlet and 28mm exhaust, both 88.5mm long and operated by double valve springs and held by split collets. The valves were probably in two pieces, as Albert Bold has experienced a number of motors with broken valve heads. Albert Bold also says, "I have seen many 600s with broken valve guides. The shorter intake guides would chip and deposit particles throughout the motor via the intake manifold. The longer exhaust would break off and slide around on the stem, this extra weight preventing the valve closing fast enough and causing it to hit the piston at high revs. If the guide didn't break from the pounding and get blown into the exhaust, it would peen the other part of the guide surface, causing sluggish valve action. I think the factory had a bad batch of cast iron when they built the 600. I have never seen this in any of the 750s." Despite the smaller ports, Bold also preferred the 600 cylinder head over the later 750 head for modified engines because it was a much stronger casting and less prone to warping. The 600 valve seats were 32mm on the intake and 30mm on the exhaust, and, according to the original design drawings, the 600 valves and valve seats lasted until the 750 from 14 April 1972.

The camshaft timing was relatively mild, with 8mm of valve lift, and the camshafts were distinguished by several clever design touches. Because the camshafts had narrow cam profiles – leading to high pressure on the cup tappet – they were hollow, with oil holes bored in the lobes to lubricate the narrow tappet. The cup tappets were drilled for lightness and they ran in individual bucket guides, not directly in the aluminium head. Both camshafts ran in four needle roller bearings and the worm drive for the tachometer was at the rear of the inlet camshaft.

600s had large shims on top of the bucket, as opposed to the 750's smaller under-bucket shim.

74

THE 600 (MV4C6)

Valve timing 600

Inlet opens	48° before TDC
Inlet closes	68° after BDC
Exhaust opens	70° before BDC
Exhaust closes	36° after TDC
Valve clearance cold intake	0.25mm
Valve clearance cold exhaust	0.30mm

LUBRICATION SYSTEM

The oil pump drive was from the starter shaft; the gear a press fit only on the shaft and retained by circlips. Unlike the racing engines, the oil pump was mounted horizontally rather than vertically, and the oil pump and filter were housed in a unit underneath the crankshaft. A small update was included in the bypass valve assembly after engine number 199037. From number 199038 a Ø9.5mm ball replaced the bypass pin valve. The early 600 also had smaller diameter oil pump gears.

CARBURETTORS AND EXHAUST

Further emphasising the touring nature of the 600, only two carburettors were fitted, and they were extremely small in throat diameter; 24mm Dell'Orto UB24 B2 and BS2. Although some owners in Europe had four carburettors fitted in later years at the factory, these were not a standard fitting and all 600s were initially fitted with twin carburettors. Each remote float bowl carburettor was fitted to a

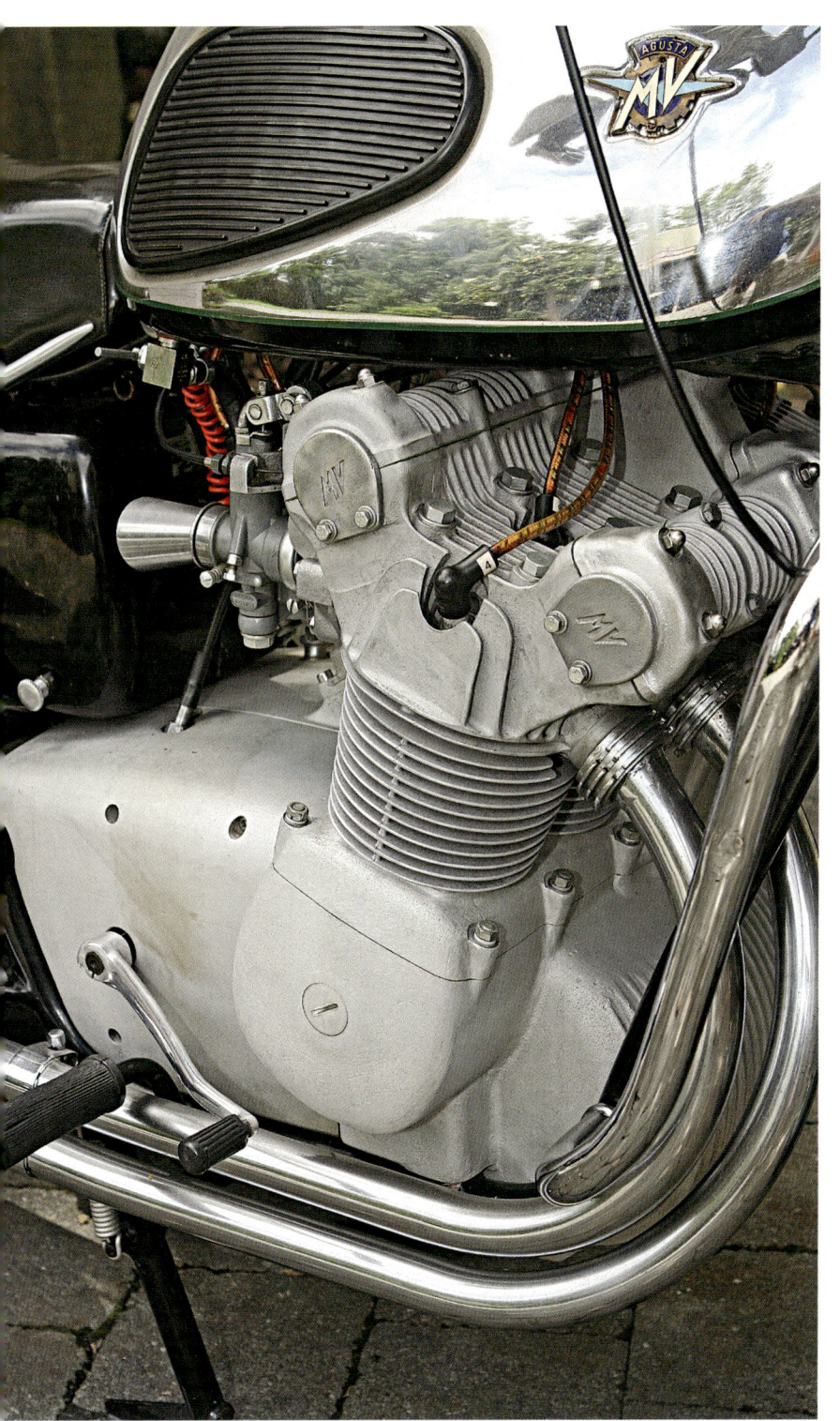

Two fins distinguished the 600 cylinder head and the outer fin cut-away. Early fours also had an inspection plug on the right of the crankcase.

All 600s had twin Dell'Orto UB 24 carburettors with open bell mouths.

75

MV AGUSTA FOURS

U-shaped 24.5mm manifold and linked by a tube. The throttle cable attached to the right carburettor and linked by a rod and lever to the left. An apparent anomaly for a touring engine was the lack of any air filtration, but this was quite common with Italian manufacturers in the 1960s and early 1970s. Both carburettors were fitted with open polished aluminium bell mouths. The exhaust system included a single muffler on each side; these mounted by two bolts either side of the passenger footpeg.

Carburettor jetting 600

Type	2x Dell'Orto UB24 B2 and BS2
Choke diameter	24mm
Main jet	125
Idle jet	45
Throttle valve	60
Needle	E 9/2 2nd notch
Atomiser	260 A
Air intake	Open horn
Pilot screw	Open 2 turns

A Bosch Dynastart was fitted underneath the engine at the rear. (Courtesy Museo Agusta)

Only the very earliest 600s had the dual point Marelli distributor.

THE 600 (MV4C6)

IGNITION AND ELECTRICAL SYSTEM

The earliest 600s included a Marelli 7K dual point distributor, located vertically instead of horizontally as on the prototype. This was fitted until engine number 199-037, as a single point Bosch distributor had become available, and from engine 199038 the distributor was a Bosch JF-4. This included a new housing at the crankcase, a longer (6x60mm) retaining screw, and a new drive gear. A 12-volt 18Ah battery powered the ignition, and the firing order was 1-3-4-2. Each distributor type had different sparkplug caps and leads: the Bosch distributor had a black lead and Bosch caps; the Marelli distributor had gold-coloured leads.

One of the most important modifications to the racing four was the addition of the Bosch Dynastart underneath the engine at the rear, near the swingarm. The drive to both the starter and generator was by one-way rubber belts; the inner driving the generator and the outer the starter. The Dynastart has always been a problematic addition to the MV (see Chapter 9), but was widely used on a variety of microcars during the 1950s and 60s (including the BMW 600 and Isetta 300/250). It incorporated an armature and two sets of field coils to provide a compact starter and generator in one unit. An indication of the problems encountered by MV's engineers in adapting the Dynastart to its racing design was the number of modifications incorporated during the 600's production life. After engine number 199-012 the roller support, washer, Dynastart shaft, and pulley support were all changed. More updates occurred after engine number 199-067. This included new pulley, bearings, washers and gaskets. According to the parts list a new pulley and gaskets were incorporated from engine number 199-0138, but there is no evidence in production records of an engine with this number.

The early 600 with the Marelli distributor had these sparkplug caps.

MV AGUSTA FOURS

Ignition and electrical system

Ignition type	Battery and coil
Fixed advance	8-10°
Automatic advance	40°
Total advance	48-50°
Breaker points clearance	0.4mm
Firing order	1,3,4,2
Sparkplug	275W long thread 14mm
Sparkplug electrode gap	0.6mm
Battery	12V 18Ah
Dynastart	Bosch 12V 135W

GEARBOX

The 600 gearbox design was inherited from the racer but was characterised by an inferior gear profile that was prone to eroding and bending of the teeth. The design was basically continued throughout the life of the engine; the 600 and 750 main and layshafts were identical, as were the selector forks. Needle roller bearings were used throughout; the only plain bearing in the gearbox was the 3rd gear on the mainshaft, running directly on the shaft with only splash lubrication. First gear was also manufactured integrally

The factory supplied this set of tools for the four-cylinder engine. (Courtesy Dorian Skinner)

on the mainshaft. Some gearbox updates were introduced early on. After engine number 199013, a 17x28x6mm gasket was added to the output bevel gear, with a new 5th gear on the mainshaft. A new internal gear selector cover was also introduced from engine 199013, and this continued on the 750. The gear selector mechanism provided a traditional Italian right side gearshift (one up and four down), via a rocking lever.

Gear ratios 600

Gear	Ratio	Teeth
1st	2.38:1	30/15x25/21
2nd	1.69:1	27/19x25/21
3rd	1.29:1	24/22x25/21
4th	1.09:1	22/24x25/21
5th	0.92:1	20/26x25/21

Although not the strongest drive train component, the gearbox was very compact.

THE 600 (MV4C6)

CLUTCH
The 600 clutch comprised six driven plates (3.5mm) and six steel driving plates and, until engine number 199023, the clutch basket included a straight cut primary gear. Five screws held the clutch together and the clutch basket was riveted to the clutch gear. This was a weakness and a source of potential disaster if the engine was tuned and used hard. Clutch actuation was by a set of rods and balls, the setup changing early in the production series. Until engine number 199012 there were two rods and two balls, this changing to three rods and three balls from engine 199013. The 600 (and early 750) clutch cover was shaped slightly differently to later versions, and tapered at the rear.

FINAL DRIVE
Drive was transmitted from the gearbox via a bevel gear with an intermediate ratio of 1.066 (16/15), the driveshaft running through the right leg of the steel swingarm to a cast aluminium final drive unit. The 600 final drive casting had slightly thinner fins than later versions, and the bevel drive early examples had a 10/30 tooth (1:3) final drive ratio. Later versions featured 12 and 36 teeth.

Gear	Ratio
Intermediate transmission	1.066:1
Transmission shaft to wheel	3:1 (10/30 or 12/36)

To deter their conversion to racers, all production MVs had shaft final drive. Drive from the output shaft to the drive shaft was by a bevel gear. (Courtesy Giovanni Magni)

FRAME, WHEELS, TYRES, BRAKES AND SUSPENSION
The black-painted frame was specially designed for the 600; a double cradle supporting the engine with a single top frame tube arched to allow cylinder head removal whilst in situ. The frame number was stamped on the rear subframe, beginning at MV4C6*199001*. The last frame number was 1990136 (built with engine 199-0104 on 21/7/69), and there were several gaps in the numbers. No frame numbers were allocated to bikes 1999109, 199113, 199121-124, and 199128. 600s didn't have a frame homologation stamp, and the rear subframe was rectangular in section as the seat hinged backwards.

18in wheels were fitted front and rear, with identical Borrani WM3 2.15x18in aluminium rims. These early rims didn't carry any specific markings and the painted silver spokes were Alpino 3.3mm, marked A. Metzeler tyres were fitted as standard; a 3.50x18in ribbed on the front and a 3.50 or 4.00in patterned on the rear. As a different speedometer drive was required to suit each tyre, a 3.50x18in rear was fitted from engine number 199001-199004, 199008-199027, and from 199061. The 4.00x18in tyre featured on engine numbers 199005-199007, 199028, and 199038-199060.

The tapered 600 clutch cover differed to the later 750.

MV AGUSTA FOURS

The 600 final drive casting had deeper fins than the 750.

One of the most unusual features of the 600 was the front brake – a pair of mechanical Campagnolo discs. The hub was stamped 'Campagnolo,' as were the 216mm rotors. These were first tried on the racing 350 back in 1966, but, even by 1967, disc brakes were rare on motorcycles. Four leading-shoe drums remained de rigueur for racing, and the mechanical Campagnolo discs were an unproven design. Unfortunately, they were tricky to set up, and from most accounts very ineffective. Although it has been written that some later 600s were fitted with a Grimeca drum from the 750, this is not substantiated, and 600s with front drum brakes appear to have had them fitted at

The frame number was stamped on the rear subframe. Note the relieved cable tie, a feature of all production MV fours.

The rear frame section was square to accommodate the angular mudguard.

THE 600 (MV4C6)

Each brake calliper had two small circular pads operated by a cable and lever.

a later date. But, as one example was built in 1971 and another in 1973, it is possible these could have had a 750 S Grimeca brake.

The rear brake was a full width 200x45mm single leading-shoe drum that was rod operated, not cable as on the prototype. A 35mm telescopic fork graced the

The Campagnolo double front disc setup was unique to the 600.

MV AGUSTA FOURS

front end, with twin shocks at the rear. As was usual for the time, the springs were enclosed on both the fork and shocks. Both the front fork and swingarm were ably supported by tapered roller bearings; 25x52x16.25mm at the steering head and 15x42x14.25mm at the swingarm.

Wheels, tyres and brakes

Front wheel	WM3x18in Borrani,
Front brake	Campagnolo 216mm dual disc
Front tyre	3.50x18in ribbed S-rated
Rear wheel	WM3x18in Borrani,
Rear brake	200x45mm Drum
Rear tyre	3.50x18in or 4.00x18in pattern S-rated

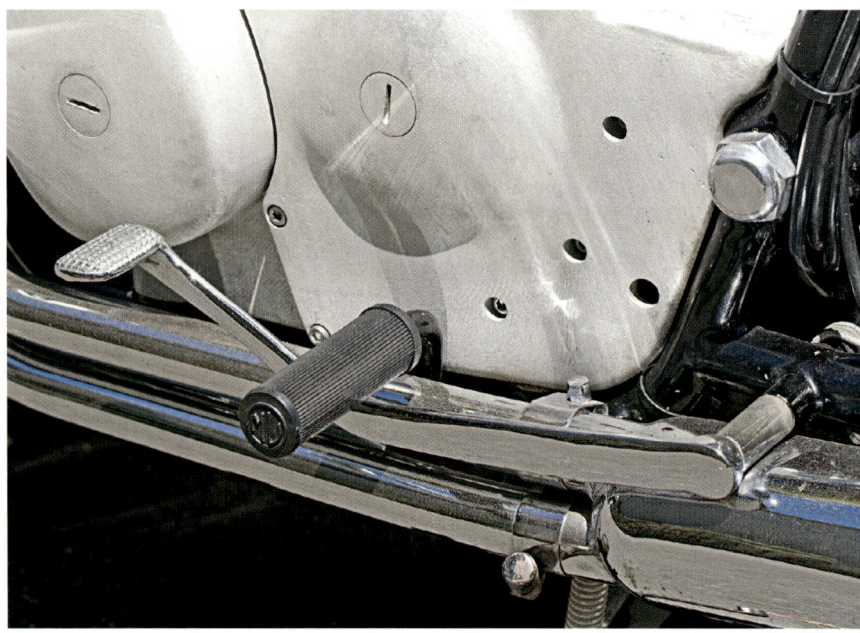

Rear brake actuation was on the left.

INSTRUMENTS, LIGHTS, SWITCHES, HANDLEBAR, CRASH BAR, FUSE BOX, HORNS AND CONTROLS

Another unusual feature that characterised the 600 was the large rectangular headlight and fibreglass nacelle that incorporated the instruments. It is believed Count Agusta stipulated these features to accentuate the 600's touring profile, and that the large Carello 45W headlight was an automotive unit. Unlike the later MV fours, this rather ugly headlight also housed much of the electric wiring. The instrument nacelle housed a pair of Veglia instruments and the ignition key. The speedometer read to 220km/h and incorporated two warning lights, while the tachometer read to 12,000rpm but didn't include a redline.

The rear shock absorbers featured enclosed springs, and the rear brake was rod operated.

THE 600 (MV4C6)

The large Carello headlight dominated the 600's frontal aspect.

A Pair of Veglia instruments sat in the headlight nacelle.

No redline was provided on the tachometer.

The speedometer included blue and green warning lights for the headlight and high beam.

More conventional than the headlight arrangement was the CEV taillight and Aprilia handlebar switches. The high handlebar was a large diameter (one inch) and a specific item for the 600 as it incorporated the front brake lever mount. A single cable Tommaselli Super Practic B throttle was also fitted, this is quite a usual feature of late 1960s Italian motorcycles.

The Bosch fuse box and regulator were neatly located above the battery, and, while turn signals were only occasionally fitted, three horns graced the 600. Two Fiamm or Bosch horns were fitted to the crash bar (another unique 600 feature) and one Aprilia under the steering head. Fiamm horns required a different crash bar and were fitted until frame number 199050. From frame number 199051, Bosch horns were fitted to the crash bar.

83

MV AGUSTA FOURS

The CEV rectangular taillight was standard issue for Italian motorcycles during the 1960s.

An Aprilia switch on the left operated the horn, lights, and indicators (the switch underneath, if fitted).

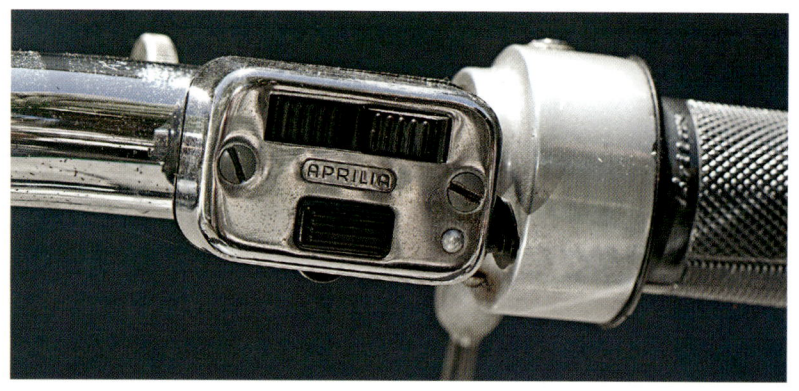

On the right was another Aprilia switch, this one incorporating the starter and light flasher.

The 600 had a Super Practic B single cable throttle unit, and the front brake lever and cable support was incorporated with the handlebar.

The fuse box and regulator were neatly positioned above the battery.

THE 600 (MV4C6)

Early 600s had 2 Fiamm horns mounted on the crashbar.

An Aprilia horn was fitted underneath the steering head.

MV AGUSTA **FOURS**

This later 600 has Bosch horns mounted on the crashbar, but still only a single rib on the front mudguard.

THE 600 (MV4C6)

The 600 crash bar mount to the frame was quite different to the later 750 GT.

FUEL TANK, SEAT, SIDE COVERS, MUDGUARDS, AND TOOLKIT

Even when it was introduced the 600's styling was criticised, and it hasn't improved over time. The arched 20-litre fuel tank had chrome panels, rubber kneepads, and screwed badges. The fuel taps were a small 12x1.50mm, and the decal fitted for 1967 pronounced 25 Constructors' World

The wide crash bar with twin horns presented an imposing front profile.

87

MV AGUSTA FOURS

Championships. 1968 models had a new decal proclaiming 26 Constructors' titles.

A Radaelli scalloped dual seat was fitted to the 600, most having a passenger strap (although the *Cycle World* 1968 test bike didn't have a seat strap) and an aluminium bead. The seat shape was changed some time during 1968 and later versions were higher at the rear. The side covers were fibreglass and the front mudguard steel. The mudguard also changed during production, which saw at least three different types. Some early front mudguards had a double aluminium ring but most had a single ring. A comprehensive toolkit was located in the right toolbox.

Over the years there has been considerable speculation regarding the colours of original 600s. The only non-black 600 mentioned in factory records was a yellow 600 delivered to Australian Kym Boynton on 25 July 1968 (engine 199-063, frame 199089). Others claim a red example was delivered to an owner in Holland, but definitely a blue 600 was produced for the exiled King of Italy Vittorio Emanuele de

The tank cap was a chrome lever style.

Savoie (then living in Geneva, Switzerland). According to Vittorio Emanuele, "I was working with Corrado Agusta selling helicopters, and I managed to sell 700 Agusta helicopters to the Shah of Iran. This was a very large order considering one Chinook cost $20 million." As an appreciation Corrado arranged for King Vittorio to receive a special 600 (that he still has today). Painted blue to represent the colours of the United Kingdom, this bike (engine number 199-014, frame number 199015) was built on 3 November 1967 and carried a specific plaque between the instruments and on the front mudguard. The engine displaced 750cc, was fed by four 24mm carburettors, and was delivered personally (also on the 3/11/67) to Vittorio by MV test rider Fortunato Libanori.

Most certainly the number of 600s that survive in their original state is many fewer than the 127 manufactured. As they were unpopular, some were later converted into 750 Sport clones – an unfortunate practice that resulted in a devalued replica. Today, the 600 is appreciated for its historical importance and existing examples are, fortunately, likely to remain as 600s. Although most 600s were built in 1967, 1968, 1969, and 1970 (prior to introduction of the 750), a solitary example was made in 1971, and another in 1973.

Metal badges screwed into the chrome tank panels.

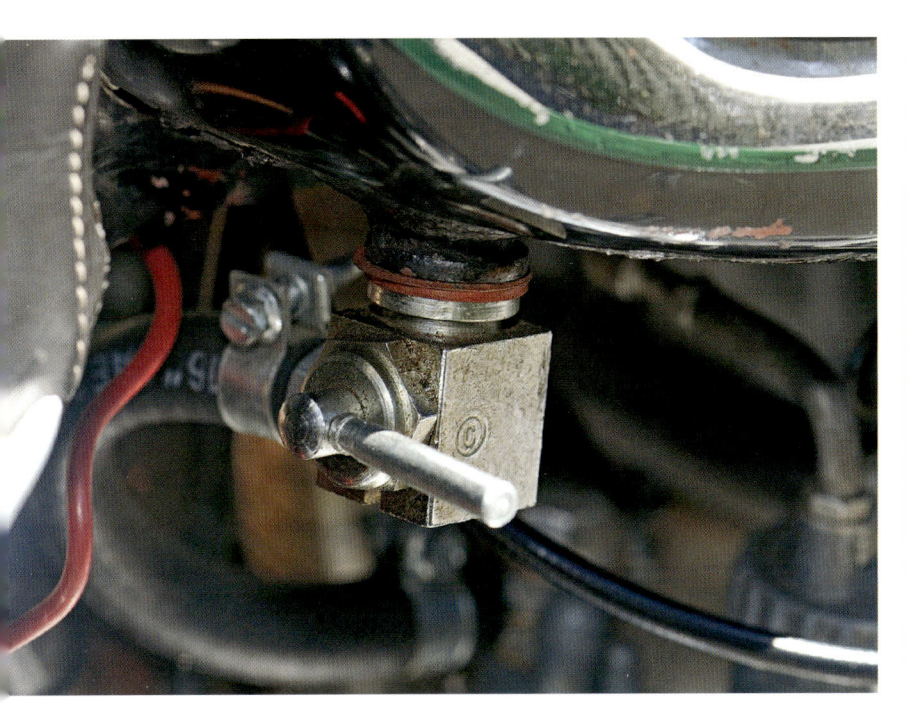

THE 600 (MV4C6)

The 600 fuel petcocks were a smaller thread than on the 750.

A Radaelli badge was riveted to the rear of the seat.

MV had 25 World Championships to its name in 1967.

A toolkit was conveniently stored in the right-hand toolbox.

MV AGUSTA FOURS

The toolkit was very comprehensive; as befitting a luxury motorcycle.

Possibly built to special order, the final example had engine 199-0127 and frame 1990101, and was sold on 6/4/73. It is also possible this final example was fitted with a Grimeca front drum brake and round CEV headlight from the 750 Sport. Richard Boshier, who has worked on many MV fours since he was a mechanic with MV Concessionaires, has seen at least one 600 with 750 wiring and a round CEV headlight.

One feature of the 600 that was indisputable was its modest performance. In its June 1970 issue *Motociclismo* magazine published a comparison test of the current crop of Superbikes, pitting the 600 against a range of motorcycles, including the new Honda CB750, Kawasaki Mach III 500, Norton Commando 750, Laverda 750 S, Harley Davidson XLCH and Electraglide, Triumph Bonneville and Trident, and

Early 600s had only one metal band on the front mudguard.

Some later 600s had twin metal bands on the front mudguard.

THE 600 (MV4C6)

Vittorio Emanuele de Savoie with his special blue 600.

This 600 was the first in Australia. Delivered in 1968 in mustard yellow, it has Bosch horns.

the BSA Lightning and Rocket 3. The 230kg MV posted the slowest acceleration figure of the entire group, covering the standing start quarter-mile in 16.3 seconds. The MV's braking performance was also the least satisfactory, requiring 60 metres stop from 100km/h. Its maximum speed of 170km/h placed it in the middle of the group. *Motociclismo* summarised the 600 with the comments, "Excellent comfort, refined mechanics, good chassis, but with completely unresponsive brakes, poor performance, excessive weight, and insufficient steering angle." The time was right for a more up-to-date replacement, and this would be the 750 S.

600 DIMENSIONS

Fuel tank capacity	20 litres (4 litres reserve)
Engine oil capacity	4kg SAE 40 Summer, SAE 20 Winter
Final drive	0.4kg SAE 90
Maximum width	810mm
Maximum length	2210mm
Maximum height	1110mm
Seat height	810mm
Ground clearance	170mm
Wheelbase	1390mm
Dry weight	221kg
Maximum speed	177km/h
Oil consumption	½kg oil/1000km

Vittorio Emanuel's MV 600 was always blue.
(Courtesy Raphael David)

MV AGUSTA FOURS

600 DISTINGUISHING FEATURES

Engine Number from 199-001 to 199-0134
Main bearings 25x52x15mm
Cylinder head with two horizontal cooling fins
Marelli 7K twin point distributor until engine 199-037
Bosch JF4 single point distributor from engine 199-038
Early versions with straight cut primary gears
Valve adjustment by shims above the buckets
9mm cam drive gears
15-fin sump
Inspection plug on left- and right side of the crankcase
Twin Dell'Orto UB24 carburettors
12-plate clutch
First gear manufactured integrally on the layshaft
Final drive with thinner fins
Frame numbers from MV4C6 199001
Campagnolo 216mm mechanical front disc brakes
Seat changed during production, later versions higher at the rear
At least three types of steel front mudguard (single and dual metal rings)
Bosch horns after frame number 199051
Rectangular headlight in fibreglass nacelle
Fibreglass side covers

600 PRODUCTION NUMBERS

Year	Number
1967	28
1968	50
1969	36
1970	10
1971	1
1972	0
1973	1
Total	127

3 THE 750 S 1970-1973 (MV4C75)

Although Count Domenico Agusta had initially sanctioned only a touring 600 four-cylinder for production, slow sales and pressure from dealers saw him reluctantly agree to the creation of a 750 Sport. But he was still resistant, fearing a 750 may not perform to expectations in competition, so he insisted on retaining the shaft drive. And while the 750 now had four carburettors, these were still the small 24mm Dell'Orto. A 750 S prototype, built out of a 600, was shown at the 1969 Milan Show, but it was still some time before the 750 S went into limited

The 750 Sport was the sensation of the 1969 Milan Show.

MV proudly displayed the 750 Sport with the array of racing trophies.

93

MV AGUSTA FOURS

production. The show prototype was very striking styled as a sports machine, and, as expected, was the star of the show. The claimed power was 65 horsepower at 7000rpm, the top speed 225km/h, and the price 1,950,000 Lire.

Probably due to the Count's reluctance, only a small number of 750s were built in 1970. This scenario may well have continued if Count Domenico had not died suddenly on 2 February 1971. His brother Corrado succeeded him, and initially there were few changes. The racing program continued unabated, but the impediment allowing a production sporting four-cylinder MV Agusta no longer remained. As a result a few more production 750s were built in 1971 than in 1970, although this still only numbered 56. Considerable time was spent testing the prototypes by chief testers Alberto Pagani, Gianpiero Zubani, and Giancarlo Dobelli. In the winter of 1970-1971 Angelo Bergamonti also spent some time on the test 750, much of it on race tracks. According to Arturo Magni, the increase in production was probably more due to demand than any other factor. He says, "Although Corrado wasn't very interested in motorcycles, nothing changed initially."

A rear view of the 750 Sport displayed at the 1969 Milan Show.

The early 750 Sport of 1970. This is a pre-production version with a different instrument layout to later examples.

THE 750 S 1970-1973 (MV4C75)

When the 750 S went into production it differed slightly from the prototype.

THE PRODUCTION 750 SPORT (1970-71)

Early in 1970 MV invited journalist Roberto Patrignani to test at MV's Cascina Costa track, and this featured in several Italian and European magazines. The test bike differed in some details to the eventual production version, notably by the silver instrument housings and lower profile red seat without 'emmevi' lettering. This example was probably the Milan Show bike as 750 Sport production didn't commence until September 1970. The first 750 Sport was built on 22 September (engine number 214-001, frame 214008, sold to Garreau in Paris), with the next on 2 October. Only nine 750 Sports were manufactured in 1970, one (engine 214-009, frame 214006, built 27/11/70) was sold to John Taylor of Yankee Motor Corporation in the USA. This early example was tested by *Cycle World* magazine in August 1971. Another (engine 214-002, frame 214009) was sold to Circle Motors in the UK on 8/10/70, the remaining going to Switzerland, France, and Italy. Of the 56 examples built in 1971 most (28) were sold in Italy, although one went to Formula One driver Jacky Ickx in Belgium (Engine 214-043, frame 214048, on 24/11/71). Amongst the anomalies in the production, the first frame number (214001) was a prototype, not assembled as a complete motorcycle until 21 July 1972 (with engine 214-0212).

ENGINE

Initially, the 750 Sport engine was derived from the 600, but with a new number sequence beginning at 214-001. Several changes in specification separated the earliest version from eventual 1970 production examples. Although the factory organised its production data by frame number, actual production generally corresponded more with engine number. 1970 engine numbers went from 214-001-214-009, with 1971 engine numbers from 214-010 to 214-075. The final 1971 engines overlapped with 1972 production, and the first engine series (those based on the 600) finished at engine number 214-0160, these continuing into mid-1972. As with the 600, all the engines were individually built, with each component selected for a perfect fit.

95

MV AGUSTA FOURS

Early 750 Sport engines were similar to the 600's, with a right side crankcase plug, and carrier without a rib (engine 214-087).

This was probably the reason why so few 750s were built compared to 350 twins during this period. Occasionally engine numbers were also duplicated (2140103 appears in two frames), and 13 examples between 1971 and 1973 had identical engine and frame numbers (although this would be by accident).

Produced only a few months later (engine 214-0135), the crank carrier on this engine now has a rib. The crankcase is still the early type with a right side plug.

750 S engine specifications

Type	Four-stroke, four-cylinder, air-cooled
Bore	65mm
Stroke	56mm
Capacity	743cc
Compression ratio	10:1 (9.3:1 1970)
Maximum power	66hp at 8000rpm

THE 750 S 1970-1973 (MV4C75)

CRANKSHAFT, CRANKCASE AND CAMSHAFT DRIVE

On the first 750 series the crankcase castings were similar to the 600 and featured a 15-fin sump. The crankshaft still included a helical primary gear but had larger (19mm) journals at each end, requiring new 30x72x19mm C3 main bearings. In other respects the crank was as for the 600, with the same con rod and big-end dimensions. The crankshaft was unchanged during the entire production run, from the 600 until the America, with no alteration in balance for different pistons. The primary drive was still 1.75:1 (56/98). The crankshaft rack was new (to accept the larger cylinders), and the 12 studs retaining the crank in the rack increased from 8mm to 10x100mm, which required new crank 'U' fittings underneath. The crank rack design was similar to the 600, as it still didn't include a rib. The crankcase also retained an inspection plug on the right. Other similarities with the 600 included the narrower 9mm camshaft drive gears.

CYLINDERS AND PISTONS

The full circle 65mm three-ring Borgo pistons were similar to those of the 600, but were now forged and provided a compression ratio of between 9.3:1 and 10:1 (depending on the data provided) – early factory data indicated 9.3:1, while the owners' manual of April 1972 stated 10:1. The piston weight was increased slightly over the smaller 600 pistons to 200 grams. Unlike the 600, the 750 had 1.68x69.57mm O-rings installed underneath cylinder base gaskets.

CYLINDER HEAD AND CAMSHAFTS

A new cylinder head was produced for the 750 Sport, initially based on the 600 (with two horizontal fins) but with modified combustion chambers. The included valve angle remained at 80 degrees and the valves identical (29.4mm inlet and 28mm exhaust), with the same 32 and 30mm valve seats. The outer fin was still cut away around the

The sump on the early 750 Sport was a narrow type with 25 fins.

The early 750 valve shim bucket had two holes.

MV AGUSTA FOURS

sparkplug. The camshafts and valve timing were also the same as the 600. What was new for the 750 was the valve adjustment system; the adjustment shims now underneath the bucket instead of on top as on the 600. This solution was more suited to high-performance. The camshaft needed to be removed in order to replace shims and adjust valve clearance. The early valve buckets were the two-hole type, similar to the 600, and prone to cracking. The 750 also received new inner and outer valve springs.

The cylinder head and cylinders were still bolted to the crank rack (without a rib) by 12 waisted studs. These studs were now 10x169mm and included extended spacers to the bottom of the stud counter bore holes to prevent the stud shearing spacers at the top. The retaining nuts were still external hexagonal 9mm. The 600-style crank rack provided a smooth look to the engine but according to Dave Kay, "It was always a mismatch."

Carburettor jetting 750 S (1971)

Type	2x Dell'Orto UB 24 B2 & 2x UB 24 BS2
Choke diameter	24mm
Main jet	105 (115 1970)
Idle jet	45
Throttle valve	70 (60 1970)
Needle	E 8 2nd notch (E10 1970)
Atomiser	260 A (260 B 1970)
Air intake	Open horn 44xL60
Pilot screw	Open 1 turn

Valve timing 750 S

Inlet opens	48° before TDC
Inlet closes	68° after BDC
Exhaust opens	70° before BDC
Exhaust closes	36° after TDC
Valve clearance cold intake	0.25mm
Valve clearance cold exhaust	0.30mm

CARBURETTORS AND EXHAUST

Although the 24mm cylinder head intakes and manifold stud arrangement was carried over from the 600, instead of two Dell'Orto carburettors on siamesed manifolds the 750 featured four individual UB 24 B2 and UB 24 BS2 carburettors. These still breathed through open aluminium bell mouths, and a single cable operated a lever from the centre. Carburettor jetting for 1971 varied slightly from the earliest 1970 examples, as did the manifold attachment. The bell mouths were angled; the outer inwards and the inner outwards. The exhaust ports were threaded as before, but with four individual chrome-plated header pipes and seamed mufflers. An unusual feature was the way the exhaust system was hung on the bike then the frame drilled for mounts – a satisfactory solution for a new machine, but it made fitting replacement exhaust systems difficult.

Four Dell'Orto UB24mm carburettors distinguished the 750 S from the 600. There was no air filtration, and on this very early example the carburettors were attached to a plate.

THE 750 S 1970-1973 (MV4C75)

The 1971 production 750 S intake manifold arrangement included two rubber insulators.

IGNITION AND ELECTRICAL SYSTEM

The single point Bosch JF-4 distributor and Bosch Dynastart was identical to the 600, and, for 1970, so was the 12-volt 18Ah battery. During 1971 the battery was upgraded to 32Ah. The sparkplug leads were black in 1970, but changed to red during 1971. The sparkplug type also changed, from 275W to 260W, but all types retained the Bosch sparkplug caps. Unlike the 1970 prototype, the production 750 S featured an external capacitor attached to the distributor body with a coiled red wire connector.

Ignition and electrical system

Ignition type	Battery and coil
Fixed advance	18-20° (8-10° 1970)
Automatic advance	28-30° (38-40° 1970)
Total advance	46-50°
Breaker points clearance	0.4mm
Firing order	1,3,4,2
Sparkplug	260W long thread 14mm (275W 1970)
Sparkplug electrode gap	0.6mm
Battery	12V 32Ah (12V 18Ah 1970)
Dynastart	Bosch 12V 135W

MV AGUSTA FOURS

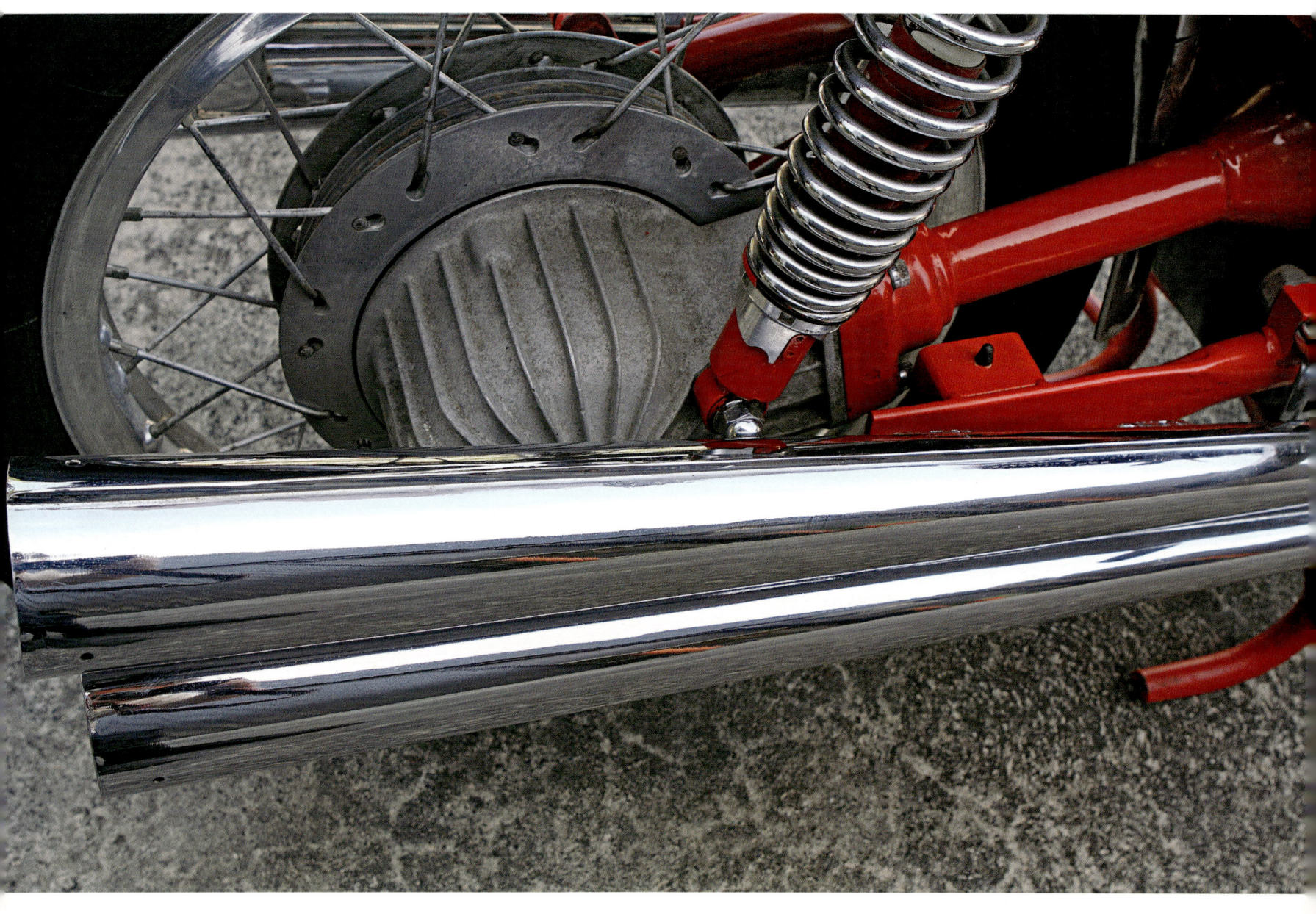

The 750 S also had four individual seamed mufflers (two each side).

GEARBOX

The 1970 750 S had a similar gearbox to the 600, but for 1971 some improvements were implemented. Previously only first gear was manufactured integrally with the mainshaft, but now the mainshaft included first and second gears. The fourth gear on the mainshaft was also new, but the layshaft and other gears remained unchanged. Apart from a direct 5th gear, the ratios were the same, but, according to Albert Bold, the gear teeth were still weak and some gears were not interchangeable with the 600 due to differing thickness.

750 S gear ratios (1971)

Gear	Ratio	Teeth
1st	2.38:1	30/15x25/21
2nd	1.69:1	27/19x25/21
3rd	1.29:1	24/22x25/21
4th	1.09:1	22/24x25/21
5th	1:1	21/25x25/21

THE 750 S 1970-1973 (MV4C75)

CLUTCH
The 750 S also had a new clutch, now with seven driven plates (3mm) and seven steel driving plates. These were the same as on the 600, except the driven plates had a different clutch centre, with triangular inner teeth. Clutch actuation remained like the later 600, with three rods and three balls, as did the five clutch springs. The clutch primary gear was also new, the unchanged clutch basket still riveted to it.

FINAL DRIVE
Although the intermediate bevel gear ratio was unchanged, for 1970 the 750 S final drive was raised to 2.54:1 (33/13). This was obviously a little high, blunting top gear performance, so the ratio was lowered slightly during 1971 to 2.67:1 (32/12).

Gear	Ratio
Engine to transmission	1.066:1 (15/16)
Transmission shaft to wheel	2.67:1 (32/12) (2.54:1 1970)

FRAME, WHEELS, TYRES, BRAKES, AND SUSPENSION
The 750 S frame was similar in design to the 600, but painted red, with numbers beginning at MV4C75 214001. Early frames didn't have an Italian frame homologation number. During 1972 the frames included DGM and OM stamps, but still without numbers. The frame also held the large diameter engine breather hose that connects to the breather outlet near the distributor housing, running through a hole near the steering head and exiting through a hole in the tube underneath the motor. The steering head angle was 63 degrees from horizontal (27 degrees from vertical) and the headstock length 160mm.

Frame differences to the 600 included a centre stand with looped feet and a rounded rear subframe, associated brackets, and a different bolt-on battery support (for the later larger battery). Borrani aluminium 2.15x18in wheels were still fitted front and rear, but now carried the markings 'BORRANI WM3 18 RECORD RM01 4470.' 36 Alpino (3.3mm marked A) spokes were fitted front and rear, laced to a Grimeca 230x30mm four leading-shoe front drum and cable-operated 200x45mm single leading-shoe rear brake (the same as on the 600). The front axle was enlarged to Ø16mm. MV wanted

The early 750 S frame didn't include a homologation number.

The 750 S final drive ratio was different to the 600.

The Borrani rims on the 750 S were stamped with identification numbers.

101

MV AGUSTA FOURS

to maintain the impression that its 750 was the fastest motorcycle available so V-rated tyres were specified, and the only ones available at the time were Metzeler; a 3.50V18 Rille 10 on the front and 4.00V18 Block C6 on the rear. The suspension was also new: the front a Ceriani 35mm fork with polished alloy legs and exposed tubes; the rear by a pair of BREV Sebac 259032 shock absorbers, with chrome springs and length of 320mm. The shock bodies were painted red, and on the early 750 S spring preload adjustment required a tool. Soon after production commenced the lower spring collar was modified to include an adjusting handle.

Wheels, tyres and brakes

Front wheel	WM3x18in Borrani,
Front brake	230x30mm double drum Grimeca
Front tyre	3.50x18in ribbed V-rated
Rear wheel	WM3x18in Borrani,
Rear brake	200x45mm drum
Rear tyre	4.00x18in pattern V-rated

The 1970 production 750 S had a fibreglass tank with the filler on the right side. This example (engine 214-009, frame 214006) was built on 27/22/70. (Courtesy Cycle World)

The instrument panel didn't have any warning lights. This is a very early example with a fibreglass tank and a centrally-mounted early style cap.

The instrument housings were Crinkle Black on the early 750 Sport.

INSTRUMENTS, LIGHTS, SWITCHES, HANDLEBARS, HORN, AND CONTROLS

The 1970 prototype had the Veglia instruments in silver housings, a 12,000rpm tachometer (without a redline), and 240km/h speedometer (without a trip meter). All production 1970 and 1971 750 Ss had black instrument surrounds with aluminium tops, mounted on an alloy plate. Frame number 214011 (engine number 214-004 built 2/10/70)

THE 750 S 1970-1973 (MV4C75)

Early 750 Sport instruments were Veglia.

MV selected premium equipment, including a Domino throttle and Tommaselli handlebars.

as shown in the owners' manual as seen in the image above. There were no warning lights on the 1970 and 1971 750 S, only a centrally-mounted ignition key. Befitting its price and status, the 750 S was also distinguished by a plethora of high quality equipment. Much of this was Tommaselli, including the kinked clip-on handlebars, Matador brake and clutch controls, with a Domino single cable throttle with black Tommaselli handgrips. Some examples had a Tommaselli Daytona throttle instead of the Domino. The handlebar switches were Aprilia, and the 40/45W headlight CEV (Made by Pagani). This was mounted on beautifully-crafted aluminium clamps. The taillight was a rectangular CEV (also Pagani) with a 5/20W stop light, but some early examples sent to the US had a round CEV taillight. A single Aprilia horn sat in front of the engine. The hollow steel footpegs were mounted

The handlebar switches were Aprilia.

Some early 750 Sports had a Tommaselli Daytona throttle.

103

MV AGUSTA FOURS

The horn on the 750 S was an Aprilia.

The rear brake switch on the very early 750 S was behind the lever.

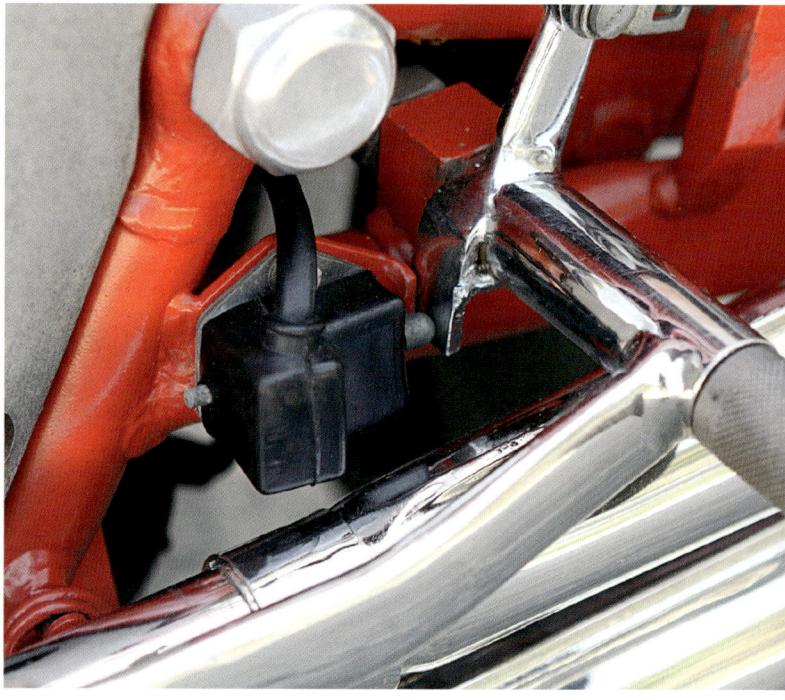

On most production examples the rear brake switch sat in front of the pedal.

THE 750 S 1970-1973 (MV4C75)

FUEL TANK, SEAT, SIDE COVERS, MUDGUARDS, AND TOOLKIT

Several types of tank were fitted, the very earliest bikes with a Vetrosina (fibreglass) tank. The fuel filler cap was a lever type; centrally-mounted on the very earliest example, and positioned on the right soon afterwards. During 1971 a steel 24-litre tank was introduced (the official steel tank blueprints were dated 20/10/71) with a new centrally-mounted flip-up chrome filler cap. The paintwork on the 1970 and 1971 750 S featured a red top section and dark blue sides with a white flash and the distinctive 'MV' cog decal. The decal on the top of the 1970 fuel tank proclaimed 30 Constructors' World Championships, and for 1971 there were 32 stars. During 1971 the tank colour scheme was changed to the red/white and blue type but the exact frame number where the transition occurred is difficult to quantify. There

This rectangular CEV taillight was featured on most early 750 Sports, although some US versions had a round taillight.

The regulator and fuse box were still under the seat on the 750 S.

on the muffler mount, providing a sporting rear-set riding position. On the earliest examples the rear brakelight switch mounted behind the lever, but this was in front on the production version. A Johnson rod linkage operated the gearshift.

This early example (engine number 214-009, frame 214006) didn't have the 'emmevi' seat logo, and the shock absorbers didn't include a spring preload adjusting lever.
(Courtesy Cycle World)

105

MV AGUSTA FOURS

was some overlap between 1971 and 1972 with the two types of fuel tank, and also with frame numbers (particularly between 214050 and 214100). Two unlinked Brev Orlandi fuel petcocks were fitted to the 750 S tank, now with a 16x1.00mm thread screwing directly into the tank. There was some inconsistency with the type of petcock used as some had an adapter for an internal 14x1mm thread. The fuel line was clear plastic, held by Jubilee clamps.

The red upholstered solo seat hinged on the left instead of the rear as on the 600, and, although the very earliest examples didn't have any inscription, the seat generally had 'emmevi' emblazoned on the rear. This was the telegram prefix for the company, in the days when a telex was the quickest means of communication. The seat was made by Gaman in Rho (Milan) and sometimes included a strap (although this was rare). An identical toolkit to the 600 was held in the seat base. Early bikes had fibreglass side covers, but during 1972 the factory built a special machine to press steel side covers. Some early examples had white '750 S' decals, but most were without in 1970 and 1971. Stainless steel 'Inox' mudguards completed the chassis specification, as did the plethora of chrome-plated fasteners. There was some inconsistency regarding the use of chrome-plated or zinc-plated bolts and washers, with sometimes a combination of both used for a specific application.

This and facing page: This MV 750 S was produced in black specifically for Australian importer Bob Jane early in 1972 (engine number 214-087, frame 214084).

THE 750 S 1970-1973 (MV4C75)

Another inconsistency in the specification of the early 750 S was a black example (engine number 214-087, frame 214084) sent to Bob Jane in Australia early in 1972. Built on 7 January 1972, the frame was also black, as was the seat. While the fuel tank was steel, the side covers were fibreglass, and underneath the black paint was the usual MV red. This example was later sold to Bill Morris, who imported it to the UK. The Italian magazine *Moto Sport* tested engine number 214-017 in December 1971; this example (frame 214018, built 15/9/71) with a steel, early paint style tank, two fin head, Veglia instruments, and the right crankcase plug.

MV AGUSTA FOURS

750 S DIMENSIONS

Fuel tank capacity	24 litres (4 litres reserve)
Engine oil capacity	4kg SAE 40 Summer, SAE 20 Winter
Oil filter	FRAM CH 803 PL Øe 59 Øi 18 L 101
Final drive	0.4kg SAE 90
Maximum width	750mm
Maximum length	2105mm
Maximum height	1020mm
Seat height	800mm
Ground clearance	160mm
Wheelbase	1390mm
Dry weight	235kg
Oil consumption	½kg oil/1000km

The early 1970 prototype with a lower seat appeared on the first publicity material.

The early 1971 advertisement proclaimed 63 World Championships.

MV was always keen to promote its victories. Its advertisement prior to the 1971 Milan Show proclaimed 67 World Championships.

THE 750 S 1970-1973 (MV4C75)

750 S DISTINGUISHING FEATURES (1970-71)

Crankshaft with 19mm journals
Crank carrier without a rib
15-fin sump
Two-fin cylinder head
9mm camshaft drive gears
Valve adjustment shims underneath the bucket
Cylinder studs with extended spacers
Right side crankcase plug
14 plate clutch
4 Dell'Orto UB 24 carburettors
4 Individual seamed mufflers
32/12 final drive ratio (33/13 in 1970)
Frame without DGM homologation number
Ceriani 35mm front fork
Sebac shock absorbers
Grimeca 230mm 4LS front brake
Ø16mm front axle
CEV headlight and rectangular taillight
Fibreglass fuel tank on early examples (dark blue with white flashes)
Decal proclaiming 32 World Championships (1971)
Fibreglass side covers, mostly without white '750 S' decals
Very earliest examples without 'emmevi' on the seat
Veglia instruments with black surround
No warning lights on dashboard
Tommaselli handlebars with Domino or Daytona throttle
Aprilia switches and horn
12V 32Ah battery (18Ah on early examples)
Chrome-plated bolts and washers used in combination with zinc-plated

The series of photos on this page depicts a 750 S with engine number 214-039, frame 214042, built on 30/10/71.
(Courtesy Roy Kidney)

109

MV AGUSTA FOURS

Striking styling and a Fontana front brake distinguished the 750 SS when displayed at Milan at the end of 1971.

The fibreglass tank was a new shape, and instrumentation included a Krober electronic tachometer. The tank shape undoubtedly influenced Ducati when designing its 750 SS the following year.

THE 750 SS

No other MV four enjoys the myth and mysticism that surrounds the 750 SS displayed at the 1971 Milan Show. This was subsequently listed as a production model, and advertised by MV in Italy and distributors outside Italy at a price considerably higher than that

The full fairing eventually became an option on the 750 S.

THE 750 S 1970-1973 (MV4C75)

Four Dell'Orto VHB carburettors were fitted, breathing through open bell mouths as usual.

The seat was a solo type, but the exhaust system was standard 750 S.

of the 750 S. The Bob Jane Corporation in Australia quoted the 750 SS for $4779, as opposed to the 750 S and GT at $3889, while in Italy the 750 SS was listed at 2,500,000 Lire, and in Germany Hansen listed the 750 SS at 17,200 DM. Hansen GmbH of Baden-Baden had been the German importer since 1970, listing the 750 S at 13,790 DM and the 750 GT 13,290 DM. However, a study of factory records doesn't indicate any production 750 SSs were actually built, and this is confirmed by Arturo Magni who said, "It was only a prototype and never put into production, although there have been several replicas made." Certainly the example on display at Milan was a very tempting offering. Actual engine details were sketchy, but carburetion included four square-slide Dell'Orto VHB27mm carburettors. The claimed compression ratio was 9.5:1, and power 60 horsepower at 7900rpm. Other specific features included a sculptured fibreglass tank, solo fibreglass seat with white upholstery, a Fontana 230mm four leading-shoe front brake, Krober electronic tachometer, Dunlop TT100 tyres, and a fibreglass full fairing. The weight was still a considerable 224kg, and the claimed top speed 240km/h. Although the 750 SS may not have made it into production, it seemed to inspire other companies. When Ducati released its 750 SS in 1972, not only was the designation the same, but it featured a similar solo seat and a similarly shaped fibreglass fuel tank.

IMOLA 200 RACE 1972

The Imola 200 race, held on 23 April 1972, was hailed as Italy's 'Daytona of Europe' and was launched with huge publicity and the promise of a record prize fund of 35,000,000 Lire (£24,000). Organised by the influential Motor Club Santerno under the direction of Dott. Francesco Costa, all the major Italian manufacturers were encouraged to build specialised racing machines to take on the best that the rest of the world had to offer. Costa was friendly with Count Corrado Agusta and he particularly wanted Agostini and MV Agusta to participate. Costa also saw an opportunity for three great Italian motorcycle manufacturers (MV, Moto Guzzi, and Ducati) to race against each other for the first time since 1957.

In early March 1972, the Motor Club Santerno arranged for a group of leading Italian motorcycle engineers to travel to Daytona to view

MV AGUSTA FOURS

The first test at Modena prior to Imola. This is Pagani's bike that differed in detail to Agostini's.

Agostini's bike had a different frame, seat, and lower tank to Pagani's.

After Pagani withdrew, his bike received Ago's No 1 plate.

Formula 750 racing at its most competitive. Arturo Magni travelled in the company of Ducati's Fabio Taglioni, Massimo Laverda and Luciano Zen from Laverda, and Moto Guzzi's Michele Bianchi. Apart from Taglioni, all had their reservations about preparing a competitive racer, and Corrado Agusta didn't decide to build an F750 racer until the end of March. With 25 days before the race, the racing department of 27 staff worked hard to build two machines; one for Giacomo Agostini and another for Alberto Pagani (son of former MV rider Nello Pagani).

There were a few stumbling blocks. Regulations required a production-based 750cc motorcycle, so MV was forced to retain the shaft drive and standard 750 gearbox. However, it was allowed to build a new frame. Arturo Magni and his son Carlo had designed a frame over the winter of 1971 as a possible replacement for the production 750 S, so this formed the basis for the racer. Each bike had a slightly different version of Magni's frame. On Agostini's bike the top tubes bent towards the swingarm as single tube, while Pagani's had straight tubes along the top of the engine with a 45-degree cut off to the seat rails. Both twin loop designs included a removable left tube for ease of engine maintenance and butt-welded seat tubes where the tubes bent downwards. Other differences between the two bikes included: Agostini's seat upholstery being held by metal fasteners as opposed to Pagani's by tape; Agostini's engine mounts were a 90-degree bent flat plate, while Pagani's were a tube; the tank on Agostini's bike curved down at the rear, following the frame tubes, while Pagani's tank was flat bottomed to follow the horizontal frame tubing. Completing the chassis specifications for both bikes were 18in Borrani wheels (a 3,25x18in on the front and 3.50x18in on the rear), a 38mm Ceriani fork and 230mm four leading-shoe Ceriani drum brake straight off the 500cc Grand Prix racer. The final drive ratio was raised to 11/32 (11:2.91), allowing the 190kg 750 to achieve nearly 290km/h.

The 750cc engine also differed considerably from the production version. As on the earlier Grand Prix racers, the cylinders were cast in one-piece instead of separately, the engine fins shaved to minimise width. This resulted in the previously rounded barrel becoming flat and one less fin near the sparkplug. The special die-cast cylinder head included special camshafts and, compared to the production

THE 750 S 1970-1973 (MV4C75)

Agostini and Magni in discussion during practice.

Although he had two bikes at his disposal, Agostini rode his original bike in the race.

The 750cc four-cylinder engine was quite special; with narrower cylinders and Dell'Orto SS1 carburettors. There was also one less outside fin on the cylinder head.

Agostini was credited with the equal fastest lap of 161.116 km/h in the 1972 Imola 200.

MV AGUSTA FOURS

In the early stages of the race Agostini led the eventual winner – Ducati-mounted Paul Smart. (Courtesy Cycle World)

When it reappeared at the end of 1973 the F750 MV was still ostensibly Agostini's 1972 Imola racer, only now with a four-valve cylinder head.

A steel box-section swingarm replaced the shaft drive.

750 the cylinder head, was angled forward, the fins not parallel with the barrel fins, plus it was a twin-fin casting. The valve angle was narrowed two degrees, larger (34mm inlet and 29mm exhaust) valves fitted, and the valve lift increased from 8.5 to 9mm. The 743cc engine retained the 64x56mm bore and stroke, but with four individual 34mm exhausts, a 10:1 compression ratio, and 30mm (bored out 29mm) SS1 Dell'Orto carbs. The power output was 85 horsepower at 9000rpm. The Dynastart was removed, and when they rolled out of the Gallarate race shop the 750 Imola bikes were painted red and white, instead of MV's usual red and silver livery.

Although there was a short test at Modena prior to Imola, official practice didn't go well for the MV team. Agostini was three seconds slower than Smart's Ducati, and Pagani six seconds down. Pagani completed only nine laps before he injured his arm and decided to leave the bike in the parking lot. His bike subsequently received a number 1 plate to be Agostini's spare, but was later withdrawn because the Elektron crankcases were not homologated. For the race Agostini found himself in an unaccustomed lowly fourth place on the grid, but at least he was on the front row. The field included 22 other factory or importer-entered machines, making the first Imola 200 one of the most competitive races ever, run in front of a huge crowd of 70,000.

When the flag fell Agostini showed his class by scorching off the line ahead of the Ducati's of Smart and Spaggiari. He led for five laps, setting the equal fastest lap of 161.116km/h

The frame was the same as for 1972, with a curved tube arching over the engine.

The shaft and final drive unit was discarded.

114

THE 750 S 1970-1973 (MV4C75)

The new swingarm allowed a larger section Dunlop racing tyre.

Double Scarab front brakes graced the front end.

with Smart and Spaggiari. By lap 40 Agostini was only 8 seconds down, with an increasing amount of smoke billowing out of his megaphones. Agostini retired with 20 laps left to run, his retirement attributed to valve failure (although others have claimed the shaft drive bevel gear failed, and another account says it was an electrical problem). There are contemporary photos of the smoking exhaust that would vindicate valve failure as the cause of retirement.

MV was quite philosophical about the Imola result, Managing Director Pietro Bertola saying after the race, "We didn't come to Imola to win, simply to show our sportsmanship by taking part, and to gain experience. This class of racing is new to us, but before long I promise you we too will be competitive." As it transpired, the 750 wasn't further developed until the end of 1973 when it appeared at a test session at Misano. Engine development saw a four-valve cylinder head, power increased to 107 horsepower at 11,500rpm, and a six-speed gearbox installed. Twin Scarab discs replaced the Ceriani front drum brake, and a box-section steel swingarm and chain drive was fitted instead of the road bike's shaft. This allowed a larger rear Borrani wheel and wider Dunlop racing tyre, and reduced the weight to 175kg. Tested by Phil Read and Pagani, it was intended to race the 750 in F750 events during 1974, but, unfortunately, that year saw the release of the Yamaha TZ700 and the F750 MV was shelved. In 1987 it passed into the hands of Team Obsolete in New York.

THE 750 S (1972-1973)

Although ostensibly still a hand-built motorcycle in limited numbers, there was gradual development to the 750 S during 1972. For categorization of the 1972 750 S it is convenient to use the 1972 factory spare parts variation list (published August 1973) as a guide. This indicates that most updates were incorporated after engine and frame number 214-0161, with further changes from engine number 214-0189 and 214-0211. According to factory production data, this would place these modifications between 8/6/72 (engine 214-0161, frame 2140163) and 4/9/72 (engine 214-0211, frame 2140267). Some engine updates were incorporated slightly earlier, with at least two known engines (214-0135 and 214-0136) using the earlier crankcases and later ribbed crank carrier.

The 750 S continued into 1973 to all intents and purposes unchanged, but early in 1973 the engine received another set of updates, this time to improve performance. This specification was

MV AGUSTA FOURS

This 1972 750 S (engine number 214-0135, frame 2140136) was built in April 1972, and was one of the last to feature the early 600-based engine (but with the later ribbed crank carrier). The side covers are steel on this example.

midway between the 1972 and 1974 engines. Mostly these updated engines were incorporated in the earlier frame, but some were also installed in the updated 1974 type frame. There was never any correlation between engine and frame numbers, with engines and frames selected at random from supply racks. Often earlier engines were installed in later frames, and vice versa, and occasionally duplicate engine numbers occurred (214-0306 was fitted to two frames). It must be remembered that only small numbers of these motorcycles were manufactured, and it is virtually impossible to classify the standard 1973 750 Sport. 750 S production peaked in

THE 750 S 1970-1973 (MV4C75)

Some 1972 750 S models featured the earlier tank colours. This is engine number 214-0251, frame 2140221 (originally sold to Gus Kuhn in London on 29/11/72).

The engine number stamp for 1972 was similar on earlier 750s.

117

MV AGUSTA FOURS

1972 (with 187 examples manufactured), but only 150 were built in 1973. This meant that, on average, around three were built each week during 1973, so it's not surprising that some variation in actual specification occurred. After September 1973 most were also built as 1974 specification, with disc brakes and the 1974 series updated engine. The official MV Agusta historical website states 335 drum brake 750 Sports were produced, although my analysis of the official records places the number of drum brake 750 Sports at 370. During 1972 more MV fours were exported than previously. Although most were still sold in Italy, France and Germany, 750 Sports were now being sent to Tokyo, Austria, Barcelona, Belgium, Australia, and Gus Kuhn in London. Australia received eleven 750 Sports and Gus Kuhn six during 1972. Most 1973 750 Sports were sold to Schneider in Germany (61), with smaller numbers in other export markets. Bob Jane in Australia received only four this year, Gus Kuhn 14, and seven went to the USA.

ENGINE

During 1972 a new crankcase was produced, and was incorporated from engine number 214-0189 (13/7/72). Now with 21 lower fins, instead

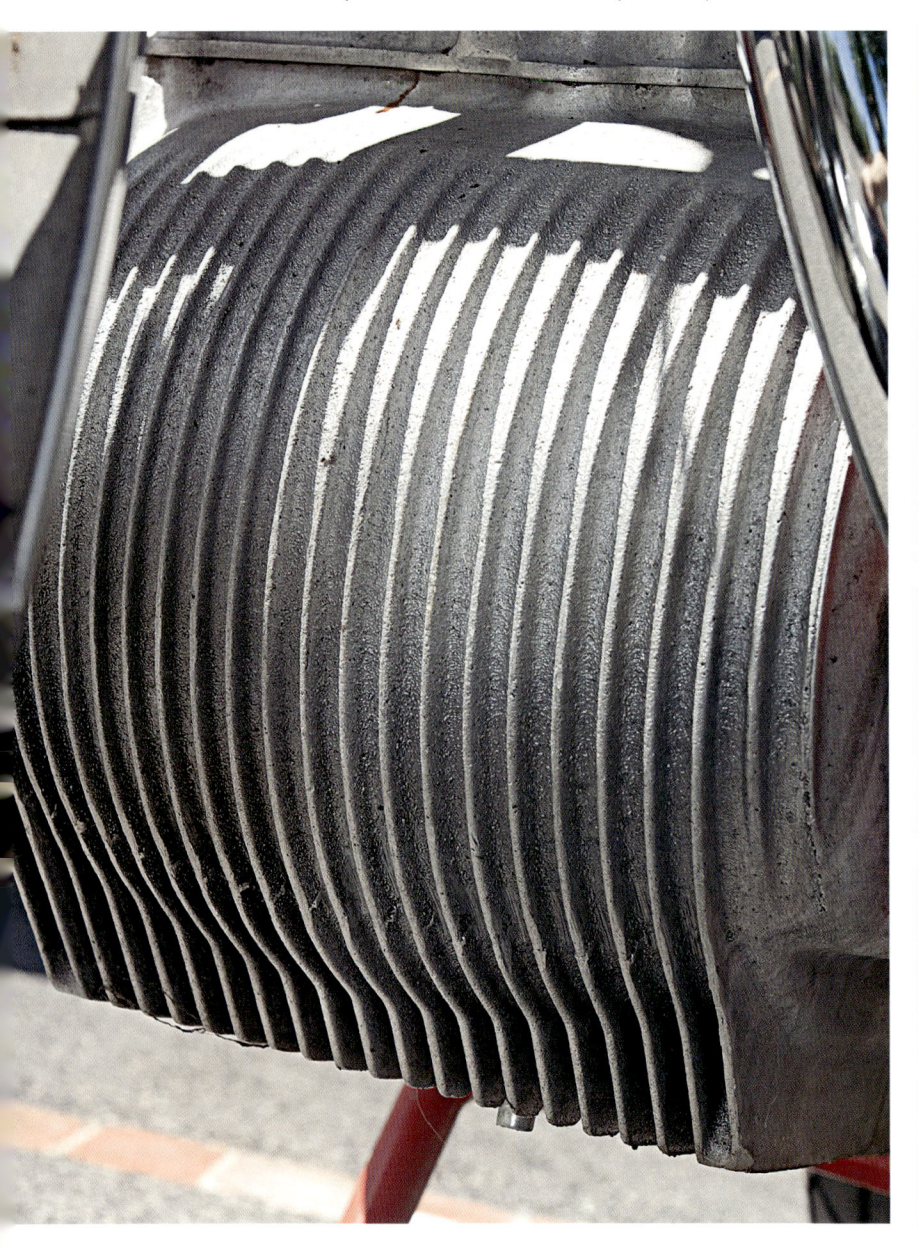

1972 engine updates included a 21-fin sump.

The right crankcase half no longer included an inspection plug.

THE 750 S 1970-1973 (MV4C75)

A single fin cylinder head casting appeared during 1972, with a reshaped outer cooling fin.

New cylinder head bolts appeared during 1972.

1972 updates included new camshaft drive gears and steel support. (Courtesy Dorian Skinner)

MV AGUSTA FOURS

The single fin casting after engine number 214-0211 was easily identifiable.

of 15 as on the 600 and earlier 750, it no longer had an inspection plug on the right, and had a new clutch cover casting and gasket. The ten screws fastening the clutch cover were increased in size to 8x20mm (up from seven 6x20mm and three 6x30mm).

Slightly earlier, after engine number 214-0161, the bushing near the intake camshaft was revised to include a smaller O-ring (1.78x21.95mm instead of 1.78x23.52mm). While the cylinder head and cylinders were still held by 12 waisted studs, there were short spacers added to the long hexagonal sleeve bolts securing the head, and the hexagon bolt

With the new cylinder head came three holed buckets and spectacle holders.

120

THE 750 S 1970-1973 (MV4C75)

Three types of pistons were used on the 750 S; the earliest on the left, the interim 1973 in the centre, and the 1974 on the right. (Courtesy Dorian Skinner)

head was now recessed. These new spacers, extended nuts, and new washers were designed to further reduce the studs' tendency to shear. New copper head gaskets were also fitted at this time. In addition, after engine 214-0161, the entire gear camshaft drive was updated, with larger (13mm) gears (although the module and number of teeth were unchanged) and new steel support box. The crankshaft supporting rack also included an outer rib, but this was also fitted to some earlier engines (from around 214-0135).

From engine number 214-0211 (4/9/72), a new cylinder head casting appeared with a single horizontal fin and reshaped vertical outer fin near the sparkplug. This was no longer cut away near the sparkplug. Inside this new cylinder head were new valve guides and paired valve guide buckets (like spectacles), with three-holed buckets (instead of two-holed), larger 8x25mm retaining screws (up from 5x20mm), and new lock washers. New studs retained the camshaft covers, and a plug and fibre washer was added at the front of the head. Although the carburettors were unchanged, on the new cylinder head the intake manifold plate was no longer required, and only one insulating plate used per carburettor. As a result, the intake mounting screws were shorter (M6x40mm instead of M6x50mm). Other earlier, small updates (after 214-0161) included a new circlip on

A new carburettor manifold appeared on the updated cylinder head later in 1972.

MV AGUSTA FOURS

A round CEV taillight appeared during 1972. This is a late 1973 bike with engine number 214-0395 (30/7/73). It probably has the interim engine specification as the exhaust system is the later type.

the distributor shaft and a new Dynastart shaft, which included an additional circlip. A valve also replaced the oil pressure relief ball on the oil pump at this time.

An undocumented interim engine update also occurred early in 1973, prior to the introduction of the 1974 specification engine. While retaining the 24mm carburettors and earlier camshafts, the cylinder head featured a combustion chamber with a semi-squish band and the larger valves (31.8mm inlet and 29mm exhaust) of the 1974 engine. The valves retained a 7mm stem; the inlet was 86.1mm long and the exhaust 84.6mm. The valve buckets were the earlier single bucket type, and the forged pistons featured a higher compression ratio with a land half-machined into the combustion chamber (unlike the

THE 750 S 1970-1973 (MV4C75)

The same bike. The frame (2140454) has the strengthened steering head of 1974 models.

1974 piston with a fully-machined land). These engines also appeared to have the 1974 type exhaust system, including lower, closer fitting, header pipes and mufflers without seams. According to the original factory drawings, these larger valves were introduced on 12/2/73. Production data indicates that the first engine number with these updates was 214-0276. A further study of engine numbers indicates the final interim 750 Sport engine number was possibly 214-0400. This was built on 26/7/73 with frame 2140416 and sold to Gus Kuhn in London.

CHASSIS

During 1972 the 750 S frame received Italian homologation number DGM10791OM, stamped alongside the frame number. Frame numbers for 1972 began at 214064, but there was always overlap between years. The final 1972 frame was 2140324, overlapping considerably with 1973. For 1973, the first frame was 2140245 and the final 1973 frame 2140469. Some of these final 1973 frames incorporated 1974 updates (such as the steering head extension). Although the basic chassis was unchanged from 1971, some small updates were incorporated after number 214-0161. The footpegs and brake and gearshift levers were new – the gear lever with a new return spring. More changes extended to the instruments, instrument housing and instrument panel. Smiths instruments replaced the Veglia, and the aluminium dashboard incorporated two warning lights; one for high beam and the other a dynamo warning light. Also new were the instrument surrounds, which were plain aluminium instead of black. The handgrips changed to brown Tommaselli, and gradually a single cable Tommaselli Daytona throttle unit replaced the Domino.

A new taillight bracket, with round CEV

The headlight mount was revised for fairing installation.

123

MV AGUSTA FOURS

A small Plexiglas screen was available on the 750 S for 1973.

The best things in life aren't free...

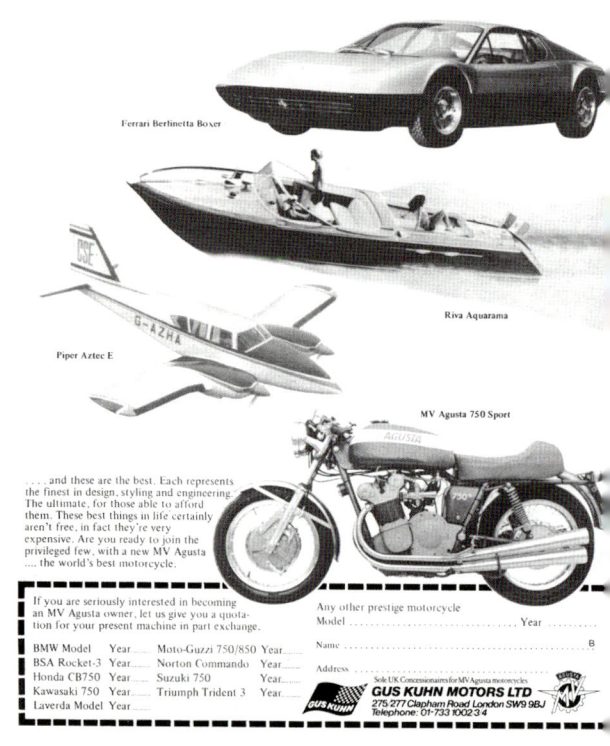

Gus Kuhn made no excuse for the price when it advertised the 750 S in Bike magazine during 1973.

taillight, replaced the earlier rectangular type, and electrical system updates extended to the incorporation of battery terminal protection caps and new wiring loom. This included wiring to the handlebar switches, headlamp, taillight, instruments, horn, Dynastart, coils, and regulator.

While the steel fuel tank was unchanged, the early style tank paint scheme overlapped for some time into 1972 and this is confirmed by period road tests. For this year the tank decal proclaimed 34 Constructors' Championships. Most 1972 750 Sports had a new tank colour scheme with large 'MV AGUSTA' decals. The red-painted steel side covers were unchanged, but invariably included a '750 S' decal, while the red seat

THE 750 S 1970-1973 (MV4C75)

cost of the 750 Sport was still prohibitive to most. In Italy, the 750 S was listed at 1,980,000 Lire, in the UK £2160 (including VAT and delivery). In the US, New York-based Commerce Overseas Corporation (COC) was the official distributor, but there was no dealer network. COC had a long association with MV through the helicopter business, and it wasn't until 1974 that it became seriously interested in distributing motorcycles.

Although the Grand Prix racing program continued as successfully as ever, MV Agusta produced only 235 motorcycles of all types in the first quarter of 1973. The motorcycle division was barely viable as a production concern, but there were other issues. The Italian government wanted more control of the aviation industry, particularly companies pursuing military contracts. In January 1973 Corrado made an agreement with state financier Pietro Sette for 50 per cent of MV Agusta to be controlled by the Government owned EFIM group. EFIM had 100 per cent control of Ducati, and early in 1973 Fredmano Spairani moved from Ducati to MV Agusta as an assistant to Corrado, who remained managing director. Spairani was one of the orchestrators of Ducati's successful 1972 Imola 200 racing effort, but was considered too extravagant by the EFIM directors that controlled Ducati. Ducati had spent a fortune on its 1971 and 1972 racing program, but was barely producing 7000 motorcycles a year and this was unsustainable. MV's racing was always subsidized by helicopter production and was a considerably more comprehensive program than Ducati's. Spairani was a racing enthusiast, but he also had conflicting business interests, most notably with the Scarab brake company in Bologna. His influence led to Scarab disc brake components being fitted to some of the 1974 Grand Prix racers and production 750 S in preference to similar patterned British Lockheed.

750 S SPECIFICATIONS (1972-73) DIFFERING FROM 1971

Compression ratio	9.5:1
Maximum power	69hp at 7900rpm
Engine oil capacity	3kg AGIP SINT 2000 20W50
Front fork oil	Shell Tellus 33 180cc per leg
Maximum width	660mm
Maximum length	2110mm
Maximum height	1040mm
Seat height	810mm
Ground clearance	150mm
Pedal height	330mm
Dry weight	230kg

The 1973 Italian advertisement was more restrained.

also included the white 'emmevi' sign. For 1973, the tank decal proclaimed 36 Championships, and a small plexiglass screen or fibreglass full fairing was an option. The wheels and brakes were unchanged. Now more widely available throughout the world, the

MV AGUSTA FOURS

750 S DISTINGUISHING FEATURES (1972-73)

Early in 1972 some engines featured a new ribbed crank carrier
After engine number 214-0161 spacers were added to the recessed hexagonal head bolts
After engine 214-0161 the gear camshaft drive included 13mm gears
After engine number 214-0189 were new crankcases with 21 lower fins
New crankcases were without a right side inspection plug
New clutch cover casting and gasket
A new cylinder head casting with a single horizontal fin after engine number 214-0211
Inside this new cylinder head were new valve guides, and paired valve guide buckets
With the new cylinder head, the intake manifold required only one insulating plate

Some 1973 engines with interim specification larger valves and higher compression pistons
After number engine 214-0161 Smiths instruments were fitted, with plain aluminium instrument surrounds and two warning lights incorporated into the dashboard
New footpegs and levers
Brown Tommaselli handgrips and Tommaselli Daytona throttle
Round CEV taillight
New fuel tank colour scheme with large 'MV AGUSTA' decals incorporated during 1972
Red-painted steel side covers introduced during 1972, with a '750 S' decal
For 1972 the tank decal proclaimed 34 Constructors' Championships, and 36 for 1973

Most 750 Sports were built in 1972, and this example towards the end of the year.

THE 750 S 1970-1973 (MV4C75)

750 S PRODUCTION RACING

Although there was no official racing of the 750 S, it was privately entered in isolated events during 1972, albeit unsuccessfully. Production racing was very important in Italy, and one of the most significant races was the 500 Kilometres of Monza, held on 25 June. The regulations were quite relaxed as, while the stock appearance had to be maintained (down to including a headlamp shell), modifications were permitted to the engine and brakes. This event drew entries from factory or distributor teams of Laverda, Triumph, Kawasaki, Suzuki, and Honda, with two privately entered MV 750 Sports. Maraccini rode a near stock 750 S, while Cipollini's bike featured a modified exhaust system and larger Ceriani front brake. Maraccini had already unsuccessfully contested the production event at Modena in April, and both MVs retired at Monza. Although they promised much, the mounted four was outclassed and the event was won by a pair of Triumph Tridents ahead of the Brambilla brother's Moto Guzzi V7 Sport.

Maraccini preparing for a wet Modena 500 race in April 1972.

Cipollini's 750 S had a racing exhaust system at Monza.

Maraccini's 750 S was nearly stock.

In Australia, Sydney dealer Brian Clarkson entered a 750 S in the 1972 Castrol Six-Hour race for production motorcycles, but retired before half-distance with clutch problems – the bike was smoking heavily under acceleration just prior to retirement, too. Clarkson also rode the 750 S at Bathurst in 1973, finishing 6th in the Chesterfield 5000 unlimited production race. Other private 750 Sport racers included a

A larger front brake was also fitted to Cipollini's 750 at Monza.

127

MV AGUSTA FOURS

Brian Clarkson at scrutineering for the 1972 Castrol Six-Hour race. (Courtesy Two Wheels)

Gus Kuhn machine entered at Silverstone in August 1974. Fitted with a half-fairing, four-into-one exhaust, and racing tyres, Dave Potter found it unsatisfactory. All these sporadic outings for the 750 Sport highlighted its inherent problems as a racing machine; predominantly the weight and modest power, compounded by the shaft final drive.

Clarkson had more success at Bathurst, finishing 6th in the 1973 Unlimited Production race.

1971-73 750 S PERFORMANCE

Sold as a high-performance motorcycle, the 1971-73 750 Sport promised more than it delivered. MV Agusta didn't readily provide test models, but Italian magazine *Moto Sport* tested an early example in December 1971. *Moto Sport*'s testing was always comprehensive but – while the MV cost 1,980,000 Lire compared to the Moto Guzzi V7 Sport's 1,460,000 Lire – the 230kg MV 750 could manage only 187.5km/h. The 225kg Guzzi Telaio Rosso, tested in the same issue, achieved 206.43km/h. *Cycle World*, testing a private 750 S in August 1971, achieved a similar top speed of 114.06mph (183.56km/h). Another early 750 S, tested by French magazine *Moto Revue* in April 1972, managed 187.5km/h at Montlhéry, with a standing start 400-metre time of 13.8 seconds. As the 1973 750 S was practically identical in specification, it

The following series of photos depicts Peter Calles' 1973 MV Agusta 750 S (engine 214-0327, frame 2140298). (Courtesy Michael Furman)

THE 750 S 1970-1973 (MV4C75)

was no surprise to see *Motorcycle* in the UK achieve a mean maximum speed of 112.34mph (180.8km/h) at the MIRA proving ground in October 1973. The standing quarter-mile was achieved in a leisurely 15.9 seconds (at 89.4mph) with the stopping distance from 30mph (48.3km/h) 30ft 6in (9.3m). Obviously, in response to these disappointing figures, the factory produced an interim updated engine during 1973. This definitely provided improved performance: testing an interim update 750 S in September 1973 *Motociclismo* managed 198.1km/h.

129

4

THE 750 GT
1972-1974 (MV4C75)

By the end of 1971 MV planned to increase production of the four-cylinder range, and announced the 750 GT alongside the 750 S and SS. The 750 GT was first displayed at the 1971 Milan Show with the 750 SS. Although the 750 SS didn't materialise, the 750 GT went into limited production during 1972. Some commentators have claimed the 750 GT was built out of left over 600 parts, but this is incorrect and the GT was more closely related to the 750 S. It also shared the 750 S engine and frame number sequence, and the differences between the 750 S and GT were largely cosmetic. Although the MV Agusta

The 750 GT – a modified 750 S – was first displayed at the 1971 Milan Show.

THE 750 GT 1972-1974 (MV4C75)

The Milan Show example featured an early engine with a right crankcase plug and twin-fin cylinder head.

historical website states 33 GTs were built, official factory records indicate 50 were produced, mostly in consecutive batches. The 1971 Milan Show bike was ostensibly a 750 S, with a special hand-beaten tank, seat, and side covers. The rear shock absorbers had spring covers, and the front forks rubber gaiters.

THE 750 GT (1972)

The first recorded 750 GT was engine number 214-054 and frame number 214045, and it was made on 6/7/72 before being sent to Schneider in Baden-Baden, Germany. Interestingly, the engine and frame numbers of this first GT were well within the 1971 750 Sport series, meaning these components were obviously sitting around for some time prior to assembly. The second 750 GT was built only two months after (15/9/72) but had a much later engine number (214-0234, frame 2140228). This was one of a batch of five consecutively numbered examples, of which four were sold to Garreau in Paris. Apart from the very first example, the 750 GT shared the updated engine specifications of the 750 S after engine and frame number 214-0161. The crankcases were then the later type; without the right side plug, and the cylinder a single fin type without a cutaway outer fin. The crank carrier was also the ribbed type. The carburettors were the same four Dell'Orto UB 24mm without air cleaners as on the 750 S, but the exhaust system included four individual mufflers without seams. The engines were identical in specification to the 750 Sport at the time. The final drive ratio was lower than on the 750 S (11/31), and while all 750 MVs were rare, the 750 GT was even rarer. Only 12 750 GTs were built in 1972, and all were exported.

CHASSIS

The 214 frame number series was shared with the 750 S, and the

131

MV AGUSTA FOURS

The 750 GT engine was identical in specification to the 750 S and featured a single fin cylinder head.

Another 1972 750 GT with early tank decals. This example has engine number 214-0275 and was built in November 1972.

This 1972 750 GT (engine number 214-0210, built on 15/9/72) had earlier 'MV' tank and side cover decals. The forks would have originally had gaiters: a crash bar was standard.

THE 750 GT 1972-1974 (MV4C75)

The mufflers on the 750 GT were without seams.

brown-painted frame was identical apart from the additional footpeg and crash bar mounts. As on the 750 S, the frame carried the Italian homologation number DGM 10791 OM. Although still including Smiths instruments, some of the earliest 1972 750 GTs featured a 750 Sport instrument panel, without holes for the throttle and clutch cables. Most 750 GT instrument panels included holes for the cables.

Much of the ancillary equipment (Smiths instruments, twin warning light dash, Aprilia switches, Tommaselli controls, Domino or Daytona throttle, brown Tommaselli handgrips, CEV lights, indicators, Borrani wheels, and Grimeca front brake) was shared with the 750 S, but many components were unique to the 750 GT. All 750 GTs were painted white and brown, and the steel fuel tank was a specific GT item, shaped quite differently to the voluptuous 750 Sport tank. The hand-beaten steel seat and tail unit were also unique. Tank

MV AGUSTA FOURS

750 GT frame number series was shared with the 750 S.

The frame homologation number was stamped after the frame number.

THE 750 GT 1972-1974 (MV4C75)

The 750 GT crash bar mount differed to that of the 600.

Most 750 GT instrument panels included holes for the cable guides. The Smiths instruments were shared with the 750 Sport. This 750 GT was originally sold with a mph speedometer for the Australian market.

specialist Primo Felotti, who also made the tanks for Grand Prix racers, built the tanks and seats for the GT. Few GTs were built because Felotti requested more money to make the bespoke tanks and seats. The Count refused, so Felotti wouldn't produce any more after the initial batch. The seat covering was quite thin so the idea of the 750 GT as a touring motorcycle was a misnomer. Fuel tank fittings, such the petcocks and filler cap, were as on the 750 S. The taillight on all GTs was the rectangular CEV, as on the 1971 and early 1972 750 S. The 750 GT also came with a specific crash bar, mounted with dual Bosch horns (in addition to the standard

Some 1972 750 GT instrument brackets were without cable guide holes. This example is engine 214-0275, and frame 2140326.

135

Although it looked impressive, the 750 GT seat covering was thin and unsupportive.

All 750 GTs had a rectangular CEV taillight.

The seat unit hinged and was specific to the 750 GT.

Twin Bosch horns mounted on the crash bar.

A single Aprilia horn, as on the 750 Sport, complemented the twin Bosch horns.

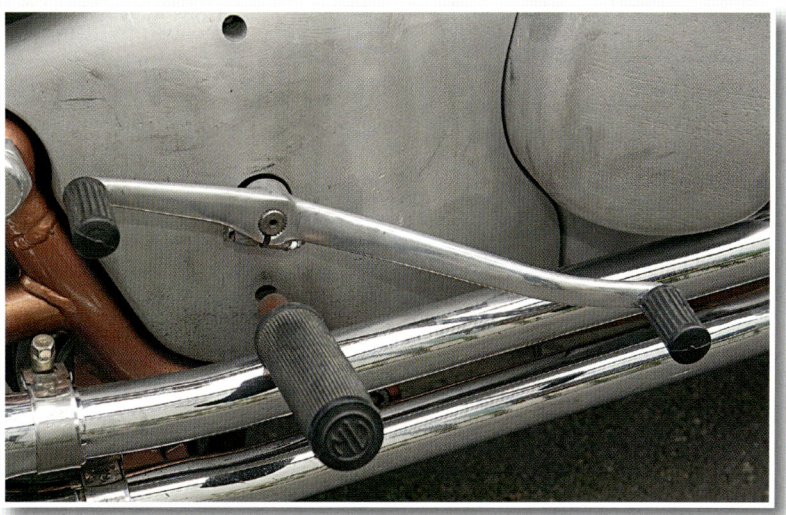

The gear lever was a rocking type.

MV AGUSTA FOURS

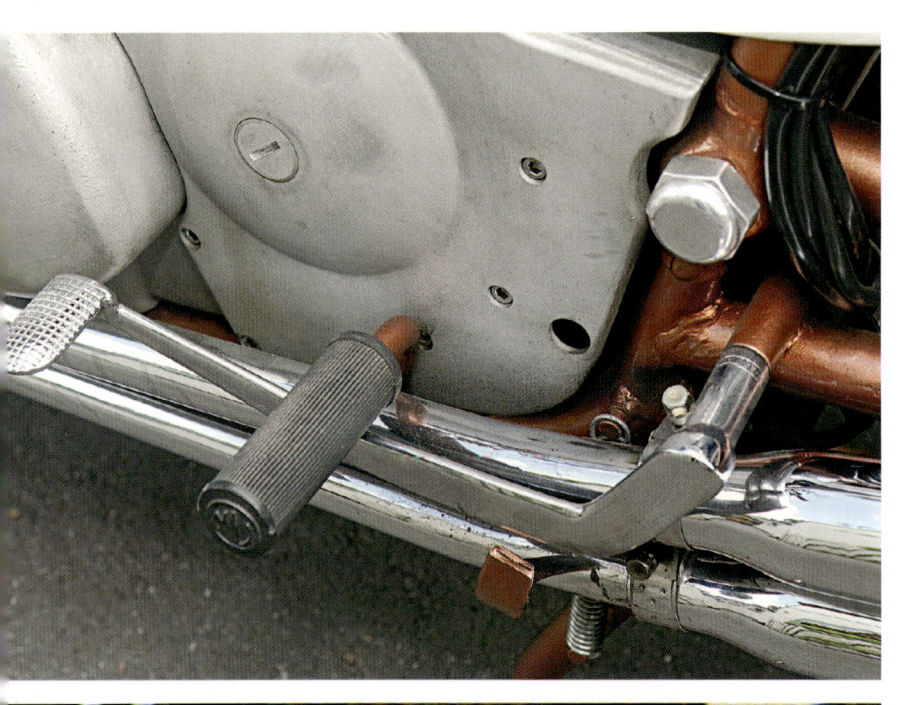

Another 750 GT specific item was the rear brake lever.

From 1973 most side cover decals were like this.

Aprilia horn), and a higher handlebar. The 750 GT handlebar was a smaller diameter (7/8 inch) than the 600 (one inch). The 35mm Ceriani front fork included rubber gaiters and frame-colour matched fork triple clamps, with the top triple clamp having handlebar mounts. Other specific 750 GT features were a rocking gear lever and rear brake pedal. The side cover decals varied, and there were at least four types (including the prototype).

Some 1972 750 GTs had '750 GT' side cover decals.

THE 750 GT 1972-1974 (MV4C75)

THE 750 GT (1973)

Most updates to the 750 GT for 1973 were cosmetic and centred on the tank and side cover decals, although it's difficult to ascertain exactly when these decal changes occurred. An example with the new decals was displayed at the Paris Show towards the end of 1972, and most 750 GTs were built the same year (23). Production was still in batches, though, and another batch overlapped 1972 and 1973. It is likely that some of the 1973 engines featured the performance updates of the interim 750 S and, thus, had the higher 9.7:1 compression often mentioned.

New tank decals distinguished the 1973 750 GT.

MV AGUSTA FOURS

The tank decal for 1973 – proclaiming 36 World Championships.

The 750 GT was on display at the Paris Show at the end of 1972.

THE 750 GT (1974)

A new version of the 750 GT was exhibited at the 1973 Milan Show, and later at Amsterdam, with a dual front Scarab disc brake replacing the Grimeca drum. Certainly, at least one of these disc 750 GTs was produced, as it appeared in US magazine tests during 1974. This bike (engine number 214-0435, frame number 2140495) was sent to Commerce Corporation in New York on 20/2/74. Because it was one of a batch of 12 bikes (from frame number 214484-214496), eight of which were built in 1974, it is possible that the eight 1974 bikes had disc brakes. The other 11 750 GTs went to Barcelona, Spain. For 1974 there was a 37 World Championships decal on the fuel tank. The final 750 GT (engine number 214-0490, frame 2140526) was built in 1974 but not sold until 20/9/75. Although 750 GT engines went beyond the 214-0401 of the updated 1974 750 Sport, all 750 GTs featured the earlier engine with 24mm carburettors. It was probable that the engine specification

THE 750 GT 1972-1974 (MV4C75)

The 750 GT seat and tail unit was unique and distinctive.

MV AGUSTA FOURS

of all 1974 750 GTs matched the updated 1973 750 Sport specification, with higher compression pistons and larger valves.

For many years the 750 GT remained in the shadow of the 750 Sport, but now earns deserved appreciation as the rarest of all 750 fours. Unlike the 750 Sport, most 750 GTs were intended for the export market, the majority of which were sold in Barcelona (15). Gus Kuhn received three, Bob Jane six, and three went to the USA.

A dual front disc brake 750 GT was on display at the 1973 Milan Show.

Another view of 214-0404. Once unappreciated, the 750 GT is now considered handsome and rare.

THE 750 GT 1972-1974 (MV4C75)

1973 750 GTs featured a Grimeca front drum brake, like this example (engine number 214-0404, frame 2140343, built 1/8/73).

MV AGUSTA FOURS

The throttle for 1973 and 1974 was a Tommaselli Daytona.

At least one 750 GT with dual Scarab disc brakes went to the US where it was tested by Motorcycle World in October 1974. This is engine 214-0435 and frame 2140495, built on 20/2/74. (Courtesy Cycle World)

The 750 GT seat and tank was hand-built by Primo Felotti.

750 GT DISTINGUISHING FEATURES

Later 750 S type crankcases without right side plug
Single fin cylinder head
Ribbed crank carrier
Dell'Orto UB 24mm carburettors
Mufflers without seams
11/31 final drive ratio (11:31)
1973 versions probably with higher compression interim 750 S engines
Brown-painted frame shared 214 series number with the 750 S
Smiths instruments; 1972 versions without holes for the throttle and clutch cables. 1973 versions with holes for cables
Unique components included steel fuel tank, and seat and tail unit
Specific crash bar with dual Bosch horns
Higher handlebar
35mm Ceriani fork with rubber gaiters
Specific rocking gear lever and rear brake pedal
Four types of side cover decals (including the prototype)
Likely that some 1973 examples featured the higher compression interim 750 Sport engine
Some examples for 1974 with dual front Scarab disc brakes

750 GT PRODUCTION NUMBERS

Year	Number
1972	12
1973	23
1974	15
Total	50

THE 750 S 1974 (MV4C75)

During 1973 the EFIM Group gradually assumed more influence over the control of MV Agusta, and at the end of 1973 Luigi Ghisleri replaced Corrado Agusta as MV Agusta's managing director. Corrado remained as honorary president and Ghisleri was given the task of expanding the motorcycle division. At a press conference at the end of 1973 Ghisleri talked of building MV into a premium performance brand, much like Ferrari in the automotive world. With this in mind, a prototype street 750 S was built in 1973 by a group of factory employees specifically for Sig. Ceriani. Based on the Formula 750 racer, this incorporated a new frame, 38mm Ceriani forks, triple disc brakes, chain final drive and cast alloy wheels. The gearshift was also on the left. Styled along the lines of the 500 GP bikes, this special 750 had black engine covers and exhaust, and a bank of racing Dell'Orto SS carburettors. Arturo Magni says, "The engine of this 750 had many special factory parts and was later sold to Germany." But the directors at MV remained unimpressed, and this 750 was destined to remain a one-off. Like most four-stroke manufacturers, MV lost interest in

This special 750 S prototype was produced by a group of factory employees during 1973.

Many features were new for a street MV, including chain final drive and magnesium alloy wheels.

145

MV AGUSTA FOURS

Formula 750 when Yamaha introduced the TZ700 early in 1974. Except for an updated engine and the option of front disc brakes, when the 1974 750 S was unveiled it was similar to the 1973 750 S. At the official 1974 Italian press release MV promised a replica of Agostini's 1972 Imola 200 750 the following year, with a chain drive 'super bomb' to follow, but, as usual, these were hollow promises.

Exact categorization of the transition to the 1974 750 Sport is difficult. While the engine updates were incorporated after September 1973,

Although built in November 1972, this example (engine 214-0266, frame 2140262) was fitted with updated engine parts at the factory in 1974. (Courtesy Marco Vittino)

THE 750 S 1974 (MV4C75)

MV also offered a double disc front brake option with the earlier interim specification engine around the same time. Bruno de Prato tested this in *Il Pilota Moto* in November 1973, criticising frame rigidity. The disc option cost an additional 115,000 Lire, and his criticism led to the strengthened steering head on production versions.

The official press release for the 1974 750 Sport in Italy didn't occur until many months later. 1974 was a difficult year for the motorcycle industry in general. The world economy was struggling and the oil crisis at its peak. The sales of expensive luxury products were sluggish, and motorcycles were not immune. MV's directors were cautious, and on 14 June 1974 MV sent a telex to selected Italian journalists inviting them to witness factory rider Gianfranco Bonera test the new 750 S on a five-kilometre straight near Malpensa airport, the same straight used for testing the factory racing bikes. MV's intention was for Bonera to set an impressive top speed, dispelling the debate that always surrounded the performance of the earlier 750 S. With Ing Di Matteo using a hand held timer, Bonera's best run yielded 214km/h, and the worst 205km/h. For the acceleration test Bonera had a 750 S available with a lower 750 GT final drive ratio. With this he managed a standing 400-metre time of 12.708 seconds at a terminal speed of 173km/h. Selected Italian journalists were then invited to test the new MV 750 S at the Pirelli establishment in Vizzola Ticino, and it was uniformly agreed the new 750 S was now a genuine 210km/h (130mph) motorcycle.

The timing for the release of the 1974 750 S was not perfect. After

A poor but original picture shows that later in 1973 MV offered a disc option for the 750 Sport with the earlier specification engine. The frame is also earlier, without the steering head extension, and the exhaust system is the earlier type with seamed mufflers.

MV AGUSTA FOURS

The author's 1974 750 S (engine 214-0513) was a representative example, produced in June 1974.

September 1974, US Department of Transport legislation called for a mandatory left side gearshift and the 750 Sport was predominately a right side gearshift model. Despite most 750 Sports still having the right side shift, after September 1974 it was possible to order it with a factory left side gearshift conversion.

ENGINE

Although the engine number sequence continued with the 214 series, there were a number of significant engine updates to ensure performance was improved. These engine updates continued after the interim 1973 updates, and were possibly incorporated after the summer break in late August 1973. The first engine after September 1973 was 214-0401. It is not certain that all engines built after this date included the updates, but a study of factory records indicates considerable consistency between engine number and date of manufacture, so it is possible. All 750 Sport engines with numbers higher than 214-0401 were built after 28/8/73.

Although the cylinder head was a carryover of the recast 1972

THE 750 S 1974 (MV4C75)

The cylinder head of the 1974 750 S was new, with larger valves and intake ports.

and 1973 750 version, with a single horizontal cooling fin from 27/12/73 (date on the official drawing), it was a new casting. Along with a larger 55mm diameter combustion chamber, the inlet ports were increased to 27mm in diameter. Valve sizes were the same (31.8mm inlet and 29mm exhaust) as the 1973 interim 750 Sport, and, although camshaft timing was unchanged, intake valve lift was increased from 8mm to 9.31mm (from 28/12/73 according to the official drawings). The exhaust camshaft was unchanged, as were the spectacle-style valve buckets, but both the internal and external valve springs were new. New pistons provided a 10:1 compression ratio, and had modified valve recesses and fully-machined lands to allow for the increased valve lift. The piston length was 70.7mm with valve recesses 33.5 and 30.5mm. The piston skirt length was 43mm. Although the pistons and 17mm gudgeon pins were new, the piston rings were unchanged.

The crankcase casting was shared with the 1973 750 S. Like the 1973 version, there was no plug on the right side, but this year a centralising bushing was fitted on a new right rear stud. A new breather hose outlet and distributor support housing were also fitted. The crankshaft 'U' fitting supports were new, the two outer fittings now differing from the four internal. Updates to the camshaft drive setup (already modified for 1972-3) included new 34-tooth camshaft drive gears, and all engines now had the ribbed crank carrier.

149

MV AGUSTA FOURS

750 S engine specifications 1974

Type	Four-stroke, four-cylinder, air-cooled
Bore	65mm
Stroke	56mm
Capacity	743cc
Compression ratio	10:1
Maximum power	69hp at 8500rpm
Maximum torque	5.9kgm at 7500rpm
Maximum rpm	9000
Inlet opens	48° before TDC
Inlet closes	68° after BDC
Exhaust opens	70° before BDC
Exhaust closes	36° after TDC
Valve clearance cold intake	0.30mm
Valve clearance cold exhaust	0.30mm

This two-into-one-into-two exhaust system was also available for the 1974 750 S.

CARBURETTORS AND EXHAUST

Along with the cylinder head modifications, also contributing to improved engine performance was a set of four Dell'Orto VHB 27A carburettors. Popular with many other Italian motorcycle manufacturers, these had square slides and the float bowl incorporated with the body. Although they retained open aluminium bell mouths, the intake manifolds were new, with a larger, circular insulator instead of a triangular type. The carburettor slide operating lever mechanism was unchanged. On at least one early example (tested by Dutch magazine *Motor*) the carburettors breathed through a black fibreglass airbox that replaced the metal side covers. The

The four Dell'Orto VHB27A carburettors and new intake manifolds of the 1974 750 S.

Most 750 Sports had a four-pipe exhaust system and mufflers without seams.

THE 750 S 1974 (MV4C75)

importer Piet van Dijk presumably fitted these, as they don't appear on other examples.

Two exhaust systems were available for the 1974 750 S: the traditional four individual pipes and unseamed mufflers, and the option of a 'two-into-one' header reverting to twin mufflers. The optional exhaust was intended to recover some of the mid-range torque lost in the engine modifications, gaining a claimed 2 horsepower between 4000 and 6500rpm but losing this at the top end compared to the four individual pipes. The four individual exhaust header pipes on the 750 S were closer to the frame for improved ground clearance, and there were new threaded exhaust header pipe clamps and new clamps where the muffler attached to the header. The mufflers no longer had a seam on top, and they sat at a different angle to the swingarm.

Carburettor jetting 750 S (1974)

Type	4x Dell'Orto VHB 27AD and VHB 27AS
Choke diameter	27mm
Main jet	128
Idle jet	45
Throttle valve	40
Needle	V7 2nd notch
Atomiser	265 M
Air intake	Open horn
Pilot screw	Open 1 turn

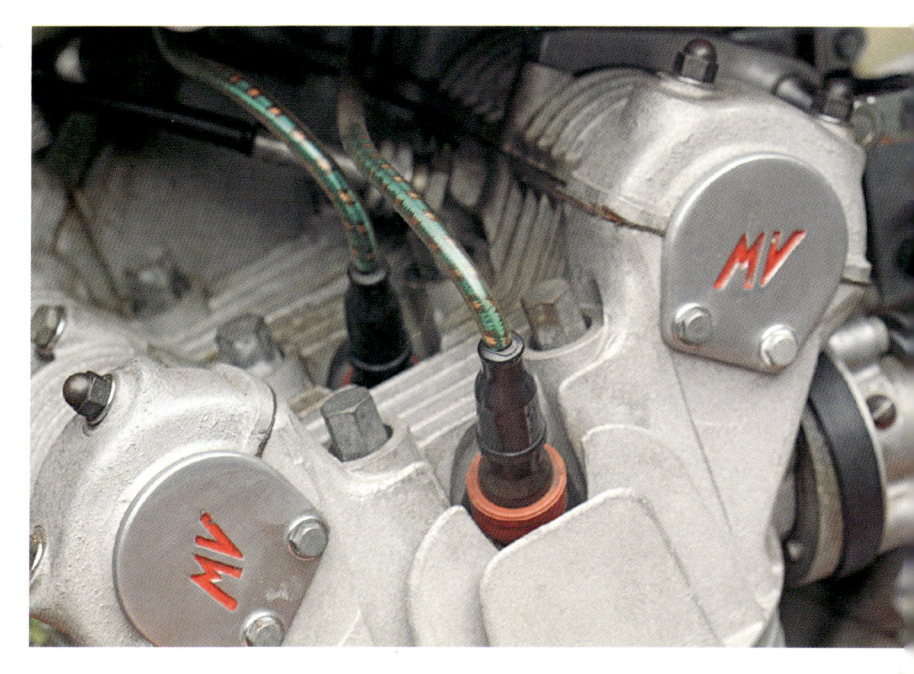

Sparkplug leads were green this year.

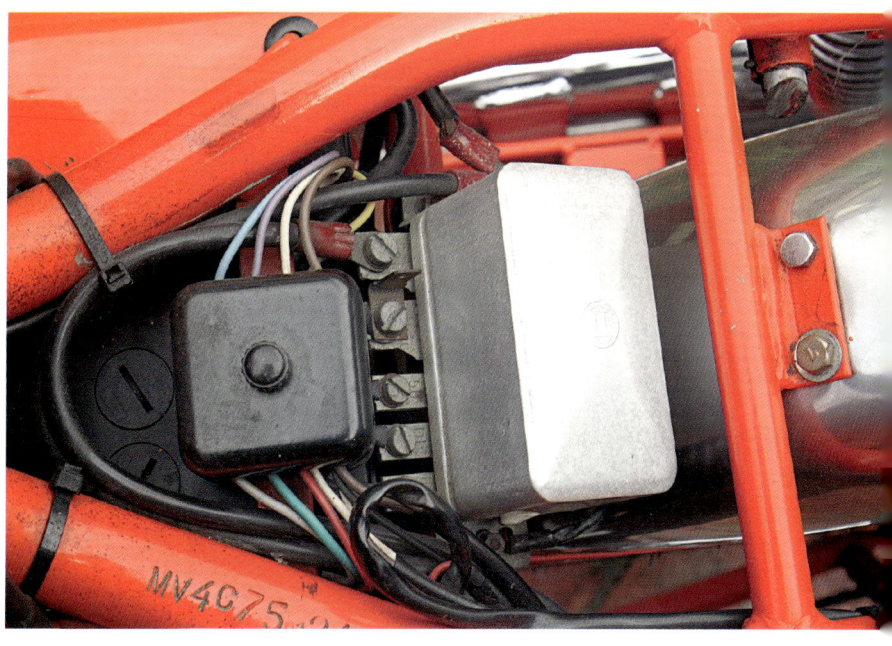

The fuse box and regulator were unchanged.

IGNITION AND ELECTRICAL SYSTEM

All 1974 750 Ss had a Bosch JF4 single point distributor and single Bosch coil. The sparkplug leads were plastic-coated green this year. There were no other changes to the electrical system, including Bosch Dynastart, regulator, and fuse box, except that a relay was now fitted on the left under the rear mudguard.

The Bosch Dynastart was unchanged for 1974.

MV AGUSTA FOURS

Ignition and electrical system

Distributor	Bosch JF4
Fixed advance	18-20°
Automatic advance	28-30°
Total advance	46-50°
Breaker points clearance	0.35-0.45mm
Firing order	1,3,4,2
Sparkplug	Bosch W260T2, Champion N3, Marelli CW260L (CW8L)
Sparkplug electrode gap	0.50-0.60 mm
Battery	12V 32Ah
Dynastart	Bosch 12V 135W
Regulator	Bosch ZAD 14Ah
Fuses	4x 8Amp

A flasher unit was mounted on the left behind the battery.

CLUTCH, GEARBOX, AND FINAL DRIVE

The 14-plate clutch, helical gear primary drive, gearbox, and final drive were all unchanged for 1974.

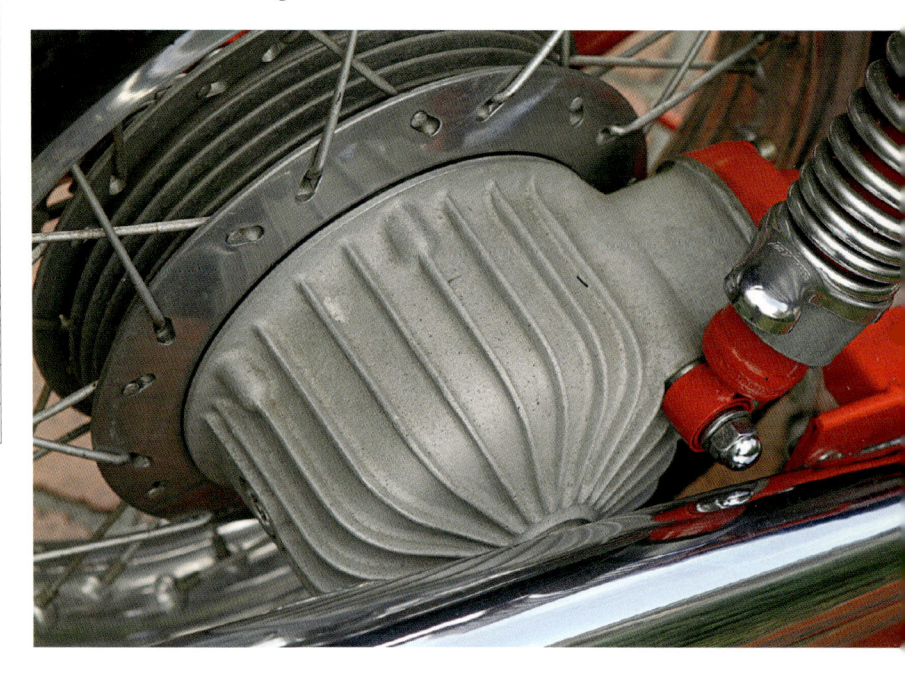

The final drive casting and gearing were unchanged.

750 S gear ratios (1974)

Gear	Ratio	Teeth
Primary	1.75:1	98/56
1st	2.38:1	30/15x25/21
2nd	1.69:1	27/19x25/21
3rd	1.29:1	24/22x25/21
4th	1.09:1	22/24x25/21
5th	1:1	21/25x25/21
Secondary	1.066:1	15/16
Final Drive	2.667:1	32/12

FRAME, WHEELS, TYRES, BRAKES, AND SUSPENSION

The red-painted frame carried the same part number as for 1973, but there was considerable overlap between 1973 and 1974 examples. As the chronology of manufacture was more closely associated with engine number, frames were selected at random. The earliest frame for the 1974 series was 2140370 (engine 214-0554), and the highest number 2140623. There were many gaps in the sequence towards the end of production, and frames carried DGM stamp 10791 OM. For the 1974 series, the headstock was lengthened to 200mm for

THE 750 S 1974 (MV4C75)

The frame number stamping on the 1974 750 S.

A distinctive feature of MV fours was the engine oil breather pipe that connected to the frame downtube.

Most 1974 750 Sports had a longer, strengthened steering head with a steering lock.

153

MV AGUSTA FOURS

added strength to cope with the improved braking provided by the optional dual front discs. On some of the earliest modified examples the headstock simply included an extra piece of tubing welded at the factory before a new frame jig was constructed. The longer headstock was braced to the front downtubes by a triangular plate. A steering lock inserted in the right side of the headstock was also new. The oil breather that vented into the front left downtube was unchanged.

Although there were a few late 1973 750 Ss produced with the Grimeca drum brake and updated engine, most 1974 750 Sports were built with the optional dual front disc brake. Those with a drum brake seem to have been sold in Italy, most export examples having the disc brake option. With disc front brakes came new lower fork legs, lower triple clamp (with provision for a brake union), and front wheel. The 36-spoke Borrani front rim was still a WM3x18in, but it had a different spoke angle with the stamps BORRANI WM3/2.15 RECORD RM-01-4782

This 750 S (engine 214-0471, frame 2140470) was built in March 1974 with EPM wheels and disc brakes. Several like this were sold in Spain. (Courtesy Raphaël David)

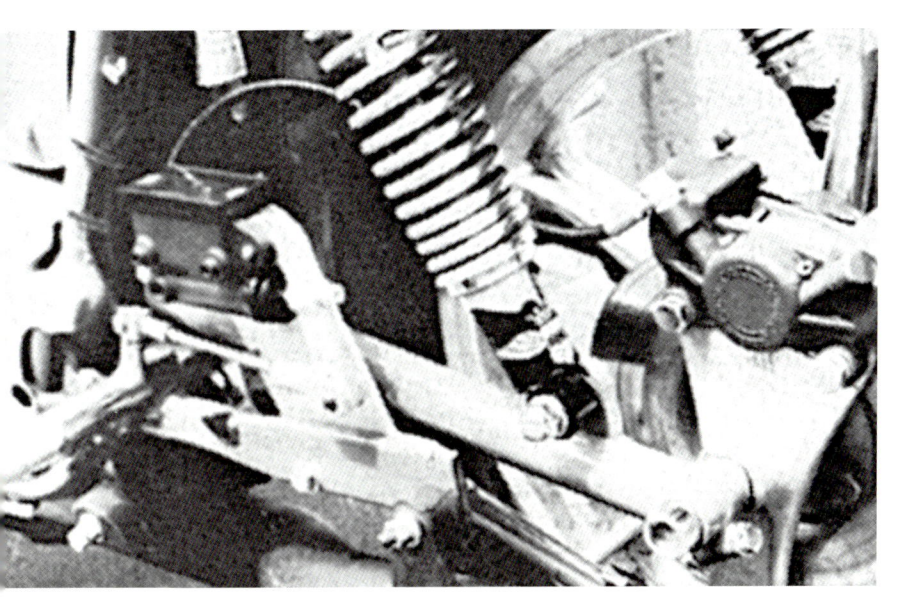

THE 750 S 1974 (MV4C75)

The Grimeca rear disc, as fitted to a few 750 Ss in 1974.

MADE IN ITALY. Spokes were painted steel Alpino, 3.3mm thick. The front fork was still a 35mm Ceriani, and the rear shock absorbers 320mm Sebac, and, apart from the lower legs, all the fork internals were as before. The rear Borrani rim (WM 2.15 RECORD RM 01 4470) and single leading-shoe brake was as before, as were the V-rated Metzeler tyres. MV was already experimenting with cast wheels, as at least two examples were sent to Barcelona with EPM wheels in March

The rear Borrani rim was as before.

1974. The rear disc, calliper, and master cylinder were by Grimeca and, although never officially listed as a spare part, the alloy wheels and rear disc brake were available for the 750 Sport. Some were included in the spares cache bought by the UK MV Owners' Club after the factory closed.

The only significant change in chassis specification was the optional dual disc front braking system, which included twin cast iron 280mm discs (7mm thick) and Scarab twin brake piston callipers. The Scarab callipers were Lockheed copies by Scarab Mozzi Motor in Bologna. While most other Italian motorcycle manufacturers were selecting Brembo brake components when moving from drums to discs in 1974, Ducati and MV Agusta used Scarab. As previously noted, this was due to Fredmano Spairani's business interest in the Scarab concern. The Scarab master cylinder included a 17.6mm piston, and the design wasn't copied from Lockheed, instead it was unusual in that the lever retained the piston. While the Scarab brakes could work well, the quality wasn't up to the standard of either Lockheed or Brembo. The callipers were prone to seizure and the master cylinder often leaked. A single black plastic covered line connected the master cylinder to a union on the lower triple clamp. US versions included a brake pressure switch at the union. While the Scarab brakes were criticised at the time, it is possible to rebuild these with modern seals and they can function perfectly. MV Agusta used chrome-plated 10mm bolts to fasten the callipers to the Ceriani fork leg, while the polished aluminium front brake lever carried finger indents to match the Tommaselli clutch lever.

The front Borrani alloy rim on disc brake models was different to the drum brake version.

155

MV AGUSTA FOURS

OTHER CHASSIS COMPONENTS

In all other respects the 1974 750 S was as for 1973. This included Tommaselli handlebars, Tommaselli Daytona throttle with brown

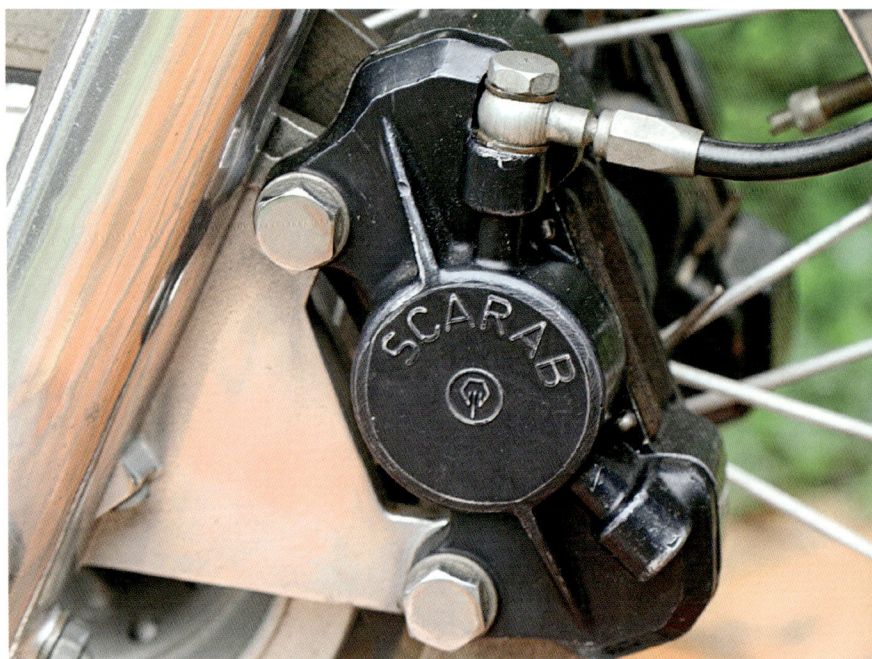

The Scarab brake callipers were Lockheed copies. Standard features included chrome-plated fasteners.

The front dual disc Scarab braking system was ostensibly an option, although it was more common than the drum brake.

The Scarab master cylinder design was compromised, but still worked well.

Wheels, tyres, and brakes (1974)

Front wheel	WM3x18in Borrani,
Front brake	230x30mm double drum Grimeca or 2x280mm disc
Front tyre	3.50x18in ribbed V-rated Metzeler
Rear wheel	WM3x18in Borrani,
Rear brake	200x45mm drum
Rear tyre	4.00x18in pattern V-rated Metzeler

THE 750 S 1974 (MV4C75)

One of the few 1974 750 Sports with a drum brake. This example (engine 214-0548, frame 2140542) was sold in Italy in September 1974.

handgrips, Aprilia handlebar switches, Smiths instruments (miles per hour speedometer for the UK, US, and Australia), CEV headlight and taillight. The dashboard retained two warning lights. Some examples also had a Voxbell horn instead of the earlier Aprilia. Although the 24-litre steel fuel tank with chrome filler cap was unchanged (the cap with a small internal seal), new this year were two fuel Brev Orlandi petcocks (different for each side) and a decal proclaiming 37 World Championships. The stainless steel mudguards carried over from the earlier 750 Sport but US examples had a longer rear section. The side covers were generally steel, although some examples did have a fibreglass type and red fibreglass side covers were offered

(Continued on page 161)

157

MV AGUSTA FOURS

Handgrips were brown Tommaselli, with the usual Aprilia handlebar switch.

The throttle was also Tommaselli this year.

158

THE 750 S 1974 (MV4C75)

The Smiths instruments and dashboard were unchanged from 1973. UK, Australia, and US versions had mph speedometers.

The chrome-plated fuel filler cap was the same as that fitted to many Italian motorcycles of this era, but included a smaller internal seal.

A new decal proclaiming 37 World Championships was affixed to the 1974 750 S.

MV AGUSTA FOURS

The front profile demonstrates the narrowness of the four-cylinder engine and sculptured fuel tank.

The taillight for 1974 was the same round CEV as fitted during 1973.

THE 750 S 1974 (MV4C75)

Later 1974 750 Sports had a new rear brake switch that also featured on the America.

A right side rear brake conversion was part of the left side gearshift option.

as a genuine spare part. Some detail components were updated during the production series, notably the rear brakelight switch. On later examples (particularly those built after December 1974), this was changed to the switch type that would feature on the America, possibly to accommodate a right side rear brake conversion as some later bikes were built to special order with a left side gearshift and right side rear brake. A CEV turn signal indicator kit that included beautiful alloy brackets was an option, as was a full fairing. Again, this was nicely crafted from very thinly laid fibreglass. Although the press release indicated that the small Plexiglas screen would no

It was possible to order the 1974 750 S with a left side gearshift.

CEV turn signal indicators were an option on the 1974 750 S.

161

MV AGUSTA FOURS

These indicators had round chrome bodies.

longer be available as it contributed to high-speed instability, it did appear on some 1974 examples.

750 S production during 1974 was haphazard, with only a few examples built sporadically each month. Although the 750 America was announced in February 1975, production of the earlier model continued into the first few months of 1975. There was no relationship between engine and frame numbers, and the highest frame number 750 S was built on 6/3/75, with engine number 214-0592 and frame number 2140623. This, as with most of the final 750 Ss, was sold to Hansen in Baden-Baden, Germany. The final six 750 Ss were sold on 6 May 1975, all going to Hansen. Although the total number of 750 Ss totalled 556, there were several gaps in frame numbers, especially towards the end of the series during 1974 and 1975, plus the 750 GT also shared the 214 number series. The number of disc brake 1974 specification examples produced possibly included 110 made in 1974, 44 in 1975, and 32 from 30/8/73-31/12/73, totalling 186. The MV Agusta historical website states 215 750 S's were built with disc brakes, but this appears optimistic and doesn't correspond with official production figures. During 1974 and 1975 six 750 Ss were sold to Gus Kuhn in London, nine to Bob Jane in Australia, and three to the Commerce Corporation in the USA. Most 1974 and 1975 750 Sports were sold in Italy (57), with another 45 examples to Schneider and Hansen in Baden-Baden. 11 were also sold to van Dijk in Holland.

As in 1973, the 1974 MV 750 Sport was an expensive motorcycle. In the UK, Gus Kuhn offered the 750 Sport for £2500 (including VAT and delivery), and in Australia it was initially $4700. Christopher Garville of the New York Commerce Overseas Corporation planned to import 200 750s, but this didn't eventuate. The asking price of $5000 was unsustainable, and

Even the cable ties on MV fours were unusual.

THE 750 S 1974 (MV4C75)

A small half-fairing was still available for the 750 S in 1974. (Courtesy Two Wheels)

even Ducati couldn't sell its 750 SS for $3000 in 1974. In Italy, the price was 2,373,000 Lire plus 18 per cent tax (427,140 Lire), with the twin disc front brake (an additional 135,000 Lire). The full fairing was available for 126,000 Lire, fitted, taking the total to around three million Lire.

Although it was expensive, the 1974 750 Sport finally offered exclusivity and the performance expected for the price. In July 1974 *Motorcycle* tested a 750 Sport, managing a mean maximum speed of 122.7mph (197.4km/h) and a best one-way speed of 127.2mph

163

MV AGUSTA FOURS

Some 750 S models were also fitted with a full fairing.

(204.7km/h). The standing start quarter-mile was achieved in 14.15 seconds at 101.17mph (162.8km/h) – quite respectable considering the weight and gearing. The Scarab front braking system was also considerably more effective than the Grimeca drum brake. The 1974 750 Sport stopped from 30mph (48.3km/h) in 28ft 9in (8.76m). These performance figures also eclipsed those of the 750 America when *Motorcycle* tested it in 1977, and at the time it was the fastest 750 they had tested. The 750 S easily bettered the Honda 750, and its speed wasn't improved upon until the Suzuki GS 750 appeared two years later.

As the final link to the 600, the 1974 750 S represented the end of

Gus Kuhn received only six 750 Sports during 1974. Here are four on display in its showroom.

164

THE 750 S 1974 (MV4C75)

A modern view. Two 1974 750 Ss, a 1972 750 S, and a 1973 750 GT.

an era for MV Agusta. Devoid of air filtration for the carburettors and fitted with mufflers providing minimal silencing, the 750 S made no concession to legislation or regulation. Turn signals were optional, only a small circular taillight was fitted, and the gearshift was still on the right (although a left shift was a later option). Many other details separated the 750 S from the next generation America. Plastic components were virtually absent on the 750 S and the chrome Aprilia handlebar switches had a vintage charm, as did the chrome Tommaselli Daytona throttle. The build quality was also considerably better than the later America. With only an average of two examples built each week there was ample time to ensure the assembly was of the highest quality. It wasn't only legislation that determined motorcycle design after 1974. Style began to assert itself as an important component, something that became much more apparent in the next generation MV four, the 750 America.

Data overleaf –

MV AGUSTA FOURS

750 S DIMENSIONS AND PERFORMANCE (1974)

Fuel tank capacity	24 litres (4 litres reserve)
Engine oil capacity	4kg AGIP SINT 2000
Final drive	0.4kg SAE 90
Maximum width	750mm
Maximum length	2105mm
Maximum height	1020mm
Seat height	800mm
Ground clearance	160mm
Wheelbase	1390mm
Dry weight	235kg
Oil consumption	½kg oil/1000km
Max speed 1st gear (9000rpm)	92km/h
Max speed 2nd gear (9000rpm)	128km/h
Max speed 3rd gear (9000rpm)	168km/h
Max speed 4th gear (9000rpm)	199km/h
Max speed 5th gear (9000rpm)	218km/h

750 S DISTINGUISHING FEATURES (1974)

New cylinder head casting with 55mm combustion chamber and 27mm intakes
31.8mm inlet and 29mm exhaust valves
Intake valve lift increased to 9mm
New valve springs
New 10:1 pistons
New breather hose outlet and distributor support housing
New crankshaft 'U' fittings and upper camshaft drive gears
Four Dell'Orto VHB 27A carburettors
Exhaust header pipes closer to the frame for improved ground clearance
New threaded exhaust header pipe clamps and new muffler clamps
Optional exhaust with 'two-into-one' header reverting to twin mufflers
Mufflers without top seam
Frame headstock was lengthened to 200mm
Steering lock in headstock
Most fitted with optional Scarab dual 280mm disc front brake

750 SPORT PRODUCTION NUMBERS

Year	Number
1970	9
1971	56
1972	187
1973	150
1974	110
1975	44
Total	556

The 750 Sport sculptured tank was unlike any other at the time and was nearly as wide as the cylinder head.

6 THE 750 AMERICA 1975-76 (MV4C75)

Although the 750 America came about from a visit to the factory by the US duo Chris Garville and Jim Cotherman in autumn 1974, the seeds for the 850 four were sown a few months earlier. At the Cologne Show in September 1974 an 850 SS was displayed, alongside a 1974 750 Sport. The 850 SS was ostensibly a modified 750 Sport, with full fairing, new tank and solo seat, and two-into-one exhaust system.

The creation of the America didn't come about through accident. Garville and Cotherman already had an association with MV Agusta; Garville through the Commerce Overseas Corporation, already distributing MV motorcycles in small quantities, and Cotherman a dealer, race tuner, and developer from Freeport, Illinois, who also bought bikes direct from the factory. They found MV's directors extremely enthusiastic when approached about developing the 750 Sport into a model suitable for the US market. During the 1960s and 1970s many Italian motorcycle manufacturers exhibited a terminal weakness for the US market when it came to developing new models. History should have taught MV to be cautious. Laverda had gone as far as making its 750 engine a Honda lookalike, as the Honda Dream was so successful in the US. Also, its subsequent American Eagle enterprise with Jack McCormack was an expensive and spectacular failure. Ducati also suffered during the 1960s and 1970s through building a plethora of unsaleable bikes for the fickle US market. After creating a range of unremarkable two-strokes and pushrod singles during the 1960s, Ducati also failed to heed warnings. In 1974 Ducati unveiled its Giugiaro-styled 860 for the US, and at the time this rode a wave of success in the press (if not the showroom). It was in this climate that MV was persuaded to invest in new equipment and create the 750 America. Fortunately they didn't engage Giugiaro to design the America, although he was responsible for the concurrent 350 Ipotesi.

The chief protagonist for the 750 America at MV Agusta was Fredmano Spairani, who had joined MV in 1973 from Ducati (as outlined in Chapter 3). Spairani was clearly convinced by Garville and Cotherman that there was

This prototype 850 SS was shown at the 1974 Cologne Show.

MV AGUSTA FOURS

Although fitted with a new tank and seat, the 850 SS was clearly built out of a 750.

an untapped market for an expensive luxury motorcycle in the US, and had MV prepare for considerably increased production of the America compared to earlier fours. It was anticipated 500 examples could be sold annually in the US at a price of $6000. In retrospect, this was a hugely optimistic figure, but it was also fraught with difficulty as the facilities at Cascina Costa simply didn't allow for such a large number of engines to be built. But Spairani didn't procrastinate, and, although updates over the 750 Sport were incorporated, MV's engineers built a running prototype within fifty days. Headed by Ing Giuseppe Bocchi this young group comprised Ing Giuseppe di Matteo, Dott. Luca Apolloni, Flavio Gallo, and Giuseppe Minervi. When testing began, primarily by Alberto Pagani, he reported to the senior engineering team led by Bocchi, Magni, Rossi, Mattavelli, and the commercial representative Bertola.

On 21 January 1975 MV Agusta held a press conference in Milan where the 750 America was officially released (alongside the new 125 Sport and 350 Sport 'Ipotesi' or Hypothesis). Next to Corrado Agusta stood Fredmano Spairani, technical, production, and racing coordinator, and general manager Luigi Ghisleri. They talked of an ambitious program, and a new era with the release of bikes derived from the Grand Prix machines. But no one

Most production 750 Americas were originally sent to the US and featured Borrani wheels.

THE 750 AMERICA 1975-76 (MV4C75)

was really fooled, the press reports stating. "For MV new means a 125 single derived from a model in production for almost twenty years, the 350 Ipotesi (new edition of the old 350 twin) and the 800 America. This has the same frame as the well known Sport, with the motor increased to 790cc and 75 horsepower, along with a different seat and a different headlight."

Ghisleri said, "These three motorcycles all have one thing in common, a high price tag. Our motorcycles are for the elite, for those truly passionate and willing to spend more for better quality. Furthermore, our bikes are expensive because they don't break. In the future MV proposes a completely new 750 and to build a 500, both four-cylinder four-stroke machines. This programme will

EPM cast alloy wheels were an option more popular in Europe and the UK.

MV AGUSTA FOURS

be developed directly with the racing division when free from commitments. With the cooperation of the best men in racing, MV wants to re-establish itself as the leader on the production front also. For 1975 the objective is 4000-4500 motorbikes, with the hope of building 10,000 units within three years." But at a time of deep economic depression (due to the energy crisis) Ghisleri's claims were unduly optimistic and, as usual, it was sometime before production examples materialised.

The first 750 America (engine number 221-001, frame number 221005) was sent to Cotherman early in 1975. Cotherman had a close association with *Cycle* magazine, providing test 750s in 1973, and made the first America available for a *Cycle* magazine test, which appeared in its May 1975 issue. Cotherman also appeared riding the bike in the test. The America impressed *Cycle*'s editors, and executive editor Phil Schilling ordered one for himself (although he later sold it as he wasn't enamoured with the high-speed stability). Soon after 750 America deliveries to the US began, MV remained positive about the future, announcing in August that it would participate in the forthcoming Superbike race at Daytona in 1976. Again, this was unbridled optimism and didn't eventuate.

ENGINE

The 750 America engine was ostensibly carried over from the 1974 750 Sport, with a new engine number sequence beginning at 221-001. Engine numbers went until at least 221-0627 (possibly beyond this as records are not available). Despite the addition of air filters and more restrictive mufflers, the claimed power was also increased over the 750 Sport.

750 S America engine specifications

Type	Four-stroke, four-cylinder, air-cooled
Bore	67mm
Stroke	56mm
Capacity	790cc
Compression ratio	9.5:1
Maximum power	75hp at 8500rpm
Maximum torque	6.62kgm at 7500rpm
Maximum rpm	9000

A line-up of new machines at the factory in 1975. After producing only a small number of 750s in 1974, production was increased significantly for the America.

THE 750 AMERICA 1975-76 (MV4C75)

The first America was tested by Cycle magazine and differed from the production version in several details. The ignition key was on the right and the horn was a chrome CEV.
(Courtesy Cycle World)

All Americas had a left side gearshift, and early examples a flat clutch cover.

Later Americas had an extended clutch cover.

CRANKSHAFT, CRANKCASE, AND CAMSHAFT DRIVE

A new crankcase assembly was produced for the America, and was similar to that of the 1974 750 Sport, except for the provision for a left side gearshift. Although the gear camshaft drive was unchanged, there was a new carrier to allow for larger cylinders. Unlike the 750 S, which included an O-ring for the oil drain spigot to the cylinder head, the America featured a larger spigot, without an O-ring. This was often the source of an oil leak.

As the gearshift was on the left, by a crossover shaft at the rear of the crankcase, the America had a new right side cover (without a hole for the shaft) and a new clutch cover with a hole. Until engine number 221-088 the clutch cover was flat around the gear shaft (as on the earlier 750s), but after 221-089 the clutch cover was extended.

171

MV AGUSTA FOURS

MV produced this cutaway 750 America engine for promotional purposes.

This later clutch cover was also retrofitted to earlier machines when later converted into 850 SSs. One other update for the America was a new oil level dipstick, with a hooked lever at the end to allow easier removal.

CYLINDERS AND PISTONS

To compensate for a quieter exhaust and more restrictive intake and maintain acceptable performance, the capacity of the America was increased to 790cc (from 743cc). The stroke was unchanged, but the bore increased by 2mm to 67mm. New individual cylinder barrels were produced, the liners thinner than on the 750 S. The three-ring Borgo pistons had a wider squish band and lower dome than the

Another view of the America cutaway engine showing the outer main bearing and Dynastart.

750 S, reducing the compression ratio to 9.5:1. This was contrary to some reports that claimed the compression ratio was 10:1, or even 10.2:1. The 67mm pistons were shorter than the 65mm 750 Sport items (63.8mm as opposed to 70.1mm), but retained 43mm skirts. The valve pockets were also unchanged at 33.5mm inlet and 30.5mm exhaust.

CYLINDER HEAD

Although some Americas featured earlier cylinder head castings re-machined to America specifications, most cylinder heads were a new casting with revised combustion chambers (to accommodate the larger pistons), retaining 27mm intake ports. The official engine drawing for the America cylinder head is dated 26/11/74. The valves were the same as the 1974 750 S, the inlet diameter 31.8mm (length 87.4mm, 7mm stem), and the exhaust 29mm (length 86.9mm, 7mm stem). Also shared with the 1974 750 S were the intake and exhaust camshafts, these carrying the same part numbers as before.

THE 750 AMERICA 1975-76 (MV4C75)

The America piston was similar to that of the 1974 750 Sport.

Valve timing 750 S America

Inlet opens	48-50° before TDC
Inlet closes	68-70° after BDC
Exhaust opens	70-72° before BDC
Exhaust closes	36-40° after TDC
Valve clearance cold intake	0.30mm
Valve clearance cold exhaust	0.30mm

CARBURETTORS AND EXHAUST

Most updates incorporated with the America were to the intake and exhaust systems. Instead of four individual Dell'Orto VHB 27mm square slide carburettors and slides by individual levers, the America had a set of four smaller VHB 26mm carburettors with enclosed tops. The new setup made it easier to obtain exact carburettor synchronisation, as the new carburettors had a crossover shaft with four individual arms, one for each

The cylinder head casting on most Americas was new.

MV AGUSTA FOURS

The Dell'Orto VHB26 carburettors with enclosed tops were new for the America, as were the rubber intake manifolds.

carburettor. The enclosed tops included lifters that provided more even slide actuation and retained synchronisation longer. The carburettors and arms were mounted to an alloy bracket as a single assembly and attached to the cylinder head with individual rubber sleeves. A racing style single cable operated the levers. Overall, it was a superior system to that on the earlier 750, the only anomaly being the smaller 26mm carburettors that didn't perfectly match the 27mm intake ports. The use of 26mm carburettors was simply due to expediency, as they were the only ones available from Dell'Orto with the

The standard exhaust system included ugly black Lafranconi mufflers.

174

THE 750 AMERICA 1975-76 (MV4C75)

enclosed lifters. When MV converted some unsold Americas to Monzas in 1977 it returned to 27mm carburettors, but with the earlier 750 S slide setup.

The America also featured a new airbox and air filter. Although the prototype tested by *Cycle* magazine had a hand-beaten aluminium airbox, the production America featured a black plastic filter box with a flat foam filter element. Completing the modifications necessary to homologate the America for the US was a set of four black seamed Lafranconi mufflers. These were siamesed, with small outlets, and, although rather ugly, were necessary to pass the 84dB limit. As an option the individual chrome mufflers of the earlier 750 Sport were also available.

Carburettor jetting 750 S America

Type	2x Dell'Orto VHB 26 DD & 2x VHB 26 DS
Choke diameter	26mm
Main jet	118
Idle jet	45
Throttle valve	40
Needle	E4 or E33 2nd notch (depending on mufflers)
Atomiser	262 AE
Start jet	50
Pilot screw	Open 1 turn (or 1½-2 turns)

CLUTCH AND GEARBOX

Although the spare parts list indicates the clutch was unchanged from the 1974 750 Sport, the clutch plates on the America were thinner, and it had an extra plate, too. The later, wider, outer clutch cover also allowed for a wider primary gear on these models. 1st, 3rd and 4th gears in the gearbox were all improved, also including a new 1st driven gear selector coupling. The ratios for 3rd and 4th gears were almost identical to before, but these had larger gears (27 and 29 tooth as opposed to 24 and 22 tooth), were finer pitched, and much stronger. The gear selector mechanism was unchanged, but the

Most Americas were fitted with the optional chrome mufflers.

MV AGUSTA FOURS

gearshift was moved to the left by incorporating two pivoting levers and a shaft at the rear of the engine. Also new was a neutral indicator switch.

The sparkplug leads on the America were mostly red.

750 S America gear ratios

Gear	Ratio	Teeth
Primary	1.75:1	98/56
1st	2.38:1	30/15x25/21
2nd	1.69:1	27/19x25/21
3rd	1.28:1	29/27x25/21
4th	1.11:1	27/29x25/21
5th	1:1	21/25x25/21

IGNITION AND ELECTRICAL SYSTEM

The ignition system with single point Bosch JF 4 distributor was unchanged, though the condenser was now connected directly to the coil by an additional wire. Some early examples retained the plastic-covered green sparkplug leads of the 750 Sport, but most Americas had plastic-covered red leads.

Ignition and electrical system

Ignition type	Battery and coil Bosch JF 4 distributor
Fixed advance	18-20°
Automatic advance	28-30°
Total advance	46-50°
Breaker points clearance	0.35-0.45mm
Firing order	1,3,4,2
Sparkplug	260W long thread 14mm
Sparkplug electrode gap	0.5-0.6mm
Battery	12V 32Ah
Dynastart	Bosch 12V 135W

FINAL DRIVE

The speedometer drive was now from the front wheel, so the America's driveshaft bearing coupling was new, as was the spacer to replace the earlier speedo worm gear.

Gear	Ratio
Engine to transmission	1.066:1 (15/16)
Transmission shaft to wheel	2.668:1 (32/12)

FRAME, WHEELS, TYRES, BRAKES, AND SUSPENSION

While the America frame was ostensibly that of the 1974 750 Sport, it was now silver painted and featured a number of different brackets and a new bolt-on battery tray. Frame numbers began at MC4C75 221001 and continued beyond MC4C75 2210600. The steering head angle was still 27 degrees, providing a trail of 110mm, and the

THE 750 AMERICA 1975-76 (MV4C75)

The America drive shaft (right) had additional reinforcing. (Courtesy Dorian Skinner)

swingarm was reinforced at the driveshaft entry. As on the 750, engine and frame numbers were not identical, but generally America engine and frame numbers were fewer than 100 apart.

Two types of wheel were offered with the America; traditional Borrani wire-spoked and gold-painted cast alloy. Both types provided the same rim width: a 2.15 WM3x18inch on the front and 2.50 WM4x18in on the rear. The front rim carried the stamp BORRANI-WM-3/2.15-18/36 RECORD RM-O1-4782 MADE IN ITALY, the rear BORRANI-250-18/36 RECORD RM-01-4863/CROSS/MADE IN ITALY EU. 'CROSS' indicated that the rim was a heavier section. The spokes were the usual Alpino (marked 'A'), 3.3mm in diameter. Also available were a set of 6-spoke gold EPM (Elaborazione Progettazione Motociclistiche) cast aluminium alloy wheels. EPM was owned by Carlo Magni and Ermanno Scaburri, and located in nearby Samarate. The EPM dimensions were identical to the Borrani, as were the standard tyres; Metzeler Rille 103.50x18 and Block C7 Racing 4.00x18.

With both sets of wheels the front brakes were as the 1974 750 Sport; dual 280mm cast iron discs with Scarab dual piston callipers

MV AGUSTA FOURS

The standard front Borrani wheel was identical to that of the 1974 750 Sport.

A larger WM4 Borrani rim was fitted on the rear.

and master cylinder. The only changes to the braking specification were rubber brake lines instead of the plastic-coated nylon type, and all front brakes had a brake pressure switch on the lower triple clamp junction, as on the US version of the 1974 750 S.

The rear brake was the usual 200mm drum with wire wheels,

THE 750 AMERICA 1975-76 (MV4C75)

EPM cast alloy wheels were optional, but all Americas had Scarab disc front brakes as standard. The Ceriani fork had larger diameter tubes.

was sometimes fitted with an incorrect spacer, and some testers complained the wire wheels weren't sufficiently strong enough to cope with the substantial weight. This was said to affect high-speed stability, and later some wheels were fitted with larger diameter (4mm) spokes.

One component that was significantly improved over the earlier 750 S was the Ceriani front fork. Now with 38mm fork tubes instead of 35mm, these stiffened the front end considerably. Fork travel was 125mm, and the fork included stronger and wider silver-painted triple clamps and a steel brace. Some updates were incorporated on the front fork after frame number 2210101, including a new lower triple clamp and stem with associated fasteners. The rear 320mm Sebac shock absorbers, with 70mm of travel, were also new for the America.

only now with a pair of inspection holes with plugs to view brake shoe wear, as required by US regulations. New with the cast wheel option was a rear disc brake – also 280mm with a Scarab calliper. The master cylinder was crudely mounted above the exhaust pipe on the right. The rear disc was not without its problems. The master cylinder was exposed and the piston vulnerable to debris dislodged by the rear wheel. There were also some cases of cracking discs. The Scarab master cylinder was also in short supply and some Americas with cast wheels were fitted with a similar Brembo unit, still mounted in the same position. The rear disc for the Scarab was a different pattern to the Brembo.

Although the cast wheels were sometimes problematic, the wire wheels also came under criticism. The America rear wire wheel

The Scarab master cylinder was the same as 1974, except for a new reservoir cap.

MV AGUSTA FOURS

Some Americas with cast wheels had a Scarab rear brake master cylinder, but this example has Brembo.

Wheels, tyres, and brakes

Front wheel	2.15 WM3x18in Borrani or alloy
Front brake	Dual 280mm disc
Front tyre	3.50x18in ribbed V-rated
Rear wheel	2.50 WM4x18in Borrani or alloy
Rear brake	200x45mm drum or 280mm disc
Rear tyre	4.00x18in pattern V-rated

INSTRUMENTS, LIGHTS, SWITCHES, HANDLEBARS, HORN, AND CONTROLS

Although MV retained Smiths as a supplier of instruments, and Tommaselli for the handlebars and controls, most of the ancillary equipment was updated. The Smiths instruments were mounted in a Ducati 750 GT-style black plastic dash with a set of LED warning lights. For some reason, the ignition switch was also relocated from its logical position between the instruments to under the front of the fuel tank (Ducati 860 GT-style). On the *Cycle* magazine prototype the ignition

THE 750 AMERICA 1975-76 (MV4C75)

The America had new Sebac shock absorbers.

A new instrument panel graced the America, but the instruments were still Smiths. This later example has a km/h speedometer.

Most Americas had mph speedometers.

key was on the right, but production examples had the key on the left. Although early reports suggested a return to the earlier instrument layout on production examples, this didn't occur. Only miles per hour speedometers (150mph) were initially fitted, but later European versions had a kilometre per hour (250km/h) instrument. Neither was equipped with a trip reset, and they had shallower bodies than those on the 750 Sport. Some Americas also had aluminium instrument holders.

181

MV AGUSTA FOURS

An LED panel was between the instruments.

A new Aprilia switch was on the left side of the handlebar.

The throttle assembly also included an Aprilia switch.

Most of the electrical equipment was Aprilia, including new handlebar switches and throttle with black aluminium bodies and plastic controls. Modelled on the Yamaha pattern, with numbers 36387 SAE QB3 on the left and 36381 on the right, these were a significant ergonomic improvement over the earlier chrome metal type. Also on

THE 750 AMERICA 1975-76 (MV4C75)

The Aprilia headlight was housed in a Crinkle Black shell.

New for the America was a black Bosch horn.

The Aprilia indicator bodies were also black, and included reflectors.

A large Aprilia taillight replaced the small CEV of the earlier 750 S.

the right was an engine stop switch. The handgrips were now black Tommaselli (instead of brown).

The 170mm headlight was now Aprilia (instead of CEV), as were the large rectangular taillight and turn signal indicators. Contributing to the dubious mid-1970s style the headlight shell and rim were matt Crinkle Black. The Aprilia indicator bodies were also black, and

183

MV AGUSTA FOURS

The America fuel tank had 'MV Agusta' badges instead of decals.

incorporated US-style reflectors. Most European models were also afflicted with these rather ugly indicators, although often distributors replaced them before sale. Completing the updated electrical equipment was a black Bosch horn instead of the earlier CEV seen on the prototype.

FUEL TANK, SEAT, SIDE COVERS, MUDGUARDS, AND TOOLKIT

New bodywork cleverly brought the venerable MV four into the 1970s, maintaining a tight, compact package that belied the America's considerable weight. As the shape was directly descended from the 1974 Grand Prix bikes, the America avoided the trend of deliberate styling that was evident in other Italian motorcycle designs. Racing design is always a result of form following function and this spared the America the angular rectilinear excesses of Giorgetto Giugiaro (Ducati 860 GT) and Alessandro de Tomaso (Benelli 750 Sei). As Giugiaro was also responsible for MV's 350 Ipotesi of the same time, it was surprising (and fortunate) MV decided to implement a racing inspired style with the America.

Holding 19 litres (including 4 litres reserve), the angular red-painted steel fuel tank was smaller than the sculptured 750 S tank. It included the same chrome-plated filler cap, but new for the America were 'MV AGUSTA' tank badges and silver decals. Also shared with the earlier tank was the '37 World Championships' decal. The fuel petcocks (with

THE 750 AMERICA 1975-76 (MV4C75)

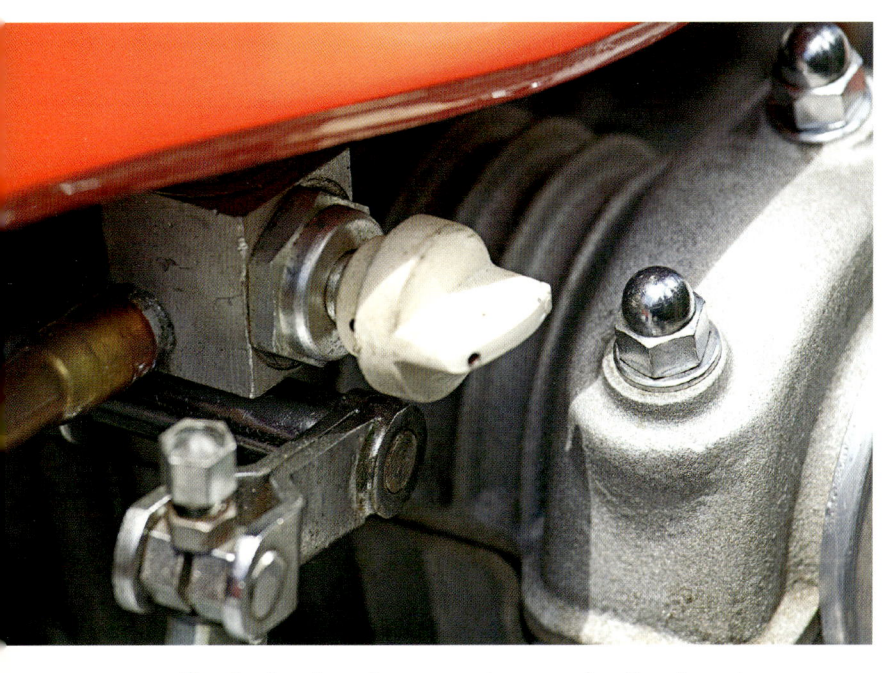

The fuel petcocks were also new for the America.

Side cover badges instead of decals proclaimed the 750 America.

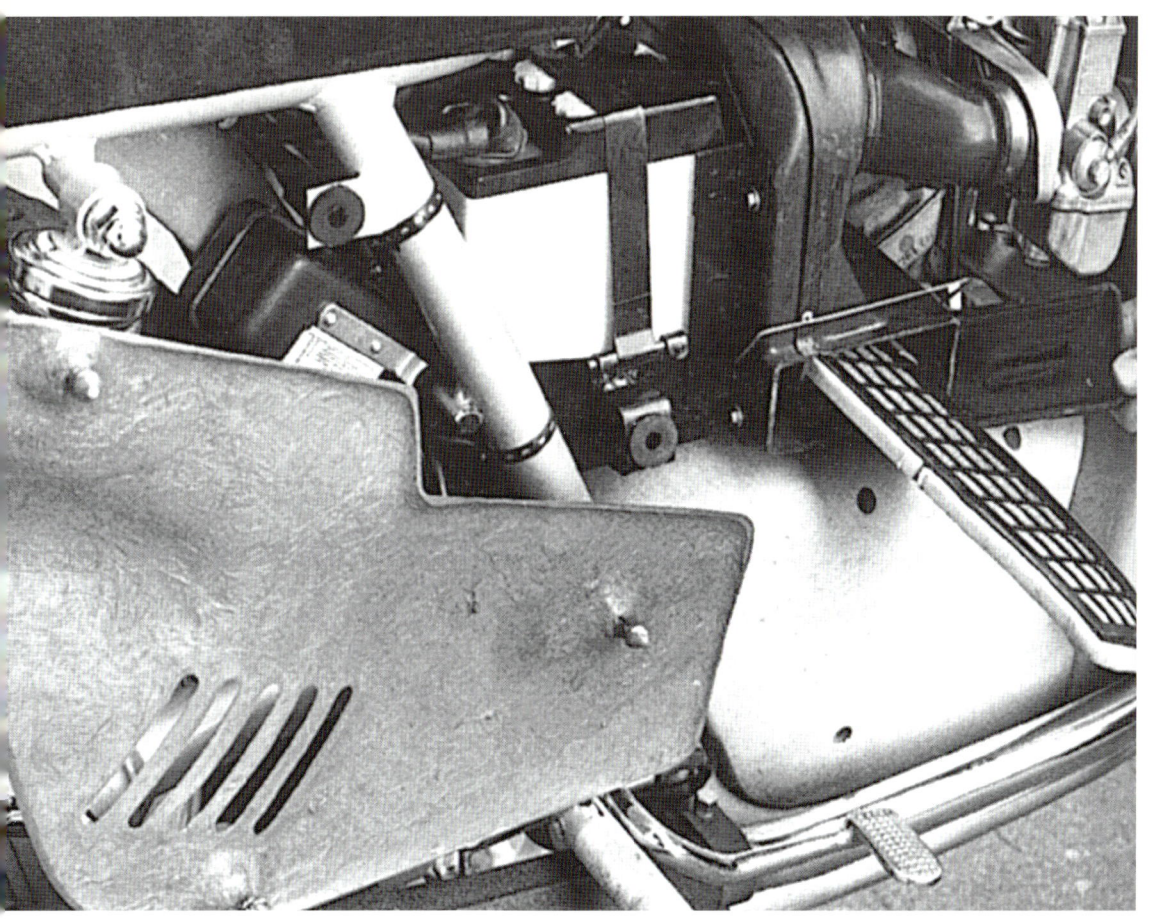

The America's suede seat was unique.

white plastic valves) were also a new design, and, although it was anticipated that ignition switch solenoid activated fuel taps (similar to the Moto Guzzi V7 Sport) would be fitted, these didn't eventuate. The side covers were fibreglass (not pressed steel) and had air

Side covers were now fibreglass instead of steel.

185

MV AGUSTA FOURS

An MV decal was placed on the seat tail.

Like the 750 S, a full fairing was available for the America. (Courtesy Roy Kidney)

The rear mudguard was the stainless steel 750 Sport item, painted red. Unlike the earlier 750 Sport, the quality of the America's paintwork was not of a very high standard, and the red colour varied considerably. An America with matching red on the tank, side covers, seat, and front mudguard was unlikely as the paint changed colour depending on the composition of the base. This inconsistency in colour also indicated the haphazard assembly of many Americas.

Like the 750 Sport, a fibreglass full fairing was also available for the America. This was painted red and silver and, apart from including turn signals and a new steering head bracket, was ostensibly the same as that of the 750 Sport.

750 S AMERICA DIMENSIONS AND PERFORMANCE

Fuel tank capacity	24 litres (4 litres reserve)
Engine oil capacity	4kg SAE 40 Summer, SAE 20 Winter
Oil filter	FRAM CH 803 PL Øe 59 Øi 18 L 101
Final drive	0.4kg SAE 90
Maximum width	750mm
Maximum length	2105mm
Maximum height	1020mm
Seat height	800mm
Ground clearance	160mm
Wheelbase	1390mm
Dry weight	235kg
Oil consumption	½kg oil/1000km

intakes, and although the prototype had decals (or possibly white sign writing), and some early production versions no decals or signs, most featured '750 S AMERICA' badges. Other fibreglass components included the front mudguard and seat with opening (and lockable) compartment. At the rear of the seat was an 'MV' decal. The black suede saddle was another unusual and unique touch, as were the number of chrome-plated nuts and bolts and chrome-plated tool kit.

THE 750 AMERICA 1975-76 (MV4C75)

750 S AMERICA DISTINGUISHING FEATURES (1975-76)

Engine numbers from 221-001
New crankcase assembly and new carrier for camshaft drive gears
Larger cylinder head spigot without an O-ring
New right side cover without a hole for the gearshift shaft
Flat clutch cover until engine number 221-088
After 221-089 extended clutch cover fitted
Thinner clutch plates and one additional plate
New oil level dipstick
Cylinder bore increased to 67mm with thinner liners
Forged Borgo pistons with 63.8mm skirt and 9.5:1 compression ratio
Most cylinder heads were a new casting, with revised combustion chambers
Four Dell'Orto VHB 26mm carburettors with enclosed tops
Production bikes with a black plastic filter box and flat foam filter element
Four black seamed mufflers with individual chrome mufflers an option
New 1st, 3rd and 4th gears. 3rd and 4th gears larger and finer pitched
Neutral indicator switch
Ignition condenser connected directly to the coil
Early examples with green sparkplug leads but most with red leads
Speedometer drive from the front wheel
Silver painted frame with numbers from MC4C75 221001
Choice of Borrani wire-spoked or EPM cast alloy wheels
Rear rim width 2.50in WM4
Dual Scarab front disc brakes with rubber brake hoses
Rear Scarab disc with cast wheels
Rear drum brake with two inspection holes
38mm Ceriani front fork
Smiths instruments in plastic dash unit
Ignition switch on left under the tank
Black Aprilia handlebar switches
Black Tommaselli handgrips
170mm Aprilia headlight in black shell
Rectangular Aprilia taillight and indicators with black bodies
Black Bosch horn
New steel tank, and fibreglass front mudguard seat and side covers
37 World Championships decal on the tank
Black suede seat covering

With no factory records available there is much speculation regarding the number of 750 Americas produced, but according to the official MV Agusta historical website the total was 540. This figure seems reasonable considering the known engine and frame numbers. Thus, the America's production in two years almost matched that of the 750 Sport in six years. This increase in production undoubtedly contributed to the reduction in quality of the America compared to the earlier 750. Every MV specialist interviewed commented that the assembly of the America didn't match that of the 750. It was rumoured 200 machines were sent to the US, and, shortly after production stopped, another 50 assembled from spares by workers from the helicopter division. These final bikes were apparently shipped to Cosmopolitan Motors in the US, and the quality was even more variable; some with badly heat-treated components, generally with poorly finished bodywork.

Another factor that contributed to making these bikes difficult to document was the low availability of spare parts from the factory during the 1970s. This resulted in non-original parts sometimes being produced by dealers, and in some cases complete bikes were disassembled for spares. Piet van Dijk, the Dutch distributor, disassembled at least five new Americas for spare parts.

Ultimately, despite the optimism of Garville and Cotherman, the Americans weren't ready for a $6000 motorcycle and a number remained unsold. During 1976 MV cultivated its other traditional markets, including Australia, Holland, Germany, Switzerland, and the UK. In Australia WH Lowe in Melbourne was the new importer, Hansen in Baden-Baden continued to distribute in Germany, and Garage Meyer in Switzerland. In Germany, Hansen sold the standard 75 horsepower America (titled the 800 S America) for 11,986 DM in 1977, but offered a range of modified versions (with Magni parts) alongside it. The basic modified America was the 800 SS Super America, selling for 17,315 DM, while the 800 SS Super Daytona America was listed at 21,950 DM. Both the 800 SS Super America and 800 SS Super Daytona America retained the 790cc engine with 26mm carburettors. The Super America was fitted with a set of black Magni 'banana' pipes, and the Super Daytona included a full fairing and four-into-one exhaust system. The power of the 800 SS Super America was 82 horsepower at 9000rpm, and the Super Daytona America 90 horsepower at 9000rpm. Both models featured EPM wheels, but, as they were ostensibly Americas, the brakes were still Scarab (though often with Brembo master cylinders). Generally, Schneider fitted smaller diameter rear disc brakes (either 225 or 240mm) with a Brembo calliper. The price of the 800 S America had climbed to 15,384 DM by 1978, with the 800 SS Super America 19,046 DM and the 800 SS Super Daytona America 24,178 DM.

Gus Kuhn had relinquished the British distributorship in 1975, and towards the end of 1976 a new importer was established. Called Agusta Concessionaires GB and owned by the Bate family of Slough, the company originally imported Saab cars to the UK, until Saab took over its own import operation. The Bate relationship with MV

MV AGUSTA FOURS

Very few Americas remained standard. This example has a Magni exhaust and Brembo brakes. (Courtesy Roy Kidney)

Agusta began extremely positively, with a dealer presentation at the Mallory Park circuit in Leicestershire in December 1976. Of the 100 dealers present, 30 signed a letter of intent to distribute the bikes, but, unfortunately for Agusta Concessionaires, the troubles back in Italy became apparent almost immediately. Although the enterprise was doomed, Bate imported 99 Americas into the UK. The standard model with spoke wheels and black exhaust retailed at £3187, and the more popular cast wheel version at £3617. With a fairing fitted this climbed to £3764.17, making it the most expensive motorcycle in the UK. One was sold to Bill Lomas, and another was lent to Phil Read.

Compared to the 750 Sport, the America was much more widely reviewed in magazines and thoroughly performance tested. Generally, the performance was as expected, too. *Cycle* magazine, in its May 1975 issue, achieved 13.06 seconds for the standing start quarter-mile, with a terminal velocity of 105.14mph (169.21km/h). This was a particularly impressive time considering the curb weight (252.9kg) and high first gear. *Cycle* went on to say that in any top speed contest the America would leave comparable motorcycles, such as the Kawasaki Z900, above 80mph (129km/h). In February 1977 *Motorcycle* in the UK found the fully-faired 750 America almost as fast as the half-faired 1974 750 Sport. The mean top speed as tested was 120.24mph (193.51km/h), with a best one-way of 122.14mph (196.56km/h). New *Motorcycling Monthly* also subjected the America to a full performance test in January 1978, managing a top speed of 132.6mph (213.4km/h) – an extremely impressive speed without a fairing. On a cool day at Malpensa airport in early 1976, *Motociclismo* magazine managed 208.69km/h from its unfaired example. With the optional fairing it achieved 219.120km/h, and the standing 400 metres was achieved in 13.032 seconds at 166.67km/h. Hansen in Germany was always forthcoming in providing test bikes to *Motorrad* magazine, the unfaired 800 SS Super America with Magni exhausts managing 209.5km/h.

However, despite all the press interest, all was not well within MV Agusta during 1976. From the outside everything may have looked healthy, but, under the EFIM directorship, the dismantling of the MV motorcycle division was already under way. In December 1975 Spairani left MV Agusta for a similar position at SIAI Marchetti (light aircraft), which was also controlled by EFIM, his replacement Alberto Armeni also coming from Ducati. At the same time, Corrado resigned and MV was left without a figurehead. MV managed to mount an impressive display at the 1975 Milan Show, including a new 350 touring machine alongside a Borrani-wheeled America, but the display was misleading. In February 1976 Ghisleri was moved to another part of the EFIM Group, and when MV closed the racing team and sold the race bikes early in 1976 the writing was on the wall. The space assigned to MV Agusta at the 1976 Milan Show was desolately empty.

Hansen in Germany offered the 800 SS Super America; ostensibly a standard America with a Magni exhaust system.

THE 850 SS (MONZA) 1977

By the end of 1976 MV Agusta was in trouble. Its reign on the racetrack ended in 1974 with Phil Read taking MV's final 500cc World Championship, and by 1976 there was no longer an official factory racing team. Rumours emanated about a merger with Ducati, with MV motorcycle production moving to Bologna. There was also talk of Alessandro De Tomaso buying both MV Agusta and Ducati, and the newly appointed British importer Agusta Concessionaires optimistically announced production of the four-cylinder models would continue for at least 15 years. Operating on behalf of a third party, Peter Bate in the UK tried to buy the manufacturing rights to continue production of the road MVs, but negotiations with the EFIM directors broke down.

Despite this uncertainty, during 1975 and 1976 several new projects were contemplated, with possible production anticipated for 1977. After the Imola race in 1972, up to 12 new engine configurations were considered. A four-valve 750, with chain final drive and steeply inclined cylinders and an integral crank carrier and hanger, was installed in a racing frame and tested towards the end of 1973 (see Chapter 3). In addition, according to Arturo Magni, "Around 10 four-valve 750cc engines were produced, but only for racing." These were distinguished from the two-valve cylinder head by a cam cover with oil feeds. During 1976 a standard America engine in a racing frame (as on the 1972 Imola racer) was readied for production, but this didn't eventuate.

During 1975 Ing Giuseppe Bocchi, another recruit from Ducati, set to work on the new four-cylinder production engine and a racing 500cc boxer four. For the production four, Bocchi envisaged a capacity between 750 and 1200cc, and, to simplify production, he incorporated a chain drive for the exhaust camshaft, with the

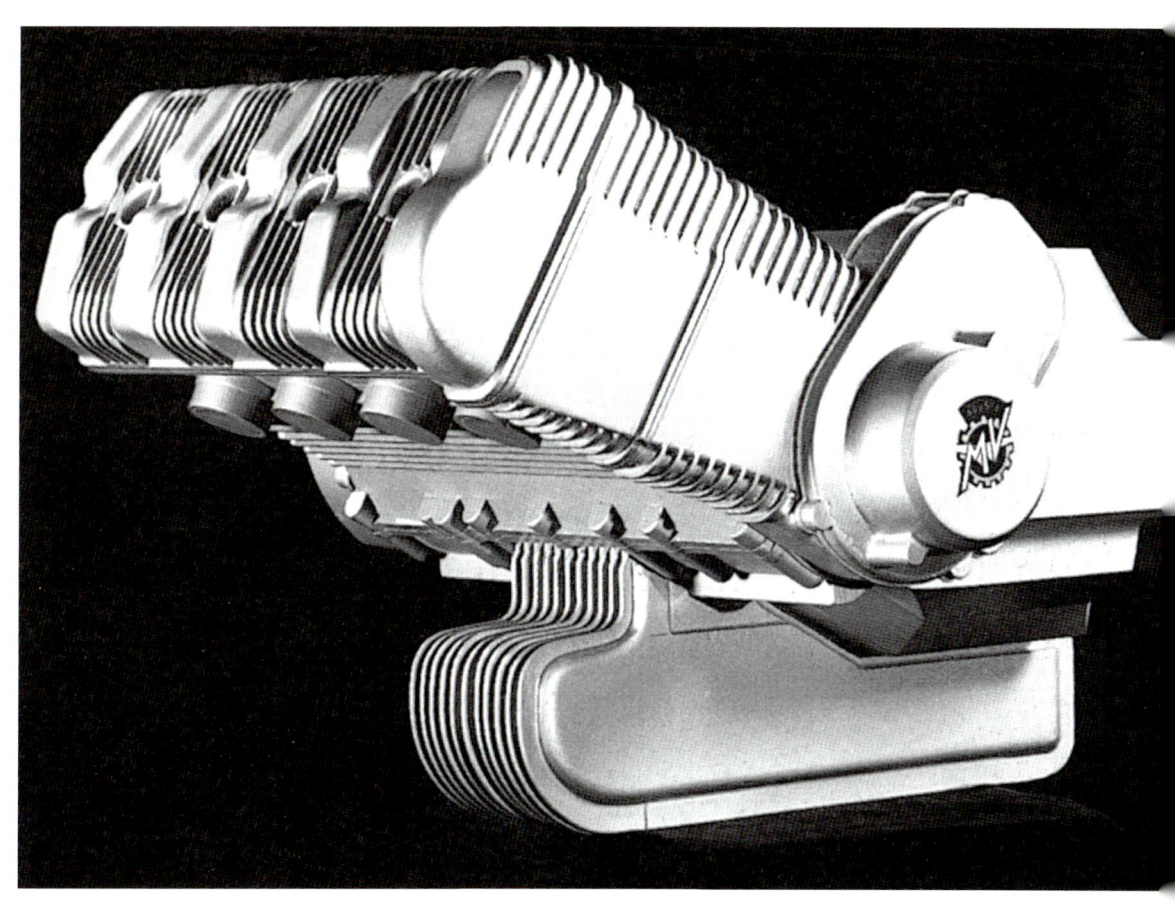

This prototype four-cylinder engine designed by Giuseppe Bocchi was considered as a replacement for the America unit during 1975.

MV AGUSTA FOURS

Another prototype four mock-up, with angular styling and chain drive.

inlet camshaft driven by a gear from the exhaust. The cylinder head design included four-valves per cylinder, with a narrow included valve angle to keep the design compact. Still air-cooled, the cylinders were steeply angled to improve airflow, but there was some doubt as to how this long, low engine could be integrated into a normal motorcycle frame. This engine didn't make it beyond the design and mock-up stage, but another plastic model of an angular 750 was produced during 1975. This was a strange mixture of early 750 S running gear, a racing frame with chain drive, and angular engine castings. Another unusual feature of this mock-up engine was a kickstart. Another engine design that made it to the prototype stage was a four with belt-driven double overhead camshafts. This included three external pulleys, with the belts covered by an outer cover similar to the Ducati Pantah. Bocchi had assisted in the design of the Pantah at Ducati, but after 18,000 kilometres of testing this was also discarded.

Although Bocchi also designed a new flat-four double overhead camshaft four-valve 500cc Grand Prix engine, it was rumoured during 1975 that MV was considering building a rotary valve 500cc two-stroke Grand Prix machine. This was another Spairani initiative, and involved Dutch technician Jorg Moller, who was responsible for Morbidelli's successful 125cc Grand prix racers. Although, as Corrado Agusta was committed to four-strokes, the idea was abandoned. Bocchi's flat-four four-stroke did make it to the prototype stage, but the initial results were unimpressive and this costly exercise was soon shelved.

Although Bocchi's new production four-cylinder engine was only a dream, the Imola 750 with a dry clutch and chain drive could have been released in 1976. However, the reality was that the aeronautical side of MV made a far more profitable concern than its motorcycle division. EFIM already had one unprofitable motorcycle company, Ducati, and its directors decided to close the MV Agusta motorcycle plant early in 1977. Some unsold Americas were converted into the 850 SS, or 850 Monza, and these were the last official four-cylinder versions available from the factory. The Monza was initially called the Boxer (after Bocchi's ill-fated new racing engine), but the factory soon changed the name. It has been suggested the name change was due to an objection by Ferrari, though this is unlikely as Ferrari also

THE 850 SS (MONZA) 1977

Arturo Magni with an America at Cascina Costa early in 1977. This has probably been converted into an 850 SS, but it retains the America's 26mm carburettors. The photo was taken in the racing department, as racing bikes are clearly in the background.

had several models using the name Monza. A more likely scenario is that Hansen in Germany – by this stage MV Agusta's most influential distributor – suggested a name change to Monza as the boxer Grand Prix racing engine was never going to materialise after 1977. In an interview at the time, British importer Peter Bate was quoted, "Ferrari call one of its cars the Boxer – why shouldn't we? The idea is that the Ferrari image should rub off."

Some mystery surrounds the 850 SS, or Monza. Certainly, a number of unsold Americas were still at the factory in 1977, but the amount converted into 850 SSs appeared to be very small. According to Mario Rossi, "We 'sweated seven shirts' to sell the final 42," and other reports indicate that 27 Monzas were officially built. They were also built to order for distributors or individuals, so the exact specification was inconsistent. Further confusion occurred as distributors in several countries modified Americas with Monza kits. In Giovanni Magni's words, "The America is the last official model produced and homologated, and after the end of production there were some unsold units. Some of these were modified at the factory, at the request of the buyer. I don't consider these a different model, just another modified America." Giovanni actually went further, saying, "The specification of all the modified

MV AGUSTA FOURS

The first 850s were titled the Boxer, but this was soon changed to Monza.

Americas differed depending on the importer; either Hansen, Bates, or Commerce Corporation." Arturo Magni, who presumably oversaw the conversions, doesn't recall the exact number, or even consider these a special model. Certainly, a small number of 850 SS were available from the factory during 1977 to those who had the contacts and finances to arrange it, and the specification of these appears quite consistent. But the exact number remains a mystery.

ENGINE

As the Monza was a modified America both models shared the 221-series engine number sequence. The numbers were quite random, with some Monza engine numbers quite low. This was not surprising, considering engines and frames were selected at random

This 850 SS (engine 221-080) is still much as it left the factory in October 1977.

THE 850 SS (MONZA) 1977

The Dell'Orto VHB 27A carburettors were the same as those on the 1974 750 Sport.

during America production. Despite some variation in equipment, the engine specifications of known 850 SSs appear to be consistent. The cylinder head ports were enlarged and 69mm pistons with shorter skirts installed. The

The 850 SS engine had individual cylinders and displaced 837cc.

MV AGUSTA FOURS

Each carburettor had an individual choke operated by a white plastic lever.

compression ratio was claimed to be 9.5:1, but was possibly higher. The individual barrels (not paired as in later Magnis) were thinner than on the America, also requiring a new gear carrier, while the top of the crankcase was machined to accept the larger cylinders. Displacing 837cc (although for some reason it was always referred to as 832cc) the Monza was the largest capacity factory-produced four-cylinder engine. It was also significantly more powerful than any earlier fours, producing an estimated 85 horsepower at 9500rpm (with some claims of 95 horsepower). Much of the power increase was due to the installation of two America inlet camshafts (another inlet replacing

The 850 Monza instruments were identical to the America, here with a mph speedometer.

194

THE 850 SS (MONZA) 1977

the exhaust), and, on non-US versions, a set of four unfiltered Dell'Orto VHB 27A carburettors (as used on the 1974 750 Sport) and less restrictive chromed mufflers (but with seams). The larger carburettors were better matched to the intake ports than on the America and no longer had enclosed tops, with the operating linkage as on the earlier 750. 850 SSs built for the US market retained the original 26mm carburettors with enclosed tops and air cleaners, along with more restrictive black mufflers, to conform with US regulations. The chrome mufflers were included in the crate with the bike. It is rumoured that fifteen 850 Monzas were US spec.

The Brembo front brake master cylinder was an improvement over the Scarab.

Other features unique to the 850 SS included a dual-point Marelli 7K distributor, as fitted to the earliest 600 in 1967. This provided a reduced dwell angle, allowing the coil to charge more quickly at higher rpm, and also included a heavier duty coil. All 850 SSs (even those with early engine numbers) appear to have the extended clutch cover fitted.

850 SS (Monza) engine specifications

Bore	69mm
Stroke	56mm
Capacity	837cc
Compression ratio	9.5:1
Maximum power	85hp at 9500rpm
Inlet opens	48-50° before TDC
Inlet closes	68-70° after BDC
Exhaust opens	68-70° before BDC
Exhaust closes	48-50° after TDC
Carburettor type	4x Dell'Orto VHB 27AD and VHB 27AS (VHB 26A on US versions)
Ignition	Marelli 7K dual point distributor
Fixed advance	8-10°
Automatic advance	40°
Total advance	48-50°
Breaker points clearance	0.4mm

Brembo brakes replaced Scarab on the 850 Monza.

195

MV AGUSTA FOURS

CHASSIS

As the 850 SS running gear was ostensibly that of an America there were few updates, and it seems the 850 SS was quite consistent in chassis specification (if not badges and model recognition). All 850 SSs had gold six-spoke EPM wheels and triple disc brakes, with Brembo brake callipers replacing the America's Scarab. The 38mm Ceriani front fork and 280mm brake discs were identical, and the front Brembo callipers retained the Scarab mount, so they were interchangeable. The Brembo callipers included metal brake tubes connecting to the rubber hoses, while the rear Brembo brake calliper was mounted on an EPM bracket, with the Brembo master cylinder on the right. The rear disc was also 280mm. Although bodywork was that of the America,

The rear Brembo brake calliper was mounted low and under the disc.

The rear Brembo master cylinder was mounted on a bracket on the right.

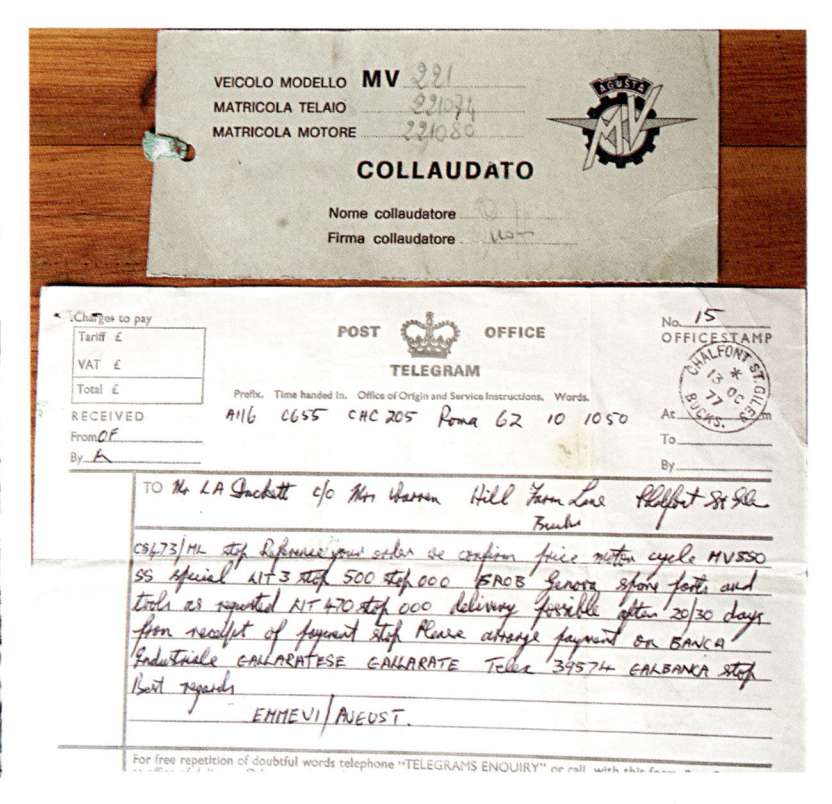

The original documents for the sale of an 860 SS to Mr LA Duckett of Melbourne in October 1977.

THE 850 SS (MONZA) 1977

some early 850 SSs had 'Boxer' decals on the side covers. Others had '750 S America' side cover badges, and some were without any model recognition. 'Monza' or '850 SS' decals were also evident on some examples, but these were dealer or distributor fitment. Some had plastic tank badges while others had MV decals. Most US 850 SSs had the MV Agusta badge on the side cover and a simple logo on the tank. Other variations included aluminium instrument holders, and the few US examples had higher handlebars. Certainly, distributors could determine the actual specification of the 850 SS, which is why there was some variance in badges and model recognition. And while the 750 S America was offered with an optional full fairing, it doesn't seem this was fitted to the 850 Monza at the factory.

850 SS 'MONZA' DISTINGUISHING FEATURES (1977)

Engine and frame numbers shared with the America
69mm pistons with 9.5:1 compression ratio
Individual barrels and new gear carrier
Extended clutch cover
Most with four Dell'Orto VHB 27mm carburettors
Four individual seamed chrome mufflers
Dual-point Marelli 7K distributor
EPM cast alloy wheels
Dual Brembo front disc brakes with metal tubes and rubber brake hoses
Rear Brembo disc brake
Early examples with 'Boxer' side cover decals
Some with '750 S America' side cover badges
Some without any model recognition
US versions with higher handlebars
Some with aluminium instrument holders

With so few genuine 850 SSs built, and many distributors converting Americas with factory-supplied kits, the myth surrounding the Monza has become accentuated. At the Earls Court Motorcycle Show in August 1977 the Boxer was on display for £3973 (plus £210.60 for a full fairing), but only two Boxers were imported into the UK. The Earls Court show Boxer had a

Visually, there was little to distinguish the 850 Monza from a 750 America. This example also has 750 America badges.

197

MV AGUSTA FOURS

right side gearshift and was lent to Phil Read. It was also used as a test bed for rear suspension developed by Hughenden. The other Boxer (with left side gearshift) was sold to John Safe, one of the founding members of the MV Agusta Owners' club. It is not known how many other 850 SSs went to the UK, but one was tested exhaustively by a series of magazines (SRX833S). Dealers also created several Monzas out of kits. One of these was subsequently tested by *Motorcycle Sport* magazine in August 1977 and had Borrani wheels and a rear drum brake. During 1978, Magni supplied an 861cc kit to the British distributor Bates, which included black twin barrel cylinders, Dell'Orto 30mm carburettors with accelerator pumps, and a Magni exhaust system with upswept curved mufflers. Richard Boshier worked at Station Garage in Taplow and converted two Americas into Magni specials, listed at £4990. At the 1978 Earls Court Show MV Agusta Concessionaires had the 750 America (with cast wheels) at £3617, and the Monza from £4498 (depending on specification). However, there was no future for such expensive motorcycles, and in October 1978 MV Agusta Concessionaires (GB) Ltd closed down. Only three 850 Monzas were sold to buyers in Australia, and possibly 15 to the US (although some claim only 4 or 5). Most 850 Monzas probably went to Germany, where the 850 SS was also initially titled Boxer before it was changed to Monza during 1977. As in the UK, Hansen offered versions with Magni's 862cc kit and, in cooperation with Roland Schneider, modified standard Americas at the customer request. Hansen also built several larger capacity versions (covered in the next chapter).

Although expensive, the performance justified the price, as the 850 SS was easily the fastest production four to leave the factory gates at Cascina Costa. When tested by *Motorcycle* on a gusty day in October 1977 the 850 Monza was also the fastest motorcycle to ever be put through the speed trap at the MIRA Midland proving ground. Even without a fairing, the mean top speed was 140.5mph (226.1km/h), with a best way speed of 144.4mph (232.4km/h). The Brembo braking was also impressive, the 850 Monza stopping from 30mph in 26½f (8.1m). But, ultimately, the 850 SS was left as something of an enigma. Undeniably exclusive, because it retained the shaft final drive it didn't offer significant functional superiority over other modified Americas. The Monza was fast, but it was also heavy. In reality, the Monza was a pragmatic response to liquidating unsold stock, and it would be left to a series of talented individuals outside the factory to create the ultimate performance MV fours.

Another US 850 SS with the same carburettors. (Courtesy Peter Calles)

As not all 850 SS models were identical, determining a genuine one can be difficult. This US-delivered 850 had 26mm carburettors with enclosed tops. (Courtesy Roy Kidney)

8 MODIFIED MV FOURS

The fact that the production MV four was intentionally created as a compromised sporting motorcycle has always encouraged the construction of specials. According to specialist Dave Kay, "An MV four was really all about the engine and the rest was peripheral." Kay also says, "The crank was too high in the frame as the oil pump sat in the bottom of the engine with a long automotive oil filter. The large crankcase was essentially an oil cooler with a filter, so the engine was deep and high. The result was the standard MV never really handled as well as expected. Under power they handle well, but it is suicidal to go into a corner too fast and brake."

Although the 600 was designed to deter customers converting them to racers, in 1969 Swedish rider, Sven Gunnarsson, built a 500cc racer out of a 600. Gunnarsson replaced the shaft final drive with a chain and created a double cradle frame. Four 26mm Amal Concentric carburettors fed the engine, and the exhaust system consisted of four individual pipes. A stout Rickman Metisse front fork, Borrani front wheel with single Lockheed brake, and 200mm Fontana twin leading-shoe rear brake completed the specification. Gunnarsson's effort was impressive, but it wasn't particularly successful.

In 1970 Fausto Pirelli of Milan built a sporting special out of a 600. Inspired by Agostini's

Swede Sven Gunnarsson was the first to create a private solo racing machine out of the 600.
(Courtesy Raphaël David)

199

MV AGUSTA FOURS

In 1970 Milanese owner Fausto Pirelli created this special out of his 600.

Grand Prix triple, Pirelli's 600 featured four carburettors, four individual exhausts, four leading-shoe Ceriani front brake, and special bodywork. Other specialist Italian companies followed Pirelli's example, with Massimo Tamburini's first special of 1971 also built out of a 600. This

Massimo Tamburini with his first special, based on a 600 MV Agusta.

was purchased from an owner in Cuneo through an advertisement in *Motociclismo* magazine. Tamburini always admired four-cylinder engines and his MV special was extremely impressive, incorporating chain final drive and a low dual cradle frame. Tamburini also enlarged the engine to 750cc and installed four racing Dell'Orto carburettors, later becoming one of the founders of Bimota. Other Italian companies offered kits, notably Menani's replacement bodywork. Hans A Muth in Germany also used a 750 S as the basis for an early design effort for his company Target Design. Muth's 750 S featured a 1974 series engine in a 1973 chassis, and he fitted a 260mm Yamaha four leading-shoe front brake, wider rear wheel rim and four-into-one exhaust. His modifications shed 15kg from the weight of a standard 750 S.

The styling of Pirelli's special was heavily influenced by Agostini's Grand Prix racers.

MODIFIED MV FOURS

Tamburini's MV was beautifully executed.

As the 600 and 750 fours were always expensive and rare, apart from some 600s converted into 750 Sports, not too many of these early bikes were made into specials. It wasn't until the wider availability of the America that the MV special became more popular. Not only was the America built in larger numbers, it was more modern in many aspects than the earlier bikes. Compared to the earlier 750 GT and Sport, the America had a stronger front fork, disc brakes, and many were fitted with EPM cast alloy wheels. With some examples still available after the factory closed, they were ideal candidates for modification.

Italian specialist Menani offered this fairing, tank, and seat kit for the 750 Sport in 1974.

201

MV AGUSTA FOURS

Hans A Muth created this radical styling exercise out of his 750 Sport.

Factory originality is generally considered the epitome for most classic motorcycle collectors, but some of the most desirable MV fours are specials by MV experts Magni, Hansen, Kay and Bold. Seeing as there are several hundred MV four-cylinder specials in existence, and all are different, it's only possible to give an overview of these bikes.

ARTURO AND GIOVANNI MAGNI

The most well-known MV four-cylinder specials are by Arturo and Giovanni Magni. Arturo Magni was MV Agusta's long-term racing team manager, and after MV folded its racing tent at the end of 1975 he remained with MV; fettling the old racers for demonstrations, but also preparing 750 Americas to special order. As early as 1974 the Magnis (Arturo and sons Carlo and Giovanni) established two companies offering performance parts for MV fours and selling EPM wheels to MV Agusta for the America. Magni also had a direct association with Hansen in Germany, and one machine created from this association

Giovanni and Arturo Magni with their frame and chain drive conversion for the MV four.

Giovanni Magni's personal machine. This has Lockheed brakes and a dry clutch.

was the Hansen 900 S 'Arturo Magni Cento Valli' built early in 1976. In 1977, Magni created his company Elaborazioni Magni with son Giovanni. Initially it offered big bore kits, chain drive conversions, and EPM wheels for the MV fours, and in 1979 Giovanni produced a

MODIFIED MV FOURS

Another view of Giovanni Magni's MV.

MV AGUSTA FOURS

frame patterned on that of the 1972 Imola 750 racer. Most Magni MVs were based on the America, and all differed slightly in specification to accommodate owner preferences. Some were built with standard frames, some with shaft drive, while most featured a chain drive conversion. They were all characterised by spectacular specification and wonderful attention to detail, and it is no coincidence that Magni MVs are coveted and highly sought after. Magni MVs represent the end of the artisan era. Every component is manufactured in-house at its workshop in Samarate (near Cascina Costa). Giovanni himself manufactures the frames, chain drive conversions and aluminium fuel tanks. Unfortunately, there is no record of the number of Magni MV conversions. When asked about this Giovanni said, "It was not

This early Magni is similar to the 1972 Imola racer. It retains the shaft final drive but includes a racing frame.

Early Magnis sometimes had a drum front brake and straight exhausts.

Many Magnis had full fairings, but this example has a half-fairing to show the engine.

possible to record the numbers because in many cases only engine parts or frame kits were sold. Then, maybe a year later, more parts would be sold for the same bike. As most of our sales are for parts and not complete bikes, we have no way of knowing how many Magni MVs there are in total."

ENGINE

The first engine items offered by Magni for MV fours were big bore kits, mostly 69mm but also 70mm. On early engines Magni used individually cast barrels, and, with 69mm cylinders, the capacity matched the

Another Magni with the half-fairing. This example has Scarab brakes. (Courtesy Giovanni Magni)

205

MV AGUSTA FOURS

The Magni chain drive conversion.

The Magni Dell'Orto carburettor kit. (Courtesy Giovanni Magni)

Monza, 837cc. These 837cc Magnis with separate barrels are quite rare, as Magni soon increased engine capacity to 862cc, with 70mm pistons. Weighing 220 grams, these pistons were slightly heavier than the standard 750 items, and their 70mm length meant it was no longer possible to use individually cast barrels – the increase in bore reduced the thickness of the cylinder wall to an unacceptable size. The cylinder studs (1-2, 5-6, 7-8, 11-12) were very close to the liners, so it was necessary to cast the barrels in pairs. Magni subsequently used the paired barrels for various engine capacities, from 837 to 1000cc. These barrels were distinguished by having 9 fins instead of 11 (as on the standard factory barrels and Magni's individual cylinders). At this

The Magni dry clutch conversion (Courtesy Giovanni Magni)

Magni's distinctive banana pipe exhaust system.

MODIFIED MV FOURS

time, Magni only offered 70mm pistons (for 862cc), with a 9.5-10:1 compression ratio.

Depending on specification, the crankshaft was lightened and balanced, sometimes with straight cut primary gears. Magni tried several cam profiles over the years, but, generally, camshafts were shared with the 850 Monza, sometimes with an extra 10-degree opening, often with a higher lift (9.5mm). A standard inlet camshaft was used on the exhaust, and Magni favoured standard valves. "The America cylinder head was really quite good in terms of performance," says Giovanni. The four carburettors were Dell'Orto, and, dependent on what was available at the time, specified by the owner. These could be either the standard VHB or PHB with accelerator pumps, usually 30mm but occasionally 32mm. More recently, Magni has preferred to use a Dell'Orto PHF 30A carburettor kit with a beautifully-crafted linkage, including three Heim joint connectors. "These are better than the 27mm, and more suitable for the road than the 32mm," says Giovanni. He also supplied a linkage arrangement for the Dell'Orto VHB 27mm carburettors fitted to the 1974 750 S and 1977 850 SS Monza. Magni initially favoured the Marelli dual point distributor, but later developed an electronic distributor with Marelli. Later he offered external dry clutch conversions, with an aluminium or magnesium housing, and magnesium camshaft covers and camshaft caps. The special clutch plates were 7 driven and 7 driving.

Magni's exhaust system was also distinctive, usually four black-painted 'banana pipes' but sometimes four straight pipes. There were three versions of the 'banana' pipe, ranging from totally open to more baffled. The final four-cylinder MV Grand Prix machines of 1974 inspired the shape of 'banana pipes.' Most Magnis had a chain drive conversion, and Magni also sold the chain drive as a kit, although installation was far from straightforward and required a certain degree of engineering skill.

FRAME

The Magni MV generally included a special twin tube frame (similar to that on the racing 750 of 1972), manufactured by Giovanni in their workshop in Samarate from lightweight chrome molybdenum

The Magni frame was based on earlier racing versions. (Courtesy Giovanni Magni)

MV AGUSTA FOURS

FORKS, WHEELS, BRAKES, AND BODYWORK

Magni preferred a Ceriani or Forcella Italia fork and, even though there were several different types, the triple clamps were always Magni – again, manufactured in-house at Samarate. The wheels were usually six-spoke EPM cast aluminium or magnesium, but wire-spoked Borrani alloy rimmed wheels were also fitted. Magni's eldest son Carlo, a mechanical engineer, designed the EPM wheels, which were either cast in aluminium or magnesium. Magni usually fitted Brembo disc brakes, either a fixed plasma-coated disc or fully floating, with Gold Series twin- or four-piston callipers. An alternative Magni-

Later Magnis had eccentrics for chain adjustment.

tubing. The twin top tubes were very close to the inlet camshaft cover, so valve adjustment was impossible without removing the engine from the frame. The frame included a removable left side down tube and lower rail (held by 6 bolts) to facilitate removal of the engine, and the upper sections were sleeved for strength. The swingarm was constructed of box-section steel and there were two types: later ones used plain Teflon bushes with the rear axle carried in an eccentric mount for chain adjustment; while earlier ones included taper roller bearings with the axle held in sliding blocks by a draw bolt and locknut. The frame had a steering head angle of 27 degrees, provided 110mm of trail, and had a wheelbase of 1450mm.

The Magni front drum brake was a four leading-shoe, this one cast in magnesium.

MODIFIED MV FOURS

Another variation on the Magni. Many Magni MVs kept the standard America Ceriani front fork.

MV AGUSTA FOURS

This Magni MV has four-piston Brembo front brakes.

manufactured Ceriani-style drum brake could also be specified. The front brake was a 230mm four leading-shoe with magnesium hub and side plates, while the rear was 180mm. Several different designs of seat and fuel tank were also available; the tank either in steel or aluminium, the fibreglass seat usually a solo type, and the fairing full or half. Like the aluminium bodywork, Giovanni Magni manufactured all the fibreglass in-house.

Although Magni subsequently branched out into BMW and Moto Guzzi specials, the MV Agusta kits are still available. These include the chain drive conversion, external dry clutch, magnesium camshaft covers, 862cc pistons and cylinders, three types of exhaust system, Dell'Orto PHF 30A carburettors, frame and bodywork (including three fairing and five seat variations). With all the various options there was no standard Magni MV, and these bikes were true artisan-built individual creations. For more information on Magni visit the company's website at http://www.magni.it/

HANSEN

Michael Hansen was the long time distributor for MV Agusta in Germany. Having begun selling MVs in 1970, he knew the market for four-cylinder MV Agustas very well. Hansen (together with his mechanic Roland Schneider) was the largest importer of MV Agusta motorcycles for many years, and in 1976 and 1977 Hansen sold the standard America alongside various modified versions. These were all built by Schneider and initially were only lightly modified (the 800 Super America and 800 Super Daytona America), but during 1976 Hansen commissioned Arturo Magni to build a special 900cc version, the 900 S Cento Valli. According to Arturo Magni, Hansen subsequently bought many chassis parts from Magni for his special MVs, while Schneider built the engines.

In 1976 Hansen offered the Cento Valli for sale at 25,400 DM, this increasing to 28,400 DM in 1977. With a claimed 105 horsepower at 9500rpm this 893cc four featured a 2mm longer (58mm) stroke, with a special German crankshaft and 10.5:1 70mm Mahle pistons with 11-fin Magni individual cylinders. Valve sizes were 31.8 and 29mm, and the engine breathed through four Dell'Orto PHF 30A carburettors with accelerator pumps and four individual cables, without any lever arrangement. The exhaust system was either a four-into-one, similar to that of the prototype

Without the fairing the racing frame is clearly seen.

MODIFIED MV FOURS

The 900 Cento Valli retained the MV frame and shaft drive. (Courtesy Roy Kidney)

850 SS of late 1974, or a set of individual curved Magni pipes. The chassis of this early Magni/Hansen America special was ostensibly stock America, including shaft drive, EPM wheels, and Scarab front disc brakes. The rear brake was changed to a smaller (240mm) diameter disc with Brembo 08 series calliper and locally supplied carrier, while a set of Koni shock absorbers replaced the Sebac. About ten 900 S Cento Valli bikes were built, and, as with all the Hansen/Schneider bikes, were either made from customers' own machines or from surplus Americas and parts.

After the 900 S Cento Valli, Hansen and Schneider developed the similar 1000 Corona, also with the MV frame and shaft final drive. A new crankshaft provided a stroke of 62mm, and with the 70mm bore capacity was now 954cc. The rest of the engine specifications were similar to those of the 900 S, including 10.5:1 Mahle pistons, 31.8 and 29mm valves, open Dell'Orto PHF 30A carburettors, and either a two-into-one exhaust system or Magni's curved individual pipes. The cylinders were now 9-fin paired Magni, and the intake valve lift increased to 8.8mm. Power output was still 105 horsepower, only now at 10,200rpm. The frame was sometimes painted red, and the brakes were Brembo or Scarab, often with a larger 280mm rear disc (as on the America). With a claimed top speed of 221km/h the 1000 Corona provided the expected performance for the 26,000 DM asking price, but it was still a heavy machine at 255kg with a full tank of fuel. Despite the cost, there was sufficient demand for Schneider to build 25 examples of the 1000 (and 1000S with racing camshafts) Corona between 1978 and 1982.

In March 1978, Hansen announced the release of its largest version of the MV four, the Grand Prix (GP) 1100. With a special crankshaft

The 1000 S Corona, also with the MV frame and shaft drive. (Courtesy Roy Kidney)

211

MV AGUSTA FOURS

This 1000 S Corona and GP 1100 were in the collection of Japanese industrialist Yoshiyuki Hayashi before being sold in the Peterson Automotive Museum auction of 1996. (Courtesy Roy Kidney)

the 74x62mm four displaced 1066cc. Special 9-fin paired barrels and a new crank carrier were built to accommodate the 10.6:1 74mm forged Mahle pistons. Carburetion was by four Dell'Orto PHF 30A carburettors, the exhaust system Magni's 'banana' pipes, and final drive by chain. Ignition was by a Marelli twin point distributor, and the claimed power output was 119 horsepower at 10,200rpm. On the first example, the front brakes were Scarab and the rear a Brembo 280mm disc. With EPM

The earliest GP 1100 models, like this, retained the MV frame, but had a chain final drive. (Courtesy Roy Kidney)

212

MODIFIED MV FOURS

Another view of the GP 1100 – possibly the fastest of all MV fours. (Courtesy Roy Kidney)

wheels the claimed weight was 202kg. The price was a staggering 29,600 DM. The Grand Prix 1100 was astonishingly fast for a production motorcycle in 1978; *Motorrad* managing a top speed of 236.8km/h at the Hockenheimring without a fairing in its May 1978 test.

Following the close of MV Agusta, early in 1979 Hansen obtained permission from MV's directors and the family to use the MV name to continue building a limited number of four-cylinder MVs. These were built through until 1982, and included the aforementioned 900 Cento Valli, 1000 Corona, and GP 1100. Only a few GP 1100s were built (possibly only five engines), two with chain drive versions of the MV frame and two with a Magni frame. A fifth engine was also built and only recently installed in a chassis. The GP 1100 tested by *Motorrad* in 1982 included a Magni frame and a Forcella Italia front fork with magnesium fork sliders. The 1066cc engine was now fed by a bank of Dell'Orto PHF 32A carburettors and power increased to 125 horsepower at 10,500rpm. With aluminium disc rotors and EPM wheels the weight was 205kg, and top speed 245km/h. The price in 1982 was 35,000 DM.

After the GP 1100 Schneider's next MV creation for Hansen was the 1000 Ago, a development of 1000 Corona. Released during 1979, this retained the Corona's 70x62mm 955cc engine, and, with a 10.5:1 compression ratio and four Dell'Orto PHF 30A carburettors, produced 99 horsepower at 10,200rpm (or 105hp with racing camshafts). Unlike the Corona, the Ago included chain final drive and a chrome-molybdenum Magni frame with box-section swingarm. As with all these specials, the specification varied, but sometimes the front brakes were a pair of 280mm aluminium plasma-coated discs with Brembo callipers. One was tested by *Motorrad* in May 1980. The weight (with

After 1979 Hansen also used the Magni frame with chain drive. This is the 1000 Ago of 1980.

213

MV AGUSTA FOURS

a full 26 litres of fuel) was 228kg, and its top speed was 221km/h. The 1000 Ago sold for 27,600 DM, and only about four were built.

Hansen and Schneider continued building MV specials to order until 1982, with something like 60 created altogether. While there were reports of unreliability with some of the larger capacity Hansen machines, this is unsubstantiated. In 1985 Hansen planned a new 16-valve 1100 MV-based superbike in cooperation with Arturo Magni, but this didn't eventuale as Hansen died prematurely and Schneider lost interest.

DAVE & MARK KAY

Although Dave Kay is one of the more controversial figures in the MV world, he and his son, Mark, have been responsible more than most for the continuation of the MV legend. The Kay relationship with MV Agusta began with the purchase of an 850 Monza in 1978, but Dave Kay's love for the marque (and the similar Gilera four) began earlier, following the exploits of the great British riders of the 1950s and 1960s (Duke, McIntyre, Surtees, Hocking, and Hailwood). A founder member of the MV Agusta Owners' Club in 1979, Dave Kay was also solely responsible for early editions of *MV News*, the club newsletter, the first edition of which appeared in September 1979. Over the past 30 years the Kays have worked on more than 240 four-cylinder MVs – a staggering number that represents 20 per cent of the total number produced.

KAY MV SIDECAR RACER

Nottingham born Dave Kay began his working career as a heating and ventilation engineer and moved to Birmingham to manage such a company. In 1970 he fabricated a kit car that won a magazine award, and by the 1980s established MVA Engineering Ltd in Sandhills, Staffordshire, specialising in MV Agusta. By 1984 he owned six MVs – the Monza, a Magni, 750 America, 600, 750 GT and 750 Sport – and would have had another if the second 750 Sport hadn't been stolen while in Italy in 1983. One of Kay's first projects was to build an MV four sidecar outfit for CRMC (Classic Racing Motorcycle Club) racing. Kay had a

Dave and Mark Kay with their replica MV 500cc three-cylinder racer.

MODIFIED MV FOURS

The controversial Kay MV sidecar as it was at the end of 1987. (Courtesy Mark Kay)

The Kay sidecar racer was powered by a 750 Sport-based engine. (Courtesy Mark Kay)

long association with sidecar racing (with Laverda and NSU outfits), and an MV-powered unit seemed a logical step. Following its debut at Cadwell Park in April 1985 Kay had a problem with CRMC officials over the MV's eligibility in a class with a 1972 cut-off year. The engine was basically that of 1972 750 Sport, but he had installed a Magni chain drive conversion that CRMC claimed wasn't available in 1972. While it was true that Agostini's 1972 Formula 750 racer retained shaft drive, Passamonti and Ricci's sidecar racer of 1969 included a chain drive. Other contentious features included the original sheet steel fabricated swingarm and heavily gusseted steering head, and every time Kay introduced a new feature CRMC seemingly altered the rules to disallow it. Dave took 16 wins from 25 starts in 1984 with his passenger Richard Battison, and when Mark took over he managed another 18 victories against the established Hillman Imp-powered competition. In 64 starts the MV sidecar never finished outside the top three and never broke down on the race track. In 1988 the Kay outfit was banned from CRMC racing, but this didn't prevent the Kays entering in the 1988 pre-TT Classic sidecar race at Billown near Castletown on the Isle of Man. Here, Mark Kay and Richard Battison provided MV Agusta with its first TT victory in more than a decade.

Kay's 750 S sidecar engine was fitted with higher lift (9.5mm inlet and 8.5mm exhaust) Magni camshafts adjusted by vernier (with 320-degree duration), and Magni high compression pistons. The heads were further skimmed to raise the compression to around 10.8:1, with minimal valve-to-valve clearance of only 1mm and an almost nil squish-band. Carburetion was by four Dell'Orto PHF 30A

215

MV AGUSTA FOURS

Mark Kay and Richard Battison on their way to victory at the Isle of Man in 1988. (Courtesy Mark Kay)

carburettors, and Midland engineer Dave Kerby made a four-pipe exhaust system. Complaints about the noise from the ACU saw a two-into-one system fitted during 1987. This was 6mm larger in diameter than standard and, with a Marelli distributor, the power at the crank was around 90 horsepower at 9500rpm.

Regulations prohibited straight cut primary gears, so the standard MV crank was retained, along with a Magni chain drive conversion. As the output drive of the MV motor was close to the centre, to accommodate the wide rear wheel with the final drive chain a crossover shaft was constructed. This was later banned and the second version required the rear wheel to track 25mm inboard of the front to line the chain. This wasn't a perfect solution and it caused some instability on fast left-hand corners.

John Derbyshire built the long-wheelbase chassis from T45 tubing, with small bracing tubes instead of gussets. The design held the engine in seven mounts, and allowed easy engine access. Leading link front forks carried a pair of Koni shock absorbers, while the rear swingarm was initially box-section with a single Koni shock absorber, mounted on eccentric bushes. Complaints about the eligibility of the swingarm led to its replacement by an earlier 1970s setup of a tubular cantilever version compressing a rubber 'donut' from a Mini car, and including a single hydraulic damper with a single hydraulic damper. This kept the overall height low, and the platform was raised at the rear in order to fit a secondary fuel tank – the primary fuel tank was contained within the rear of the wheelarch. Running on three 10in Windle wheels with Dunlop 145xL10 'greenspot' tyres, the Kay racer was stopped by four Lockheed 9in discs. The handlebar lever operated one front disc, the other three were by a foot lever. The original version included a

MODIFIED MV FOURS

dustbin fairing, but a small handlebar fairing later replaced this. The dry weight of the Kay racing sidecar was only 190kg, and it was capable of around 210km/h. Although dogged by controversy, Mark Kay campaigned the MV sidecar for several years, finally retiring it when he could no longer find a passenger.

500 SS

In 1989 Dave Kay formed a new company, Eiger MV, and expanded his activities to include building complete replicas. The first was a 500 SS for his son Mark to replace a stolen Kawasaki 600 commuter bike. 500cc was chosen because it fell into a lower insurance bracket for the then 21-year-old Mark. The basis of the engine was a set of crankcases the Kays were already offering as a replacement. These required 30 hours of machining from a bare casting, and were sloped in shape rather than round so they couldn't be accused of making fakes. A set of 10.5:1 53mm Asso pistons were used with a standard 56mm MV crankshaft. The 53x56mm dimensions were similar to Les Graham's 1952 500 racer, and the 500 breathed through a set of four Dell'Orto VHB 27A carburettors.

The frame was a modified 750 Sport item, with the lower rear cross tubes relocated to accommodate a chain drive conversion, and the Sport fuel tank was narrowed 50mm. Most of the rest of the running gear was similar to the early 750 Sport, including the Grimeca front brake. The 500 SS won the 1989 Classic Bike of the Year at Stafford, and this bike was later sold and converted to 750cc. "It was far too heavy for a 500," Dave commented.

At the same time, Dave Kay continued to prepare racing MV fours. In 1989 he built an 832cc solo machine for the Classic Bike/Norman Hyde

Mark Kay's 500 SS won the Classic Bike of the Year award at Stafford in 1989. (Courtesy Mark Kay)

EIGER (MV) LIMITED
The Hallmark of Quality

EIGER's Classic Bike of the Year 1989

Our reputation speaks for itself: -

Winner of 19 Concours 1st Awards including
Classic Bike of the Year 1989

32 Race Wins including 1st I.O.M. Classic Sidecar Race

In 1989 Dave Kay formed Eiger (MV) Limited and offered complete replica MV motorcycles.

series, and in May 1990 entered rider Pat Sefton in the 1300cc Classic TT at the Billown Southern 100 course. It had a bored version of the engine from the sidecar racer in a Magni frame. On the last lap Sefton crashed while in fourth, but the team returned in September 1992. This time Sefton lined up for the 750cc Manx Grand Prix on the Mountain Circuit against a field of modern machinery, coming home 40th out of a field of 105. Sefton's race average was more than 150km/h, but for

217

MV AGUSTA FOURS

The Kay Ferrari now resides in a private museum in England. (Courtesy Mark Kay)

KAY FERRARI

In 1990, after completion of the 500 SS, Dave Kay established new company Meccanica Verghera and set about building a larger engine. This 72x62mm engine displaced 1010cc and would form the basis for his next project, the Kay Ferrari. Kay obtained permission to use the Ferrari 'prancing horse' logo from Piero Ferrari and the bike included a number of individual features. The camshaft end caps were cast with the Ferrari logo, and the fuel tank badges and filler cap were genuine Ferrari. The engine was still ostensibly an MV four, retaining two valves per cylinder, but was fed by a pair of automotive-style dual throat Dell'Orto carburettors. The magnesium crankcases

Dave Kay the result was immaterial. "Just seeing and hearing an MV four flat out on the island again was enough for me," he says.

A bare casting for the Kay cylinder head.

218

MODIFIED MV FOURS

The Kay MV crankshaft, manufactured in England.

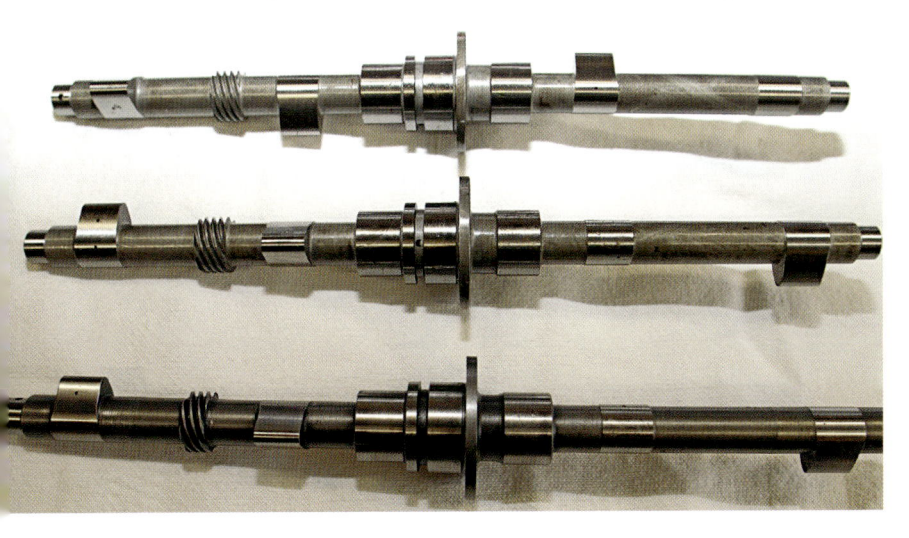

The Kay selector drum (underneath) was considerably lighter than the stock MV item.

A pair of Kay camshafts, with the standard 600 and early 750 type MV underneath (with narrower tacho worm drive).

were black and cast to include a larger and deeper sump extension. Kay cast special 11-fin cylinders in a single block and included a chain final drive conversion. The power was reputed to be around 118 horsepower, but as push-starting was the only way to start the engine it wasn't a very practical road machine.

Dave Kay commissioned Denny Barber to build a tubular steel double cradle frame that allowed easy engine removal, and included a box-section steel swingarm. He fitted a pair of White Power upside down forks, 17in Astralite spun-aluminium riveted

The Kay clutch on the left is a reverse of the factory clutch on the right.

wheels, and six-piston front brake callipers. Inspired by the Ferrari Testarossa and 288 GTO, the hand-beaten aluminium bodywork was supplied by Terry Hall, with digital instrumentation from Demon

MV AGUSTA FOURS

A Kay-built Grand Prix replica. (Courtesy Mark Kay)

Dave Kay also redesigned the MV clutch. "The clutch design was the wrong way round, with the friction plates stationary and the plain plates moving," maintains Dave Kay. "We convert the friction plates to driven plates, exactly as the factory did with the 1972 750 Imola racer." The Kays make their own clutch plates of paper friction material soaked in mineral oil. "These are slipped by burning the oil on the paper, and in 15 years they have proved unproblematic," says Kay.

By subcontracting Peter Kyte for alloy bodywork and Clive McCarthy for fibreglass, the Kays were able to produce MV specials comparatively quickly. Around 30 complete Kay MV specials have been built, and Dave Kay quotes a price of £35-40,000 for a complete Magni 862cc special depending on specification. The Kays also offer Gilera four-cylinder replicas, and currently produce a replica of the 1972 500cc MV racing triple to special order. Visit http://www.mv-agusta.co.uk/ for more information.

ALBERT BOLD

Operating out of an historic 1805 barn in Kimberton, outside Philadelphia, Albert Bold's Twekes. The weight was 225kg, and top speed 240km/h. The project was very time-consuming and not complete until 1995 when it was displayed at the Stafford Classic Bike Show and Festival of Speed. According to Dave Kay, "this was my interpretation of what a motorcycle would look like if Ferrari built it." The Kay Ferrari was later sold to Rodney Timpson in the UK.

In 1997 toolmaker Mark Kay found he was spending more time in his father's workshop than at work, so he set up his own company to build engines for the complete motorcycles assembled by his father Dave. The Kays believed the original MV design was flawed, particularly the cylinder head that was prone to distortion, leading to leaking cylinder head gaskets and difficulty with cylinder head removal. The Kays redesigned the cylinder head, incorporating three horizontal fins for improved cooling, and used superior heat treatment to minimise distortion. They commissioned a small foundry, GPD in Nuneaton, to sand-cast crankcases, cylinder heads, and one-piece cylinder blocks.

Paddock Engineering in nearby Tamworth did the gear cutting, Alpha Bearings built the crankshafts, and Arias supplied the pistons.

Albert Bold working on an America in his workshop in Pennsylvania.

MODIFIED MV FOURS

Bold's first MV racer was based on a 600 and he used it to win the 1982 and 1983 WERA over 500cc vintage titles.

background as a machinist extraordinaire began at five-years-old when his father taught him simple drill press operations in the family's machine shop. At the age of 19 he brought home a 1968 MV 600 in boxes and set about building it into a club racer. In 1982 and 1983 Bold won the National WERA (West-End Roadracing Association) over 500cc Vintage Championship on his MV Agusta special. At the time, apart from a lone contestant in the Spanish Superbike series, Bold was the only competitor in the world racing an MV four.

Without the benefit of a large budget, his racer was very much a home-built special. The stainless steel exhaust system was created out of a ladder from the local high school and, unable to afford a set of Brembo disc brakes, Bold patterned some discs from cast iron

The 600cc engine was enlarged to 750cc and a Magni chain drive conversion was fitted. The frame essentially remained stock.

221

MV AGUSTA FOURS

Albert Bold's second generation racer was much more radical and included mechanical anti-dive.

manhole covers that were being replaced in Philadelphia. The stock frame was strengthened with chrome-molybdenum gussets, and Bold built a box-section steel swingarm to suit the Magni chain drive conversion. He also outlaid for a set of 18in EPM wheels and installed Marzocchi remote reservoir shocks. The engine received a set of 67mm America barrels and pistons, two stock 750 inlet camshafts, and Manley stainless steel valves. Top Pro drag racer Frank Giardano flowed the heads and four Dell'Orto PHF 32A carburettors were installed. The bottom end was stock, and a Vertex magneto replaced the original distributor and Dynastart. The clutch consisted of 600 basket with 750 spline gear and America clutch, with an extra plate.

The frame was a rigid trellis type and the carburettors earlier Dell'Orto SS.

MODIFIED MV FOURS

This modification required an additional alloy spacer in the side cover to prevent it fouling the thrust plate with clutch actuation. The power of the 790cc four was around 70 horsepower at 8700rpm, but the weight was a substantial 215kg.

Although Bold concentrated on the WERA Vintage class, he also raced the MV in Superbike and Formula 1 with impressive results. But the limitations of the single loop 600 frame were becoming apparent. The braking forces kept cracking the front downtubes, and the short-wheelbase and high centre of gravity provided twitchy handling. During 1985 Bold decided to build a bike around his own frame, this time conceiving a hybrid that could be quickly converted to suit the rules for vintage or Superbike classes. Thus, the brakes could be disc or drum, and the exhaust four pipes or four-into-one.

Inspiration for the frame came from the factory 430cc Grand Prix triple, but instead of a full cradle tube Bold decided to use the engine as a stressed member. He built engine mounts out of 7075 aluminium billet, and the triangulated tubular frame from 4130 chrome-molybdenum. To provide maximum rigidity the frame tubes ran as close to the engine as possible. Eccentric adjustments at the axle and swingarm pivot allowed for a variable wheelbase, which was mostly around 1450mm, up on the 1370mm of his earlier racer. The cylinder head was raked out to 26 degrees (from the original's 24 degrees) and the frame structure weighed only 6.8kg.

The suspension was Marzocchi. The front a magnesium Marzocchi 35mm racing fork (from a Ducati TT2), offset 60mm and fitted with a set of 7075 billet Bold triple clamps that also incorporated the clutch and brake fluid reservoirs. A mechanical anti-dive was also added to the front end. With titanium arms this setup was similar to that used by Udo Gietl on John Long's BMW R90S Superbike in 1978. A set of 18in Akront rims laced to Bold's billet hubs completed the chassis specification.

This Bold special has a Bimota-style frame.

MV AGUSTA FOURS

The engine came from Bold's earlier racing bike, with capacity increased to 788cc and a set of America barrels. Considerable effort was spent lightening internal components, in particular the cam drive, and on developing the cylinder head. A set of Honda V65 Magna valves were installed (intake 36mm and exhaust 32mm) with stock America 67mm pistons machined to provide a 9.8:1 compression ratio. The camshafts were a Magni racing inlet, and stock MV inlet camshaft for the exhaust. The stock America five-speed gearbox was retained, but Bold lightened the gears by about 60 per cent and cut the width because the Bosch Dynastart was eliminated and the load on the gears reduced. He fitted a Scintilla magneto, while the con rods and six-bearing 56mm crank were standard MV. With a set of early style 28mm Dell'Orto SS carburettors the power was estimated at around 95 horsepower at 11,500rpm.

The hydraulically actuated clutch still consisted of a 600 basket with 750 spline gear, and much modification was required to retain a right side gearshift with Magni's chain drive conversion that was designed for a left side gearshift. The attention to detail was quite staggering, and Bold managed to reduce the weight from the earlier racer by 40 per cent, to 151kg with a 50/50 weight distribution. Individual components included a handmade exhaust system, a hand-beaten tank and tail section from 3003 aluminium, and a set of individual lightened sprockets. Later a newer style tank and seat were built. Unfortunately, on its second outing, at Daytona in 1989, it threw a con rod, punching a hole in the right crankcase. Since then it has been hanging in Albert's shop, awaiting a rebuild.

Another Bold special originated in Italy with a Bimota-style monoshock frame, but was unlikely to be an actual Bimota creation. The 862cc chain driven Magni-modified engine was originally from an earlier 750 S, and the mild steel frame included a single De Carbon shock absorber. While the original wheels were wire-spoked, Bold installed a set of Morris 18in seven-spoke aluminium wheels. The front fork was a 38mm Marzocchi, with Brembo brakes. Today, Albert Bold continues as the premier specialist for older MV models in the US. More information can be found online at http://www.boldprecision.com/

OTHER MODIFIED MV FOURS

Dave Kay wasn't the first to build an MV four-cylinder sidecar racer. In 1968 the Swiss pair Edgar Strub and Hans-Peter Hubacher built a 500cc sidecar racer out of a 600 MV four. Hoping to take on the all-conquering BMWs, the Strub-Hubacher MV retained the shaft final drive and breathed through four 27mm Dell'Orto SS1 carburettors. But by 1968 Strub was 52-years-old and at the end of his career, so the MV never realised its potential. Italian sidecar specialists Luigi Passamonti and Spartacus Ricci also built a sidecar racer out of a 600cc MV. This appeared in Italian events during 1969 and was notable for its chain final drive. Fitted with four Dell'Orto SS carburettors, Passamonti had some moderate success during the early 1970s, although Giuseppe dal Toè's BMW generally outclassed the MV.

Outside the established MV experts, other companies were also involved in the creation of MV specials. At the 1976 Bologna Show Segoni of Florence displayed a 750 MV four with a special frame and chain final drive. The spine frame was an Egli-style, with 100mm

Luigi Passamonti and Spartacus Ricci raced this MV sidecar in Italian events from 1969. This was one of the earliest chain drive conversions for the 600.

Segoni had this MV 750 special on display at the 1976 Bologna Show.

MODIFIED MV FOURS

During the 1980s the Rossi brothers continued to race MVs and build specials like this with a Magni frame.

Three of the Team Firenze racing fours. The 900 in the foreground was the successful TT1 machine, and the 16-valve four is in the centre.

backbone and 30 and 32mm down tubes. Rolling on a wheelbase of 1420mm, the bare frame weighed only 14kg, and, with EPM wheels and a 38mm Ceriani fork with Fontana disc brakes, the weight of the complete bike was only 185kg. Segoni advertised this frame kit at a considerable 5,500,000 Lire.

During the 1980s a pair of enthusiasts, the Rossi brothers, formed Team Firenze and built a small number of specials and racing bikes. With their series of special four-cylinder racing machines they competed in the Italian Superbike series in 1982 and 1983. Although they used Magni frames and twin shock rear suspension, the engines were quite special, as the Rossis cast one-piece cylinder blocks and installed Wiseco pistons. Their 900cc TT1 racer included separate crank hangers like the road bikes, and breathed through four 34mm Dell'Orto carburettors. Wheels were EPM; a 16in on the front and 18in on the rear. As well as the TT1 machine, Team Firenze also built a 16-valve 750 for historic events. This engine had the cylinder barrel cast with the crankcase hangers like the racing bikes, so was probably one of the prototype factory 16-valve engines. Another two-valve 750 four had integral cylinders and carrier like the racing bikes. The crowning glory for Team Firenze was Sauro Biondi's victory in the 1983 Italian TT1 race at Maggiore in 1983, on the 900. But this was an isolated victory as the days of racing domination by air-cooled in-line fours were now over. The Team Firenze collection was sold to British MV collector Peter Jones in 1988.

9 LIVING WITH AN MV FOUR

Although many MV fours are no longer ridden regularly, they remain a reliable and viable classic motorcycle. The engine may be a six-decade old racing design, but with careful and regular maintenance it will still last a long time. According to Dave Kay, "The basic 600 was very close in specification to Surtees' 500, and for a 50 horsepower street engine was over-engineered. MV tried to make it bulletproof." Kay also says, "An MV takes around 15 miles to warm up and must be run at 2500-3000rpm on a steady throttle. It takes a minute to get the cambox full of oil, and the most catastrophic thing for a crank is to rev it when cold." This chapter offers a brief guide to some of the problems encountered when living with an MV four. It must be emphasised, though, that the MV engine is a complicated design and requires careful and knowledgeable assembly. Although from this brief rundown of troubles it may seem the MV Agusta four-cylinder engine is problematic, in reality the MV engine is extremely strong and reliable. These are some of the problems that can appear through poor assembly and maintenance, or unsympathetic use.

ENGINE
CRANKSHAFT

The crankshaft oil spigots that transfer oil from the carrier to the split bearings can become loose if the engine is revved hard and suddenly shut off. This can cause the steel pegs to elongate the holes in the carrier, and ultimately result in no oil to the main bearings. Dave Kay found this fault in 90 per cent of engines he examined and overcame the problem by making stepped dowels with the larger end to the carrier. The little end oil holes were sometimes not countersunk correctly, resulting in the piston pin receiving insufficient oil at high rpm. The con rod can also pick up metal from the pin. Missed gears and accidental over-revving (above 8500rpm) can result in a twisted crank. A correctly built crank should also have less than 0.025mm

**Although nearly 40-years-old, the 750 S is still a fine riding machine.
(Courtesy Peter Calles)**

LIVING WITH AN MV FOUR

The MV crankshaft is very robust if treated sympathetically. (Courtesy Dorian Skinner)

run out across its length. According to Dave Kay, "Forget running the engine at 10,000rpm. Even running to 9000rpm on every gear change will eventually see the gearbox or clutch acting up. If you use 7500-8000rpm they will last forever."

VERTICAL TIMING CASTING
This was secured to the crank carrier with bolts and split washers. Eventually the split washers open out and the bolts slowly loosen until the casing is located only by the cylinder head. If a bolt got caught in the gears the result would be catastrophic. Dave Kay recommends replacing the split washers with plain thick washers and securing the bolts with Loctite.

CYLINDER HEAD, BARRELS, AND GASKETS
The exhaust port is close to the gasket, so, when hot, the head can bow into the exhaust port, causing the top of the barrels to warp. A solution is to weld the bottom of the exhaust port, creating a D-shape. Before bolting down the cylinder head, check the timing tunnel gasket is correctly located and the oil transfer spigot is in place. Bolt the head down sequentially, starting at the inner studs and working sequentially outwards. When converting a 750 S to 790cc, the 750 Sport barrels can't be fitted to the America carrier because the liners are thicker. America barrels can be fitted to a 750 Sport carrier, but the fit is loose and requires careful positioning of the base gaskets and the 'C' rings used to centralise the barrels. Monza barrels (larger but

The vertical timing casting was secured to the crank carrier by bolts and split washers. (Courtesy Dorian Skinner)

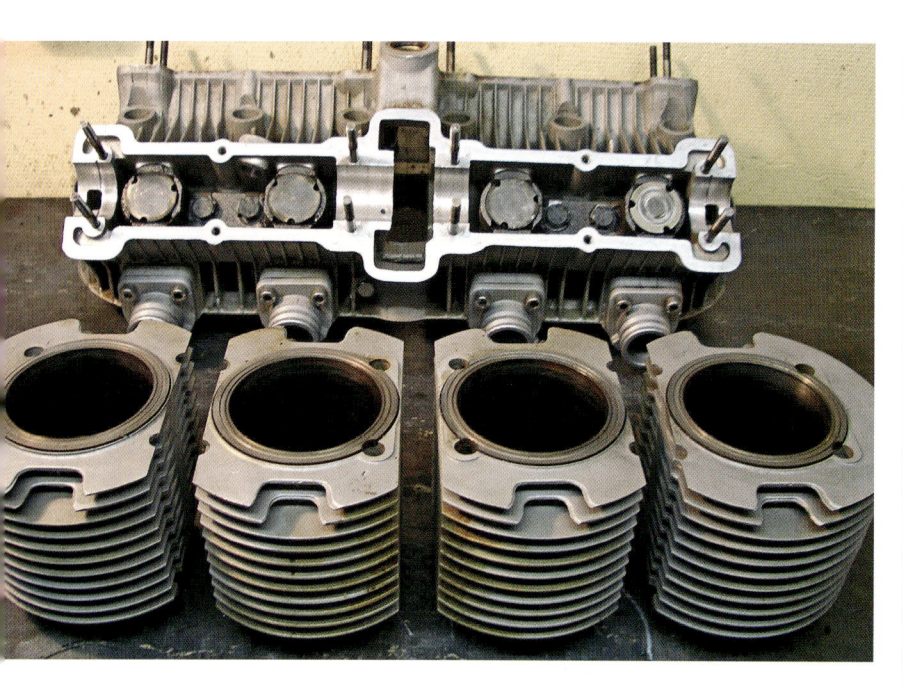

MV AGUSTA FOURS

The four separate cylinders and the cylinder head of the MV four. (Courtesy Dorian Skinner)

The cam gear teeth have red paint marks that are invaluable when it comes to assembly and disassembly. (Courtesy Dorian Skinner)

All MV engine parts carried specific numbers. (Courtesy Dorian Skinner)

with thinner liners) will fit a 750 Sport carrier but not the America carrier, which needs to be machined to accept the Monza liners.

Cylinder base gaskets can be tricky to install, as two barrels have to be fitted over each gasket. This often tears the gasket so it can be easier to cut the gasket in half, position onto the barrel and (on 750s) place the O-ring outside the liner to keep the gasket in place. Before bringing the next piston to TDC, temporarily retain the first barrel with nuts and spacers to stop the O-ring being displaced. A suitable replacement O-ring is shared with the float chamber of Dell'Orto UB 26mm carburettors.

Correct engine head gaskets are crucial, and need to be 0.5-1mm larger than the bore to allow the gasket to squash down when torquing the head. If the gasket is too small, the piston will hit the head when shutting down at high rpm – a problem evident particularly with 832cc, 69mm bore engines with America 67mm head gaskets. A useful tip is to always check and ensure the gaskets used during the rebuild match the engine: the 67mm bore America requires 68mm gaskets; the 65mm bore 750 Sport 66mm gaskets. On 837 and 862cc conversions, packing the barrels to reduce the compression ratio will detrimentally increase the squish band. The result is piston and combustion chamber overheating and, ultimately, detonation. The correct squish clearance for converted America engines should be 0.75mm.

CAMSHAFTS AND VALVE CLEARANCE

On the 750 GT, Sport, and America the camshafts need to be removed to reset valve clearances, a procedure that requires some care. Prior to engine dismantling or valve shimming, turn the engine to TDC on the No. 1 cylinder (clutch side) and on the compression stroke (noting the positions of the red marks on the cam gear teeth). Take particular note of their relationship to the machined cam box mating surfaces on the head. When viewed from the side of the engine, the coloured red teeth should show completely. This should be done before removing the cams. Take a digital photo of the position of the gears, too,

LIVING WITH AN MV FOUR

Valve clearances can be more easily adjusted if the cylinder head is removed. (Courtesy Dorian Skinner)

as it is easy to reinstall the camshafts one tooth out (18 degrees). This is caused when tightening the cam hangers; the cam tends to rotate when it meshes with the timing gear. The red mark needs to be located slightly higher than its final position. When installing cams it is also advisable to remove the tachometer drive, as this can be damaged when tightening the cam hangers.

When adjusting valve clearances do not mix buckets or shims. Measure each with a micrometer and compensate by adjusting shim thicknesses. Shims will need to be ground on an oilstone or surface grinder, as an unparallel surface can result in the shim displacing and the valve remaining open. The recommended valve clearance is reasonably large (0.25mm inlet and 0.30mm exhaust for the 750 S, and 0.30mm for both on the America), but if the inlet is too loose pocketing will result (and a loss in performance). Valve clearance can vary 25 per cent from the recommended value before adjustment is critical. If the cylinder head is removed, it's easier to shim the valves before the head is refitted. Install the cam in the head with valves 1 and 3 fitted, shim and then remove. Shim 2 and 4 separately. Although this means removing the cams and valves twice, it makes measuring the clearances simpler. Remove and mark the cams, buckets, and shims so they can be replaced in the correct sequence. To seat the collets tap the retainer at the top of each valve spring, not the valve stem.

To avoid bending valves when installing cams with the No. 1 piston at TDC, the cam apex should be aligned at 7:05 for the No. 1 exhaust and 4:55 for the No. 1 inlet. The timing marks on the flat teeth should be aligned with the flat surfaces either side. When checking valve timing the valve clearance needs to be correct, as incorrect shimming will affect valve timing. With standard shimming, a 8mm lift standard America inlet cam has 300 degrees crank opening, but a 0.2mm clearance will provide 330 degrees and 0.4mm clearance 285 degrees. Ensure the cam gears are fitted to the correct side of the cam flange. If fitted incorrectly, the camshafts will not receive any oil. It is also recommended to fill the engine with oil before installing the cam covers, and turning the engine by hand to ensure oil is getting to the cams. If the bearing caps are not secured correctly, or the engine runs too hot, the camshaft inner needle roller bearings can move outwards. Although the valve bucket guides stop these bearings falling out, it is useful to Loctite them. The 750 inner and outer valve springs are interchangeable with the 350 twins.

LUBRICATION

The oil pump is formed from a complex gravity casting and cracks are known to appear in the wall of the chamber that houses the paper element. This can potentially lead to oil passing back directly to the sump. Another problem with the oil pump is that it first appeared on the 50 horsepower 600, and was later asked to serve up to twice that in an 862 Magni. Oil pumps vary in efficiency; the flow rate regulated by ratings of the relief and bypass springs, and the gear endplay to the cover plate. Endplay should be minimised and within the limits of wear (0.150mm). Faulty relief valve springs can also result in the oil returning to the sump. The oil pump unit should be fitted without the gearbox outer cover in place, otherwise problems can occur because it will be fitted blind. Dave Kay has come across several near catastrophes caused by poorly fitted oil pumps, in particular the omission of the oil transfer bush from the pump to the crankcase oil ways. This will result in extreme overheating and a serious loss in performance. A troublesome oil leak on Americas from the timing tunnel to the front of the cylinder head can be solved by enlarging the oil way in the timing tunnel and installing an aluminium dowel with O-rings. As MV engines run very hot, synthetic oil is recommended, as well as genuine oil seals, which have a higher lip pressure than most replacement types to prevent oil leaks.

Replacement oil filters can also be problematic. The original (pre-1980) paper oil filter elements were malleable and sealed easily in the chamber as they had a cardboard top. Newer replacements with metal tops and bottoms don't seal well at the top, and the 3 small centring dots on the filter housing need to be removed for a modern filter. These centring dots guide the cardboard filter, and the spring under the cartridge forces the cardboard to fit the housing. On filters with metal tops this spring isn't strong enough to force the filter onto the 3 centring dots, which can result in a 1-2mm gap between the top of the filter and the housing. According to Dutch MV expert Erik Hakstege, it's important to check this with some grease on the cartridge. "On 99.9 per cent of MV's I have seen without the modification, the filter wasn't working as the oil didn't go through the element." This observation is echoed by Albert Bold who says, "... massive damage can be done to the motor if the filter is not carefully fitted. The engine was designed for a paper element filter, not metal ended. The metal end will prevent the element from seating properly against the end of the oil pump, as the three ramps that centre the element will prevent the filter seating. Three reliefs need to be ground

MV AGUSTA FOURS

into the end of the filter. If you do remove the pump, it is vital the oil pump collector or oil manifold (part# 199.09.016.0.00) be replaced into its original position." Albert goes on to say, "When these motors are oil starved, the No. 3 cylinder will seize. But only the wrist pin is usually damaged. The rollers and balls in this motor are great and will last a while with little oil feeding them. I would rather replace a piston than a whole crank or other expensive parts." Replacement oil filters should not have metal ends, and the dimensions should be height 104mm, OD 55mm, and ID 13mm.

Alternative oil filters include:
AC 165, 61
Baldwin 106, 106 HD
Ford 5000674, 675, 676,
Fiam FA 4018 and A
Fram CH-4461, CH-5576, CH 803 APL and PL
General Motors 5577966
Hastings LF182
Knecht AF12/1, EH 268, EH 268/1 and 2
Motocraft EFL 063, EFL 069, EFL 087
Purolater H27122, L27122, MF 103 A, MF 108 A, P221, P23
Volvo 349619, 349619-1
VW 0400700504, 400700504

ENGINE BREATHER

The original engine breather is incorporated into the engine casting, allowing water to penetrate. Erik Hakstege recommends an engine breather hose rubber; the rubber fitting on the outside of the engine casting, sealing the crankcase from water and dirt.

GEARBOX PROBLEMS

As the gearbox originated on the 600 and continued unchanged through to the final 850s, some problems have surfaced over the years. Most problems occur when a bike is ridden hard, and an Achilles heel of the gearbox is the 15x42x13mm layshaft bearing in the outer cover. This deep groove ball race was never designed to take side loads, but can be replaced by an angular thrust type if necessary. Another ball bearing not designed for side thrust is the 30x62x16mm bearing on the mainshaft behind the bevel gear. The additional side thrust imposed by the bevel gear causes the bearing to wear, allowing the mainshaft to move sideways and damaging the selector forks. If the wear is excessive, the gears will slip out off mesh under load as the shafts are pushed apart. In an extreme case (not unknown), this loads the tip of the gears and a tooth breaks off. The broken tooth will either harmlessly drop into the sump or drop between the gears, pushing the shafts even further apart. In the worst case scenario the gearbox is destroyed and the outer gearbox bevel housing splits in two. It is recommended this ball bearing be replaced at 25,000km, or a Magni chain drive conversion installed to eliminate side thrust.

This rubber can be inserted around the engine breather tube, sealing it against dirt and water ingress.

The gearbox was quite compact, although not trouble-free if the engine was used hard. (Courtesy Dorian Skinner)

LIVING WITH AN MV FOUR

and 16x20x17mm needle roller bearings supporting the end of the mainshaft and 5th gear. Both are inadequately lubricated and, if they break, result in failure of the other gearbox bearings. These bearings should be replaced when the outer gearbox cover is removed.

Layshaft end float is critical and must be within factory tolerances. Excessive lateral movement of the transfer gear behind the clutch (secured only by a washer and circlips) can result in failure of the rollers and possible damage to the gear centre and layshaft. If the layshaft or mainshaft is replaced, the end float must be checked and the shaft re-shimmed if necessary.

CLUTCH

Clutch slip can affect some engines and is caused by a variety of factors. Dave Kay believes the way the clutch is used, particularly riding the clutch, determines the amount of slip. Sometimes the clutch centre studs were unequal in length, as were the five securing nut shoulders. When assembled on the studs without springs, the height should be the same as with the springs fitted. The flanges that locate in the end plate should not be cracked or distorted, and the eight rivets securing the basket to the primary gear should be checked for shearing. These have to transmit all the power to the mainshaft and under extreme load will shear. If the rivets fail, they end up in the transfer gear behind the clutch. If the basket and gear are welded on

Some enthusiasts raced the 750 America in endurance racing. This is at Spa in Belgium, in 1976, but the America was too heavy for such duties.

The hardened 5mm washers used to locate the mainshaft inner bearing to the crankcase inner vertical wall can also split, leaving the mainshaft and bearing to float. The factory fitted two washers per bolt, so must have been aware of a problem that could be solved by fitting a thicker mild steel washer. The only plain bearing in the gearbox was on the 3rd gear mainshaft and, with only minimal splash lubrication, under extreme use this gear can overheat; twisting on the shaft and destroying the shaft bearing surface. An occasional side effect of 3rd gear failure is mainshaft overheating, resulting in the clutch operating rods becoming welded to their ball bearing spacers inside the shaft.

Another gearbox problem evidenced on engines worked hard is failure of the 12x28x15mm

The Magni with its compact frame and chain final drive was a more efficient sporting MV four.

231

MV AGUSTA FOURS

the back (not the face), either side of the lightening holes, the basket can be easily removed later if necessary with a milling cutter spotted on the holes.

The friction plates on the fours are interchangeable (same thickness) with the 350, but the 750 plates have smaller sized friction pads (more per plate). The 350 plain steel plates do not fit the 750, but the clutch springs and clutch outer cover are interchangeable between the 350 and 750.

DISTRIBUTOR AND IGNITION

Although the stated ignition advance is 48-50 degrees (total), Dave Kay recommends 46 degrees for 5-star fuel. According to Kay, "As MVs run hotter than the norm, the total ignition advance is more critical. Holed pistons are a direct result of too much ignition advance, and the Monza is more susceptible. Both the higher compression ratio and greater overlap exhaust cam (America inlet cam) require higher-octane fuel and retarded ignition timing. If you run a high compression Magni or Monza set at 18-degrees static for a total of 56 degrees, the result will be a holed piston, or possibly two." It is important to check the contact breaker gap and set to the manufacturer's clearance before adjusting the timing. All engines must be checked with a strobe timing light to verify. Check the Bosch distributor has the same centrifugal advance as the original. Factory specifications are 18 degrees with 30 degrees centrifugal advance, but newer versions of the J4 distributor have 36-38 degrees centrifugal advance. The Marelli twin point distributor on the early 600 and 850 SS was also problematic. The springs were prone to loosening and the bob weights to jamming on full advance. The twin point distributor was also more difficult to set up for correct ignition advance.

SPARKPLUGS

Model	NGK	Champion	Bosch	Marelli
861 Magni	B8ES	N3	W260T2	CW260L
832 Monza	B8ES	N3	W260T2	CW260L
America	B7ES	N3	W260T2	CW260L, CW8L
750 S GT SS 4C75	B8ES	N3	W260T2	CW260L, CW8L
600 4C6	B8ES	N3	W260T2	W275

DYNASTART

The Bosch Dynastart mechanism is one of the more problematic aspects of owning an MV four. The combined dynamo and starter function was achieved with a second set of field coils energised by the starter solenoid inside the regulator. The Bosch Dynastart is quite powerful, although not as fast charging as an alternator, charging at about 11 amps, but still adequate for most uses. To test a Dynastart D+ is disconnected and DF to earth shorted. At medium revs D+ should rise to above 14V, with approximately 6Ω between earth and the disconnected D+. If the resistance is not 6Ω, the coils have probably shorted due to corrosion or overheating. The design is not ventilated so overheating can be a problem.

Measuring D+ over a range of rpm also checks the regulator function. When D+ is greater than the battery voltage the cut-in relay should operate, and as rpm rises and D+ increases to more than 13V the right side relay should start to lift off the earth contact. This substitutes the rear resistor instead of a short to earth, as for DF. When D+ is greater than 13.8V the right-hand-side relay should shut, providing maximum resistance to DF. Most Dynastart charging faults seem to be caused by the regulator. The Bosch regulator has a removable cover (two screws in the sides), exposing the starter solenoid to the left, the pull-in relay in the middle, and the three-position regulator on the right. Just in front of the regulator relay, near the connection terminals to D- and D+, is a 20A fuse soldered between two points. If the earth connection to the battery breaks or shakes loose, excessive voltage from the dynamo output blows the protection fuse. This is easily fixed with solder.

Other problems can occur with the Dynastart unit. The biggest cause of Dynastart destruction is over-tightening the belts. If a belt snaps the starter engaging block may break. Spraying industrial belt dressing directly on the inside of the belts with the engine running

The standard fairing sometimes led to engine overheating, but worked better on engines with 24mm carburettors. (Courtesy Peter Calles)

LIVING WITH AN MV FOUR

can cure belt slip. When replacing the belt it is important to use a standard Pirelli and not a deeper Ferodo type that can foul the crankcase. Some Dynastart shafts were not sufficiently heat-treated, and these can destroy the splines driving the Dynastart mechanism. Some components were over-hardened, including the mating five star dog that carried the five plungers and rollers, the splined dog that located the two spring-loaded ratchets, and the splined washer. All these should slide easily, and if not the shaft splines can be filed to size. The Bosch Dynastart was also used on the BMW 600 and Isetta microcars of the 1950s, and copies of it are still used on golf carts.

FAIRING

Overheating has always been a problem with the four-cylinder engine, exacerbated by the optional full fairing of the 750 Sport and America. The fairing worked better with engines with 24mm carburettors, but the outer cylinders didn't carburet cleanly on engines with 26 and 27mm carburettors. Alberto Pagani added air vents to the sides of the fairing on some examples at the factory in 1973 to deflect air to the rear of the cylinder head. Pagani also fitted larger diameter Y-shaped fuel lines to provide an improved fuel flow for the carburettors when hot.

Air vents in the fairing were factory-fitted on some examples.

An MV Agusta Owners' Club day at Mallory Park in June 1985. Seeing so many fours together is rare today.

233

MV AGUSTA FOURS

750 BEARINGS

Location	No	Size (mm)	Type
Outer crankshaft (750)	2	30x72x19	6306N C3 ball with circlip
Outer camshaft	4	15x35x11	6202 C3 ball
Inner camshaft	4	35x28x20	HK 2820 needle roller
Timing gears	3	35x62x9	16007 ball
Clutch basket	1	35x40x27 long	K35 needle roller
5th drive gear inner	1	16x20x17	Needle roller
5th drive gear outer	1	30x62x16	Ball
Mainshaft	1	25x52x18	4205 ball
Mainshaft outer	1	12x28x15	Needle roller
Bevel gear support	1	25x62x25.25	Tapered roller
Coupling support	1	25x52x16.25	Tapered roller
Layshaft	1	15x42x13	6302 ball
Layshaft	1	17x47x14	6303 NR ball with circlip
Dist. driveshaft (horiz.)	1	12x32x10	6201 ball
Dist. driveshaft (horiz.)	1	12.75x17.5x12.5	Needle roller
Dist. drive support lower	1	10x26x8	6000 ball
Dist. drive support upper	1	20x42x12	Needle roller
Stator engine pulley	2	20x42x8	6004 ball
Oil/Dynostart shaft	1	17x47x14	6303 ball
Oil/Dynostart shaft	1	15x35x11	6202 ball
Swingarm	2	15x42x14.5	Tapered roller
Steering head	2	25x52x16.25	Tapered roller
Bevel box rear drive	2	25x62x25.25	Ball
Rear bevel driveshaft	1	40x80x18	6200 ball
Rear bevel driveshaft	1	50x80x10	16010 ball

The 11-digit MV Agusta spare parts nomenclature is as follows:

Model type (first 3 digits)	Group number (2 digits)	Item number (within group [3 digits])	Assembly of parts (3 digits)
199 (600)	01 (Crankcase)	001 onwards	Most parts with 0-00
214 (750)	02 (Crank & cylinder)		1-00 first modification
221 (America)	03 (Head)		2-00 second mod.
	04 (Carburettors)		0-01 item within assembly
	05 (Clutch)		0-02 another item
	06 (Gearbox)		0-03 another item etc.
	07 Gear selector)		
	08 (Ignition)		
	09 (Starter)		
	10 (Oil pump)		
	11 (Frame)		
	12 (Tank, exhaust)		
	13 (Front fork)		
	14 (Handlebar)		
	15 (Front wheel)		
	16 (Rear wheel)		
	17 (Tyres)		
	18 (Electrics)		
	19 (Misc)		

SPARE PARTS

Although spare parts are quite difficult to obtain, many for the four-cylinder models are still available through the MV Agusta Owners' club of Great Britain. In 1991 Spares Secretary Peter Eacott negotiated the purchase of most of the remaining spares at Cascina Costa, and the classic spares service available to club members has recently reopened. For more information visit www.mvownersclub.co.uk

ALSO FROM VELOCE –

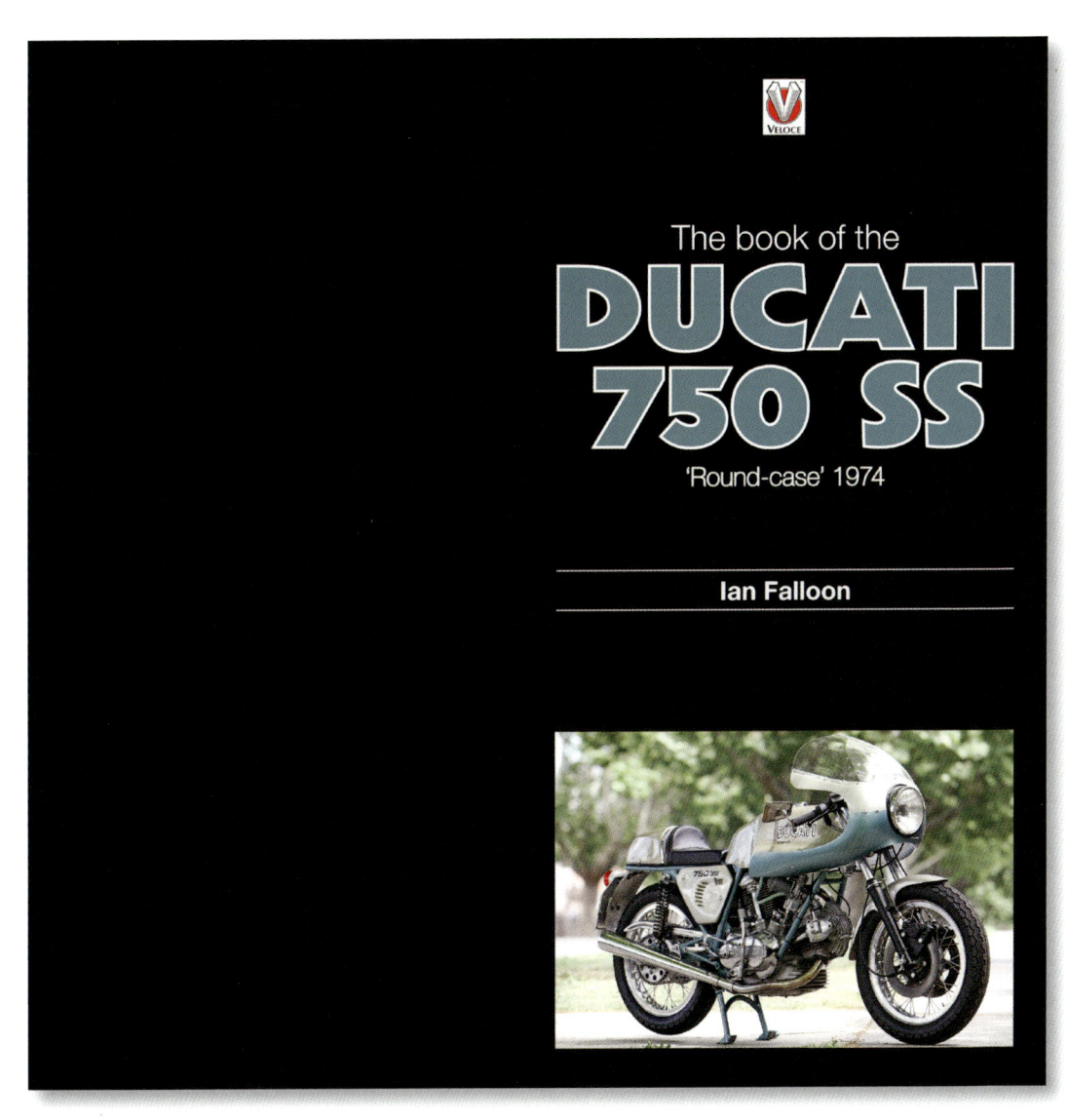

THE BOOK OF THE DUCATI 750 SS 'ROUND-CASE' 1974

Ian Falloon

- Hardback
- 25x25cm
- £40.00
- 176 pages
- 259 colour and b&w pictures
- ISBN: 978-1-84584-202-4

Although manufactured for only one year, 1974, the Ducati 750 Super Sport was immediately touted as a future classic. It was a pioneer motorcycle – expensive and rare, and produced by Ducati's race department to celebrate victory in the 1972 Imola 200 Formula 750 race; for Ducatisti, it is the Holy Grail.

For more info on Veloce titles, visit our website at www.veloce.co.uk
email info@veloce.co.uk • tel: +44 (0)1305 260068 • prices subject to change • p+p extra

ALSO FROM VELOCE –

LAVERDA TWINS & TRIPLES BIBLE

Ian Falloon

- Hardback
- 25x20.7cm
- £29.99
- 160 pages
- 222 colour and b&w pictures
- ISBN: 978-1-845840-58-7

The large capacity Laverda twins and triples were some of the most charismatic and exciting motorcycles produced in a golden era. With a successful endurance racing programme publicising them, Laverda's twins soon earned a reputation for durability. Here is the year-by-year, model-by-model, change-by-change record.

For more info on Veloce titles, visit our website at www.veloce.co.uk
email info@veloce.co.uk • tel: +44 (0)1305 260068 • prices subject to change • p+p extra

ALSO FROM VELOCE –

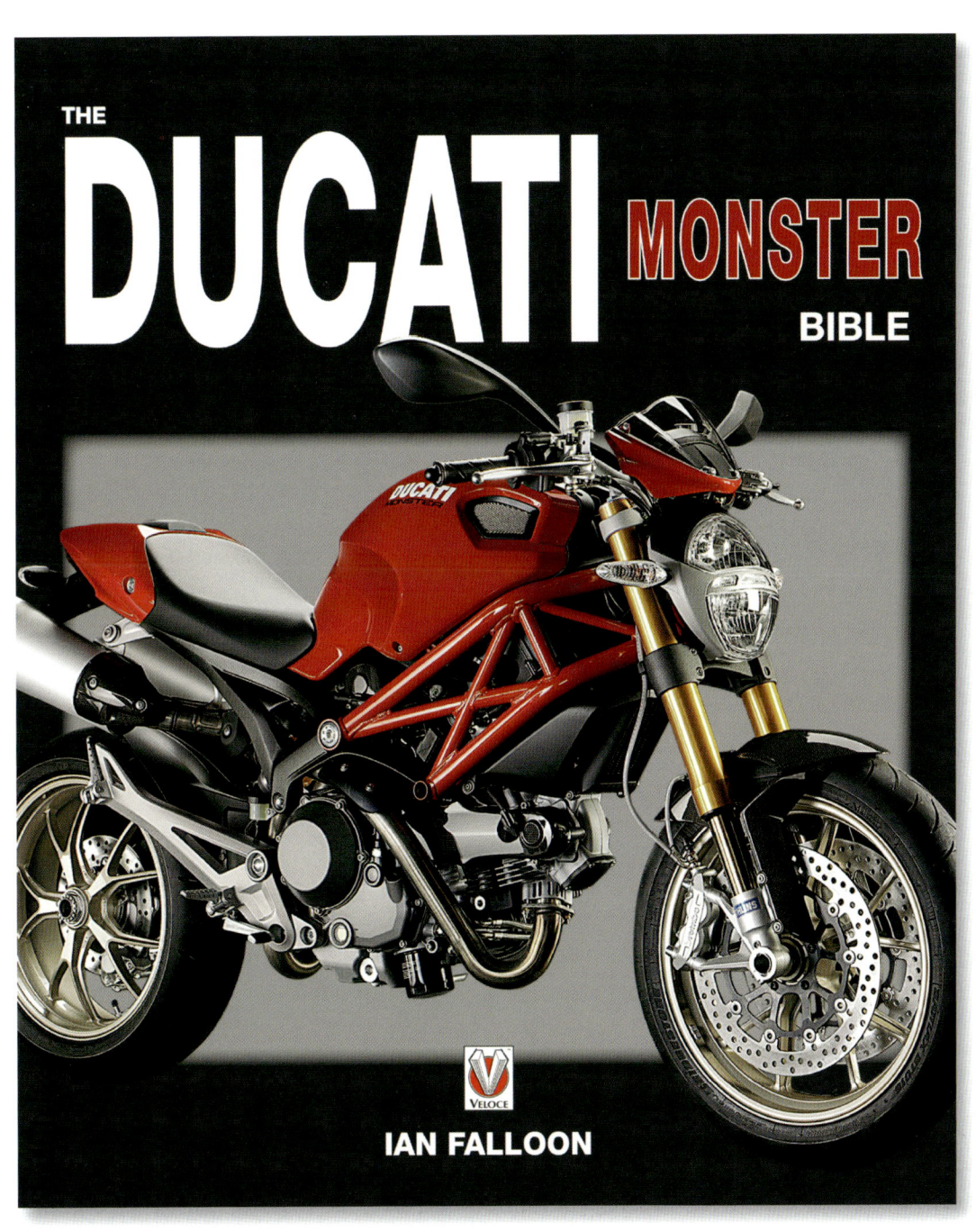

THE DUCATI MONSTER BIBLE

Ian Falloon

- Hardback
- 25x20.7cm
- £30.00
- 160 pages
- 197 colour pictures
- ISBN: 978-1-845843-21-2

When Ducati unleashed Galluzzi's Monster at the Cologne Show at the end of 1992, few expected it to become Ducati's most successful model. Dramatically styled, minimalist in stature, yet bristling with innovative engineering, the 900 Monster created a new niche market. Here is the ultimate guide to the Monster maze.

For more info on Veloce titles, visit our website at www.veloce.co.uk
email info@veloce.co.uk • tel: +44 (0)1305 260068 • prices subject to change • p+p extra

INDEX

ACU 216
Agostini, Giacomo 56-59, 61, 111-115, 146, 199, 200, 215
Agusta, Corrado 88, 94, 111, 112, 125, 145, 168, 188, 190
Agusta, Count Domenico 8-9, 14, 19, 20, 22-24, 30-32, 39, 44, 46, 48, 49, 53, 55, 56, 60-63, 82, 88, 93, 94, 135
Agusta, Giuseppina 14
Agusta, Vincenzo 14
AJS 24
Alfa Romeo 9
American Eagle 167
Amm, Ray 30-32
Amsterdam 140
Anderson, Bob 42
Apolloni, Dott. Luca 168
Arcore 9, 10
Argentina 51
Armeni, Alberto 188
Armstrong, Reg 21, 31
Artesiani, Arcisco 14, 17, 18
Assen 36, 39, 46, 48, 51, 53, 54, 57, 58
Australia 59, 91, 106, 107, 111, 118, 127, 157, 159, 162, 187, 198
Austria 118

Baden-Baden 111, 131, 162, 187
Balbo, Italo 10
Bandirola, Carlo 8, 14, 17, 18, 21, 28-31, 42, 58
Barber, Denny 219
Barcelona 22, 24, 29, 118, 140, 142, 155
Bate, Peter (family) 187-189, 191, 192, 198
Bathurst 127-8
Battison, Richard 215, 216
Belgian Grand Prix 13, 32
Belgium 13, 21, 36, 39, 40, 42, 46, 48, 95, 118, 231
Bell helicopters 8, 63
Benelli 184
Bergamonti, Angelo 94
Bertacchini, Bruno 14, 17
Bertola 168
Bertola, Pietro 115
Bertoni, Franco 8, 14
Bianchi 48
Bianchi, Michele 112

Bike magazine 124
Billown, Castletown 215, 217
Bimota 200, 223, 224
Biondi, Sauro 225
Birmingham 214
BMW 10, 43, 77, 223, 224, 233
Bocchi, Giuseppe 168, 189-90
Bold, Albert 74, 100, 202, 220-224, 229-230
Bologna 125, 155, 189
Bologna Show 224
Bonera, Gianfranco 147
Bonmartini, Count Giovanni 9, 10
Bordoni, Professor 9
Boshier, Richard 74, 90, 198
Boynton, Kym 88
Brambilla, Tino 43, 127
Brands Hatch 45
Brescia 9
Brown, Bob 36, 42, 46
BSA 91
Bugatti 10
Busto Anzio 62

Cadwell Park 215
Caldarella, Benedicto 54, 55
Calles, Peter 128
CAN 10
Caproni Aircraft Company 10
Carrano, Vittorio 51, 60
Cascina Costa 8, 42, 95, 168, 191, 198, 204, 234
Castrol Six-Hour race 127, 128
Cattolica 43
Cavaria (Varese) 61
Ceriani, Sig. 145
Chesterfield 5000 127
Cipolloni 127
Circle Motors 95
Clady course 21, 22
Clarkson, Brian 127, 128
Classic Bike/Norman Hyde series 217
Clermont-Ferrand 43, 45, 48
Cologne Show 167
Colombo 12, 40
Commerce Overseas Corporation (COC) 125, 140, 162, 167, 192
Copeta, Alfredo 8, 24

Cosmopolitan Motors 187
Costa, Dott. Francesco 111
Cotherman, Jim 167, 170, 187
CRMC (Classic Racing Motorcycle Club) 214, 215
Crystal Palace 34, 36
Cuneo 200
Cycle magazine 63, 170, 171, 175, 180, 188
Cycle World magazine 63, 64, 66, 88, 95, 128

Dale, Dickie 24, 28-30
Davies, Dickie 60
Daytona 54, 60, 111, 170, 224
Derbyshire, John 216
Dijk, Piet van 151, 162, 187
Dobelli, Giancarlo 94
Downer, Dave 52
Ducati 61, 110-112, 114, 125, 155, 163, 167, 180, 184, 188-190, 223
Duke, Geoff 36, 45-47, 51, 52, 54, 214
Dunstall Norton 52
Dutch Grand Prix (TT) 29, 36, 48, 56

Eacott, Peter 234
Earles, Ernie 20
Earls Court Motorcycle Show 197, 198
EFIM Group 125, 145, 188-190
Egli 224
Eiger (MV) Ltd. 217
Emanuele de Savoie, Vittorio 88, 91
England 32, 219
Europe 75, 169
European Championships 10, 11

Faenza 29
Fascist government 10
Felotti, Primo 135
Ferrara 17, 29
Ferrari 47, 64-5, 145, 190, 191, 218
Ferrari, Piero 218
Fiat 9
Fiera Campionara di Milano 62, 63
FIM 10, 36
Findlay, Jack 53
Finland 51, 53
Florence 224
Forconi, Tito 8, 30

238

Formula 750 146
Formula One 47, 57, 95
France 63, 95, 118
Francisci, Bruno 22, 24
Franzosi 24
Freeport, Illinois 167
French Grand Prix 43

Gallarate 8, 32, 114
Gallo, Flavio 168
Galtrucco, Renato 62
Garreau, Paris 95, 131
Garville, Christopher 162, 167, 187
Geneva 88
Genevoise 70
German Grand Prix 21, 24, 25, 27, 39, 49, 56
Germany 42, 46, 111, 118, 131, 162, 187, 188, 191, 198, 200, 202, 210
Germany, East 48
Ghisleri, Luigi 145, 168-170, 188
Gianini, Carlo 9, 10
Giardano, Tony 222
Gietl, Udo 223
Gilera 9-19, 21, 30, 31, 35-40, 51-4, 60, 70, 214, 220
Gilera, Giuseppe 10, 52
Giugiaro, Giorgetto 167, 184
Graham, Les 8, 14, 17-28, 31, 32, 35, 217
Grassetti 58
GRB 9
Guglielminetti 19
Gunnarsson, Sven 199

Hailwood, Mike 48-58, 60, 214
Hailwood, Stan 51, 60
Hakstege, Eric 229, 230
Hall, Terry 219
Hansen GmbH (Michael) 111, 162, 187, 188, 191, 192, 198, 202, 210, 211, 213, 214
Harley-Davidson 90
Hartle, John 40, 42-44, 46, 47, 52, 53
Hayashi, Yoshiyuki 212
Hillman Imp 215
Hockenheim 48, 58, 213
Hocking, Gary 44, 46-50, 58, 214
Holland 21, 42, 88, 162, 187
Honda 46, 47, 49-51, 53, 55, 57, 58, 90, 127, 164, 167, 224
Hubacher, Hans-Peter 224

Ickx, Jacky 95

Il Pilota Moto magazine 147
Imola 49, 52, 57, 112, 114, 115, 189, 190, 204
Imola 200 race 111, 113, 114, 146
Imola Gold Cup 31, 44, 50
Irwin, Bill 66
Isetta 77, 233
Isle of Man (TT) 14, 17-22, 24, 26, 29, 30, 32, 36, 38, 39, 41-46, 48-50, 52, 53, 55, 57, 215-217
Italian Championships 10, 17, 18, 21, 29, 31, 35, 36, 39, 42, 43, 56, 58, 225
Italian government 125
Italian Grand Prix 8
Italian manufacturers 40, 76, 111, 150, 155
Italy 22, 25, 42, 95, 110, 111, 118, 125, 127, 147, 154, 157, 162, 163, 224
Italy, King of 88

Jane, Bob (Corporation) 106, 107, 111, 118, 142, 162
Japan 63
Jawa 48
Jones, Peter 225

Kavanagh, Ken 23, 24, 31, 38, 39
Kawasaki 90, 127, 188
Kay, Dave 69, 74, 98, 199, 202, 214, 215, 217, 219, 220, 224, 226, 227, 229, 231, 232
Kay, Mark 214-217, 220
Kerby, Dave 215
Kimberton, Pennsylvania 220
Kuhn, Gus 117, 118, 123, 124, 128, 142, 162, 164, 187
Kyte, Peter 220

Lancelotti, Count 9
Laverda 61, 90, 112, 127, 215
Laverda, Massimo 112
Leicestershire 188
Libanori, Fortunato 88
Liberati 39
Lola 57
Lomas, Bill 20, 24, 28-30, 36, 188
London 117, 123, 162
Long, John 223
Lotus 57
Lowe, WH 187

Maggiore 225
Magi 14
Magni, Arturo 5, 8, 13, 14, 17, 18, 23, 24, 26, 30, 35, 94, 111-113, 145, 168, 187-189, 191, 192, 198, 202,

205-208, 210, 211, 214, 224
Magni, Carlo 112, 177, 202, 208
Magni, Giovanni 5, 191, 202-204, 207, 210
Mallory Park 47, 51, 53, 188, 233
Malpensa (airport) 8, 147, 188
Manx Grand Prix 217
Maraccini 127
Masetti, Umberto 21, 22, 28, 29, 31, 32, 37, 39
Matchless 53
Mattavelli 168
Matteo, Ing Giuseppe Di 147, 168
Mazzucchelli, Maurizio & Figli 69
McCarthy, Clive 220
McCormack, Jack 167
McIntyre, Bob 38-9, 48, 52, 60, 214
Meccanica Verghera Agusta 8
Menani 200, 201
Mendogni, Emilio 44-47
Mettet, Belgium 23
Meyer, Garage 187
Miami 64
Milan 8, 10, 106, 110, 111, 168, 199
Milan Show 8, 14, 61, 93-95, 110, 130, 131, 140, 188
Milan Trade Fair 12
Milano Taranto road race 18
Milano, Gilberto 39, 58
Miller 10
Minervi, Giuseppe 168
Minter, Derek 51, 52
MIRA 129, 198
Misano 115
Modena 29, 35, 112, 114, 127
Moller, Jorge 190
Mondial 8, 37, 38
Montjuich, Barcelona 21, 31
Montlhéry 128
Montoli, Mario 20
Monza 8, 9, 14, 17-24, 26-29, 31, 35, 37-39, 42, 44, 47, 49, 51-55, 57, 127
Morbidelli 190
Morini 56
Morris, Bill 107
Moto Guzzi 10, 16, 31, 36, 37, 39, 61, 111, 112, 129, 185
Moto Revue magazine 128
Moto Sport magazine 107, 128
Motociclismo magazine 63, 90, 91, 129, 200
Motom 9
Motor Club Santerno 111
Motor magazine (Dutch) 150

239

Motorcycle 129, 163, 188, 198
Motorcycle News 63
Motorcycle Sport magazine 198
Motorcycle World magazine 144
Motorrad magazine 188, 213
Müller, Hans Peter 24
Muth, Hans A. 200, 202
MV Agusta Concessionaires 74, 90, 187-189, 198
MV News 214
MVA Engineering 214
MZ 44, 53

Natal Grand Prix 50
Nations Grand Prix 14, 17, 21, 24, 37, 42, 47, 49, 55, 58
New Motorcycling Monthly magazine 188
New York 115, 125, 140
New Zealand 66
North Atlantic Pact 8
Norton 18, 23, 24, 31, 35, 42, 43, 47, 48, 90
NSU 215

OM 9
OPRA 10
Ospedaletti 17
Oulton Park 52

Pagani, Alberto 94, 112, 114, 115, 168
Pagani, Nello 9, 28-31, 37, 112
Palazzo Triennale 14
Paris Show 139-140
Passamonti, Luigi 215, 224
Patrignani, Roberto 95
Petersen Automotive Museum 212
Philadelphia 220, 222
Phillip Island, Australia 59
Phillis, Tom 50
Pirelli 147
Pirelli, Fausto 199, 200
Portovenere 9
Potter, Dave 128
Prato, Bruno de 147

Read, Phil 48, 53, 115, 188, ,189, 198
Redman, Jim 51, 53, 57, 58
Remor, Piero 9, 11-14, 18
Rhodesia 50
Ricci, Spartacus 215, 224
Rob Walker Racing Team Lotus 50
Rome 9

Rome University 9
Rondine 10, 11, 70
Rossi brothers 225
Rossi, Mario 20, 54, 61, 70, 168, 191
Rous, Charlie 60

Saab 187
Sachsenring 48, 51, 53
Safe, John 198
Samarate 177, 204, 207
San Remo 17
Sandford, Cecil 19, 20, 22-25
Sandhills, Staffordshire 214
Scaburri, Ermanno 177
Scarab brake company (Mozzi Motor) 125, 155
Schilling, Phil 170
Schneider, Roland 118, 131, 162, 187, 198, 210, 211, 214
Schotten 27
Scuderia Duke 51
Sefton, Pat 217
Segoni 224
Serafini, Dorini 10, 11
Sette, Pietro 125
Shah of Iran 88
Shepherd, Terry 39
SIAI Marchetti 188
Silverstone 36, 128
Slough 187
Smart, Paul 114, 115
Solitude 21, 37, 41, 46
South Africa 45
South America 54
Spa Francorchamps 14, 36, 48, 51, 53, 231
Spaggiari, Bruno 114, 115
Spain 17, 140, 154
Spairani, Fredmano 125, 155, 167, 168, 188, 190
Spanish Grand Prix 17, 18, 21, 31
Spanish Superbike Series 221
Stafford Classic Bike Show 217, 220
Station Garage, Taplow 198
Stockholm 28
Strub, Edgar 224
Surtees, John 32-49, 52, 57, 58, 214
Suzuka 53
Suzuki 127, 164
Sweden 63
Swiss Grand Prix 19
Switzerland 17-19, 88, 95, 187
Sydney 127

Taglioni, Fabio 112
Tamburini, Massimo 200
Tampere 53
Target Design 200
Taruffi, Piero 10
Taveri, Luigi 30, 39
Taylor, John 95
Team Firenze 225
Team Obsolete 115
Thruxton 18
Timpson, Rodney 220
Toè, Giuseppe dal 224
Tokyo 118
Tomaso, Alessandro de 184, 189
Tripoli Grand Prix 10
Triumph 90, 127

Ubbiali, Carlo 22, 24, 30, 37, 47
UK (United Kingdom) 18, 63, 74, 88, 95, 107, 125, 157, 159, 162, 169, 187, 188, 198, 220
UK MV Owners' Club 155, 198, 214, 233-4
Ulster 39, 48, 51, 53
Ulster Grand Prix 11, 20, 35-6
US (USA) 63, 64, 95, 105, 118, 125, 140, 142, 144, 157, 159, 162, 167, 168, 170, 175, 178, 179, 184, 187, 195, 197, 198, 224
US Department of Transport 148
US Grand Prix 54

Varese 18, 69
Velocette 20
Venturi, Remo 30, 43, 45, 46, 58
Verghera 22
Vizzola Ticino 147

Webster, Bill 32, 49
WERA (West-End Roadracing Association) 221, 223
Woods, Stanley 10, 44, 46
World Championships 8, 14, 19, 22, 28, 29, 32, 33, 35-40, 42, 44-47, 50, 53, 57, 58, 88, 89, 105, 124, 125, 140, 157, 159, 189

Yamaha 115, 146, 182, 200
Yankee Motor Corporation 95

Zen, Luciano 112
Zubani, Gianpiero 94
Zündapp 69